ANGLO-ETHIOPIAN RELATIONS
1869 to 1906

About the Author

K. V. Ram, after obtaining his B.A. (Hons) and M.A. degrees from the University of Mysore, he taught in Ethiopia from 1961 to 1966. A gold medallist in history, he won the Memorial University graduate fellowship and the Izak Killam scholarship respectively in 1966 and 1967. These scholarships enabled him to pursue his research degrees in Canada where he obtained his second M.A. from the Memorial University and Ph.D. from Dalhousie University after extensive archival work in London, Paris and Rome on Ethiopia's relations with the European powers. He has held faculty positions in Dalhousie University, Halifax, Canada, Makerere University of Uganda and the University of Lagos, Nigeria. He has published many articles on Ethiopian History in *The Journal of Imperial and Commo.ıwealth History,* London, *The Canadian Journal of African Studies, The Journal of East African History,* Nairobi, *History in Africa,* North Western University, U.S.A. and other academic journals of repute.

Also, he has to his credit a book entitled *Britain and Ethiopia 1805 to 1868: A Study of British Policy* (Concept, 1985).

ANGLO-ETHIOPIAN RELATIONS 1869 to 1906

A Study of British Policy in Ethiopia

K. V. RAM

CONCEPT PUBLISHING COMPANY, NEW DELHI-110059

ISBN-13: 978-81-8069-624-4 **ISBN-10 :81-8069-624-3**

First Published 2009

Published and Printed by

Since 1974

Concept Publishing Company

Regd. Office:

A/15-16, Commercial Block, Mohan Garden

New Delhi-110059 (India)

Phones : 25351460, 25351794, *Fax* : 091-11-25357109

Email : publishing@conceptpub.com,

website: www.conceptpub.com

Editorial Office:

H-13, Bali Nagar, New Delhi-110 015, India.

Cataloging in Publication Data--*Courtesy:* D.K. Agencies (P) Ltd. <docinfo@dkagencies.com>

Anglo-Ethiopian relations, 1869 to 1906 : a study of British policy in Ethiopia / K.V. Ram.

p. cm.

Includes bibliographical references.

Includes index.

ISBN 13: 9788180696244 ISBN 10: 8180696243

1. Great Britain--Foreign relations--Ethiopia. 2. Ethiopia--Foreign relations--Great Britain. 3. Ethiopia--Politics and government--20th century. I. Ram, K. V. (Krishnamurthy Venkat), 1934-

DDC 327.41063 22

Preface

Ethiopia has a unique place in African History. Not only is she one of the oldest Christian civilizations but also the only indigenous State of Africa which repulsed severe attacks made on her Independence by imperialist European powers and Egypt and emerged as beacon light of African Independence.

She was the only African State of the period which achieved equal diplomatic Status with European States and also achieved territorial gains in her frontier settlements with Britain and France relating to their colonies adjacent to her in North-east Africa.

During 1870-1906 period Britain was involved with Ethiopia to secure her strategic and political interests in that country through informal imperialism. Britain was the predominant industrial and military power of the period and a Christian nation with which the landlocked Christian Ethiopia was interested in close relations to overcome her geographical isolation, to improve her defence capabilities, end internal strife and disunity and achieve progress.

The 1869 and 1906 period was a significant period in the history of British expansion when the imperial mood swayed from withdrawal from her white colonies in Australia and Canada to colonial expansion in 1906. This comes out clearly in Britain's relations with Ethiopia from territorial disinterest and withdrawal in 1869 to the paper partition of the country in 1906 with France and Italy. But Ethiopia did not fall into the hands of the imperialist. This was due to her internal strength, religious cohesion, social and political dynamism and farsightedness of her emperors Yahannes and Menelek who had the tact and ability to exploit European rivalries for their national benefit and arm their patriotic soldiers. Britain had ignored these facts and underestimated Ethiopia until with modern weapons to the maximum extent possible she inflicted humiliating defeats on Egypt and Italy in 1889 and 1896 respectively. From then onwards Britain never lost sight of Ethiopia's strength in formulating her policies and negotiations with that country.

In looking at the Anglo-Ethiopian relations of the period the study throws light on many questions of significance for today's world including the problems of underdevelopment, the nature of 'Foreign aid', "Neocolonialism" the nature of relations between "advanced" and "backward" countries and the importance of self-reliance and internal unity and strength to preserve independence and achieve progress.

K. V. Ram

Acknowledgements

I express my gratitude and appreciation to the following Institutions which helped me in my research and preparation of this work.

1. Historical Research Institute, University of London, London.
2. The School of Oriental and African Studies, University of London.
3. India Office Library and Records, London.
4. Public Records Office, London.
5. Archives de la Documentation, Ministre Des Affaires Etrange Quaid Arsay, Paris, France.
6. Archivie dell' Ex Ministero dell' Africa Italiana, Rome, Italy.
7. Dalhousie University, Halifax, N. S. Canada.
8. Social Science and Humanities Research Council of Canada, Ottawa, Canada.
9. University of Addis Ababa, Addis Ababa, Ethiopia.
10. Concept Publishing Company, New Delhi, India.

K. V. Ram

Contents

List of Maps

Introduction

This is a study of Anglo-Ethiopian relation from 1869 to 1906. Britain was a great world power of the time with a large empire and still on the path of expansion. Ethiopia, with the exception of Egypt, is the oldest and most widely known African State. As the legendary kingdom of the Queen of Sheba and the mysterious Prester John, as the oldest Christian State of Africa, as the gallant nation which inflicted a crushing defeat on a European power during the scramble for Africa and as a beacon light of African independence during the period of European colonial rule Ethiopia has attracted considerable attention to herself. With an unbroken tradition of independence and a history spanning over two thousand years from pre-Christian times to the present there a sense of wonder surrounding her.

Perched on the Highland, an area not easily accessible to the outside world until the beginning of the nineteenth century, Ethiopian have lived in independence and dignity, proud of their indigenous culture and institutions. Though forced into near isolation by geography, reinforced by the hostile Turko-Egyptian encirclement which began in the fifteenth century, Ethiopia maintained steady commercial relation with the adjacent Sudan, Somalia, Arabia and India, religious contracts with Jerusalem and occasional diplomatic contracts with Europe. However Ethiopia never maintained continuous diplomatic relations with any state: rather they were sporadic and irregular; at times active and at other passive. After the Turkish occupation of the Western Red Sea Coast and the brief Portuguese intervention in the sixteenth century Ethiopia went into near diplomatic isolation until she was drawn into vortex of international relations in the nineteenth century by pressures of expanding European and Egyptian imperialism.

From the beginning of the nineteenth century many

European nations sought relations with Ethiopia for trade, territory or religion. The First of these was Britain which sent an official diplomatic mission to Ethiopia in 1809, established consular relations with her in 1848, fought a successful war with her in 1868 and thereafter withdrew disenchanted and dejected. This phase of Anglo-Ethiopian relations has been studied and analyzed. But Britain did not remain disengaged from Ethiopia for long. She was drawn into relations with that country first in response to Ethiopian initiatives and later to protect British Imperial interest in the region. The 1869-1906 period was a momentous epoch during which Ethiopia repulsed the several attacks made on her independence by European and Egyptian imperialists and emerged as a strong power in the Nile Valley. During this critical period the country was ably served by Emperors Yohannes and Menelek, both of whom attempted to cultivate close relations with Europe ironically as a means to contain European imperialism and promote Ethiopian interest. While Emperor Yohannes made relation with Britain the central focus of his foreign policy Menelek attached greater importance to relations with France before he turned towards Britain in his effort to contain growing French predominance. With a deeper understanding of European rivalries than Yohannes, Menelek sought to exploit them for Ethiopia's benefit. No European power was allowed to maintain a long-term predominance because as soon as one was perceived to be endangering Ethiopian Independence it's influence was ended by fearful Ethiopian rulers.

All through the 1869-1906 period Britain was involved in Ethiopia at first somewhat reluctantly, later actively. This was a significant era in the history of British expansion when the imperial mood swayed from one extreme to the other. In 1865 a parliamentary select committee recommended British withdrawal from colonial enclaves in West Africa. But the mood of withdrawal slowly gave way to expansion and by the 1890's Britain had acquired huge blocks of territory in all regions of tropical Africa. Similar extremes characterized British approaches to Ethiopia. In contrast to the earlier policy of territorial disinterestedness by 1906 Britain had concluded a virtual paper partition of Ethiopia with her European colonial rivals earmarking her share of the country. But Ethiopia did not disintegrate and fall into the hands of the imperialists. This was due to her internal strength. Ethiopia was different from other African Countries, in its heritage, structure, religious cohesiveness and socio-political dynamism. She could rely on a system of flexible socio-political structure which had stood the test of internal fragmentation and external challenges for centuries and enabled Ethiopia to mobilize and field thousands of "nationally" inspired patriotic soldiers to check external aggressors than crumble before them.

Ethiopia was the only African Country to escape from European imperial rule and survive as an independent sovereign State, like Thailand in Asia. Ethiopians like people of Thailand had been independent for centuries, believed in their internal strength to protect themselves, had a knowledge of European imperialism and used services of foreign advisors to enlighten themselves about strategies of imperialists to neutralize them. Their rulers were proud of their Independence and sovereignty and could assert their leadership at home while confident of conducting foreign relations. They had tact and ability to exploit European rivalries for their national benefit. Ethiopian ruler, like their Thai contemporaries, believed that if they "properly balanced big powers" they could ward off danger to their Independence. Indeed Anglo-French rivalries helped both Ethiopia and Thailand to some extent, to survive independently. European imperialists, including the British, had ignored these aspects and underestimated Ethiopia until she inflicted humiliating defeats on Egypt and Italy in 1884 and 1896 respectively. Britain never lost sight of Ethiopia's strength in formulating her policy towards that country in the 1896-1906 period.

One important question that arises to the student of British relations with Ethiopia of this period is what factors produced the *volte face* in British policy from the withdrawal and disengagement of the 1870 to the paper partition of Ethiopia in 1906 against the time when Ethiopia might disintegrate. What role did the British occupation of Egypt and the "ensuing scramble" play in this change? Given Ethiopia's strategic importance to Britain in the Nile Valley, in the Red Sea region and East Africa why was imperial rule not extended to Ethiopia during the scramble for Africa? We might rather ask on the contrary why Britain ceded so much territory to Ethiopia in the various frontier treaties concluded with her? There are no published studies on Anglo-Ethiopian relations which have addressed themselves to these issues though there are many studies of British imperialism in Africa, European diplomacy during the scramble and Ethiopian topics which touch upon certain aspects of Anglo-Ethiopia relations as integral to the major themes. To this category belong William Langer's Diplomacy of Imperialism, Leonard Woolf's Empire and commerce in Africa, Ernest work's Ethiopia A Pawn in European Diplomacy, G.N. Sanderson's, Britain, Europe and the upper Nile, Gebre Selassie's Emperor Yohannes IV, Harold Marcus's Emperor Menelak, Life and Times and Proflessor Sven Rubenson's. The Survival of Ethiopian Independence. This study tries to fill the lacuna.

This is a study of British policy in Ethiopia from 1869 to 1906.

It is primarily concerned with Britain's "Official Mind", official perceptions of Britain's interest in the Ethiopian region and the policies and strategies pursued to secure them. However cognizance is taken of the aims and strategies of the Ethiopian rulers as well as Britain's colonial competitors France and Italy and Germany, to be able to interpret British policy in an international perspective. Given the orientation this research has been primarily based on Britain's diplomatic correspondence housed at the Public Record Office and at the Library and Records of the Indian and Commonwealth Office, London. Italian, French and German perspectives on the issues derived from a perusal of Italian documents at Archivio Storico dell'ex Ministero dell' Africa Italiani, Rome, Italy and *Documenti Diplomatici Italiani* and *Documents Diplomatiques Francais* published by the Italian and French Foreign Ministries as well as the *German Diplomatic Documents* in four volumes selected and translated into English by E.W. Dugdale. All official documents of this time refers to the country as Abyssinia, the name by which Ethiopia was known in Europe. During my researches spanning several years I have benefited from the insights and contributions of several scholars in the field. They are too numerous to be acknowledged here individually. My indebtedness to them in indicated in the references. This study has benefited greatly by the criticisms and suggestions of Professor. J.E. Flint and comments, insights and stylistic amendments of Professor J.B. Webster who so kindly cared for me while revising this work under his roof and Dr. William Heinz for his suggestions. I am most grateful to them. I hope this study helps to understand the non-economic and strategic oriented British Policy in Ethiopia and the diplomacy and strength of the Ethiopian rulers who defended their independence from external aggressions. I express my appreciation to Vijaya my wife, who suffered loneliness and boredom during my long spells of absence while researching and drafting this monograph.

K.V. RAM

1

Reluctant Britain and Persistent Ethiopia Assertion of Sovereignty

In 1868 Lord Stanley, the British Foreign Secretary, declared in the House of Common that "We can do without Abyssinia and the Abyssinians must learn to do without us."[1] On the other hand announcing his accession to the Solomonic Throne in 1871 Emperor Yohannes IV of Ethiopia wrote to Queen Victoria "I will not forget the friendship which I have found with England... I hope You will not forget our aid."[2] The student of Anglo-Ethiopian relations is struck at once by the diametrically opposing attitudes of the two powers towards their mutual relations. While Britain pulled away Ethiopia was trying to draw closer. While both attitudes arose out of the same historical context they emanated from opposing perceptions of their past relations and expectations for the future. A brief survey of that past helps to explain this dichotomy and to understand the tortuous course of Anglo-Ethiopian relations in the 1870s and the 1880s.

By 1870 Britain had more than sixty years of relations with Ethiopia, twenty of these being consular. Seeking new markets for her manufactures and cheap raw materials for her industries Britain had entered Ethiopia in the first decade of the nineteenth century. Believing in the mutual profitability of trade and its potency to galvanize Ethiopian society and to bring about economic and social changes Britain appointed a consul to Ethiopia in 1848, concluded commercial treaty with her rulers according recognition to Ethiopia as an "equal state", a privilege that was denied to other Sub-Saharan African states of the time. Britain's expectations however failed to be realized in the harsh Ethiopian environment. A proud warlike people who praised soldiering and firearms but looked down upon trading, Ethiopians neither understood nor shared Britain's commercial hopes. Forced into near isolation by hostile Moslem powers which occupied her coast and viewing international relations in the medieval context of Christianity against Islam, Ethiopia welcomed Britain as a friendly Christian ally, a strong military and naval power which could help her with communications and firearms. However differing political perceptions unshared economic objectives and imperious wills set the industrialized patronizing Britain and medievally oriented but politically conscious Ethiopia on a course of collision. Though preaching reforms Britain did not aid the modernizing Emperor Tewodros in reforming Ethiopia; despite the common Christian faith Britain did not support Christian Ethiopia against her Moslem enemies. This was unacceptable to its highly ambitious and proud Emperor Tewodros. Attempting to coerce Britain into aiding him and avenging her negligence he forfeited Britain's sympathy. The result was Tewodros's Seizure of the British consul and other Britons, the British military expedition of 1868 to Ethiopia to release them and restore Britain's prestige, and the defeat and death of the Emperor.

Costing nine million sterling this expedition was one of the expensive British military undertakings of the century in Africa. The irony was that the total value of British trade to Ethiopia in the past three decades did not amount to the cost of the expedition! After releasing the British captives from Tewodros's fetters and leaving the fort of Magdala "a blackened rock as a warning to all who injure the subjects of Her Majesty the Queen of England" the British withdrew from Ethiopia without claiming either indemnity or concessions.[3] Ethiopia was seen as a state with no prospects for serious commercial developments. No wonder that Lord Stanley concluded that the two states must do without each other.

The British withdrawal from Ethiopia announced by the Conservative Government of Disraeli had full public and parliamentary support. Besides the traumatic experience with the Emperor Tewodros the mood of the time also favoured Britain's withdrawal. In the 1860's Britain was going through a low tide of imperialism. The Palmerstonian expansiveness was giving way to sombre reflections on possible withdrawals from burdensome colonial ventures and Britain was going ahead with devolution of authority to the White colonies overseas. Liberals under Gladstone who formed the next Government of Britain elevated withdrawal to a policy of disengagement towards Ethiopia. It was Liberal Clarendon, the one time protagonist of close relations with Ethiopia, who ordered the closure of the British consulate at Massawa "the only effective channel of communication with Ethiopia."[4]

This policy of disengagement was in conflict with British humanitarian ideals of the times. Moulded by the Mid-Victorian ideology of White man's noblesse oblige towards the "backward" African, many officials in the Foreign and India offices and in the Red Sea region opposed the abrupt ending of the civilizing mission to Ethiopia, considering the step as "unsympathetic and unnecessarily cautions."[5] Shocked as they were by Emperor Tewodros's excesses they did not like to see official channels of communications closed to Ethiopians, most of whom had nothing to do with the deeds of their late emperor and presumably needed Britain's "civilizing" influences. They also feared that the closure of the Massawa consulate would hurt British interests in the region. Not only would restraints on slave traders plying between Ethiopia and the Moslem countries on the eastern Red Sea shore be removed but also the security of the British settlement at Aden, which depended on food imports from that African coast would be adversely affected. Supported by the influential Napier of Magdala and the Secretary of State for India they urged the British Government to maintain the British consulate at Massawa in order to facilitate contacts with Ethiopia.[6]

The British experience in Ethiopia had been so disappointing that these arguments failed to win the Foreign

Secretary. With no economic interests to protect or promote in Ethiopia and that country having no control over the region bordering the Red Sea, which was of strategic interest to Britain, the British Government had no inducement to be involved with her. Nor did the closure of the Massawa consulate seem to endanger British interests as the officials had argued. Aden's security was unlikely to be hurt as its primary suppliers of victuals were Berbera and Bulhar ports on the Somali coast and not Massawa. Uninterrupted food supplies from those ports had been ensured through Britain's treaties with the Somali chiefs. Anti-slave activities might not suffer if Britain's naval presence in the Red Sea was increased and the Aden Residency strengthened to watch slave traders. Primarily the British consulate at Massawa had been established in 1848 to facilitate close contacts with Ethiopia and now with precisely the opposite being the objective Clarendon saw no reason to maintain the consulate. However to placate British Indian officials he suggested that Government of India might appoint a consul at Massawa were it deemed "expedient".[7] This suggestion did not commend itself to either the India Office or the Government of India which refused to burden itself financially. Neither the British Indian Government wanted to step in where the imperial Government was stepping out nor burden itself with new overheads.[8] Thus matters stood in 1869 with Britain disengaged from Ethiopia.

However Ethiopia regarded the situation differently. While the closure of the British consulate at Massawa did not signify to the Ethiopian chiefs any change in British policy, the British withdrawal from Ethiopia did not seem to make any significant difference to internal political processes. Emperor Tewodros's death touched off armed struggle among principal Ethiopian chiefs for the Solomonic throne. Even if Tewodros had nominated a successor to the throne a war of succession would have been unavoidable since military strength more than legitimacy determined the issue. An Ethiopian saying chillingly assumed that an Ethiopian Emperor must wade through blood to the Solomonic throne. Soon after Tewodros's death Wagsum Gobaze of Lasta, then in his thirties, commanding about 40,000 soldiers, declared himself as the Emperor taking the throne name of Habte Giorgis.[9] But his tenure was uncertain; he had to make his titles good militarily. There were other claimants to the throne with royal blood in their veins and declared ambitions. These were Kassa Mercha of Tiger and King Menelek of Shoa, each commanding large forces and waiting to realize his imperial ambitions. While the fate of the new Emperor hung in the balance the shift in the central authority had no visible impact on the people who continued to live in their home towns and villages under local chiefs who were their visible authorities.

The post Tewodrean foreign relations of Ethiopia now slipped into the Zemane Messafint pattern with each provincial chief conducting external relations without reference to the King of Kings. Though these at first had primarily to do with accepting or rejecting foreign travellers and ensuring them safe passages and protection, their scope expanded and became more purposive after Tewodros, as Ethiopian monarchs spearheaded diplomatic initiative to secure European aid or intervention to resolve the regional crisis. No matter who conducted external relations, whether the King of Kings or provincial chiefs, some concerns were common and constant to them all. These were the procuring of firearms, free trade at Massawa and passage for the Patriarch of the Ethiopian Orthodox Church. In the 1870's and the 1880's notwithstanding Ethiopia's efforts to establish close relations with Christian Europe, most European states remained disinterested in her. Of the two European powers, Britain and France which had been involved in Ethiopia while self imposed disengagement policy kept Britain aloof from Ethiopia, the Franco-Prussian war prevented France from playing active role in that country.

It was ironic that Britain was disengaging from Ethiopia just when she commanded the highest prestige and abundant goodwill in that country. Britain's voluntary withdrawal from Ethiopia after a successful military campaign had won her Ethiopia's admiration. Territorially disinterested, religiously non-interfering and militarily strong Britain appeared a desirable friend and useful ally to Ethiopian chiefs. Engaged in a contest for the Solomonic throne they desired Britain's goodwill and support. While Dejazmach Kassa of Tigre requested the British Government to supply him firearms, rockets and military experts to operate them so as to strengthen himself against Wagsum Gobaze, who had declared himself the Emperor.[10] Gobaze told the British Government of Kassa's challenge to his authority. Presumably he expected Kassa to be restrained, though he made no specific request to Britain.[11] Having distanced himself from the British during the Magdala campaign, King Menelek of Shoa was equally anxious to get back into Britain's good graces. He expressed his desire to Queen Victoria for close friendship referring to the tradition of friendly relations between Shoa and Britain.[12]

These Ethiopian initiatives showed the British Government the difficulty of implementing the preferred disengagement policy towards Ethiopia. Given the developments, what should be the level and limit of relations with Ethiopia? Lord Clarendon, the Foreign Secretary, feared that either direct dealings or frequent contacts with Ethiopia might eventually involve Britain in political embarrassments. Preferring Ethiopian chiefs to be distanced and discouraged from dealing with the British Government directly, he wanted their approaches to be limited to the British Residency at Aden. He told the Ethiopian chiefs curtly that it would be well to write to the (British) Resident at Aden than any member of the British Government"[13]. Nor was he in sympathy with their political goal of creating a strong central-state under "one man's" rule. Such ambitions of the late Emperor Tewodros had plunged Ethiopia into long civil wars, bloodshed and suffering. Preferring Ethiopia's return to the political order of the "Era of Princes", Clarendon counselled the Ethiopian chiefs "to abstain from all hostility and encroachment upon each other" and to rule peacefully in their territories serving their subjects. Tendering paternal advice and providing no aid Clarendon preferred to keep away from Ethiopia. He was in complete agreement with his predecessor Lord Stanley's policy: "It will in no way concern them (the British) what may be the future that awaits Abyssinia, what rulers may hold power in that country; what civil wars and commotions may arise... They do not consider it incumbent upon themselves to set up or support any form of Government or any particular rule under which it shall be carried out in a country in which they have no British interests to support"[14] Where neither commercial interests nor territorial aspirations existed troublesome involvement was clearly undesirable.

Understandably Clarendon's suggestions were unwelcome to Ethiopian chiefs as it encroached upon their right to conduct external relations directly with the foreign office. Ignoring the British advice Kassa of Tigre continued to deal with London directly, while Menelek of Shoa resorted to more subtle diplomacy to assert his rights. In November 1869, while requesting British intervention with the Somali chiefs to remove obstacles to Ethiopian trade at their ports, Menelek asked to be allowed to establish a Commercial Agency at Aden to promote Shoan trade.[15] Clearly Menelek's requests involved not only trade but also recognition of Shoan rights to have accredited representation in British territory. Though the British Government was unhappy about Ethiopian initiatives which militated against the disengagement policy, it had, nevertheless, not divested itself of the belief that Anglo-African contacts would promote African development through dissemination of progressive ideas. These beliefs and humanitarian sentiments strongly influenced the British response to Menelek's requests during a discussion at the Foreign Office regarding the attitude to be maintained towards him. The Under Secretary for Foreign Affairs argued that "the more you bring these semi-civilized princes into communication with the civilized world the great influence for good you have over him."[16] The British Resident at Aden and the Catholic missionary Massaja both urged the British Government to support the young Shoan King, who was thought to be amenable to progressive views, anxious to introduce reforms, suppress the slave trade and promote legitimate trade. Strongly supporting Menelek's request Lord Napier predicted that other Ethiopian princes might make similar requests. By obliging them Britain might influence them beneficially without much cost to herself.[17] While sharing the humanitarian concerns and complying with Menelek's requests Lord Granville shunned political relations with Ethiopia. The trauma of British experience with the late Emperor Tewodros still oppressed him. This dichotomy is evident in his decision on the issue. While consenting to allow Menelek to appoint a Commercial Agent at Aden, Granville laid down explicitly that "no function of political order was to be extended to the Agent.[18] These restrictions did not bother Menelek who appointed Monseiur Tiani as his Commercial Agent soon afterwards.[19]

Kassa of Tigre was more daring than Menelek in asserting his sovereign rights to international relations. He took initiatives, though somewhat unconventional, from the established diplomatic practices of Europe. Convinced that in-spite of its lukewarm attitude Britain was the only European power whose friendship was desirable to cultivate, Kassa appointed Messrs. Henry King & Co. as his consular Agent in London without seeking leave of the British Government, and sought official recognition. This was indeed a master stroke of diplomacy; a British firm to represent him in Britain would be familiar with the *modus operandi* of London and also keep him informed of British views and moves on matters of concern to him. Wishing to strengthen his relations with Britain further, Kassa dispatched an Ethiopian diplomatic mission to London with a letter and gifts to Queen Victoria.[20] The mission made of the English speaking Alequa Birru, Wolde Giorgis and Mercha Worque arrived in Alexandria en route to London. The British were very unhappy to be faced with a *fait accompli,* and stalled it, refusing permission to proceed to England.[21] The Ethiopian embassy was pressed to hand over the letter and presents for the Queen to the British Consul-General who would transmit them.[22] Strongly protesting that it would be an insult to their prince to return home without completing the mission and without a reply from the Queen the Ethiopian envoys stayed on in Cairo where they could be seen even a year later.[23] In the meantime after overthrowing the incumbent Emperor, Kassa ascended the Solomonic throne with the name of Yohannes. Announcing his accession to the Ethiopian throne and assuring Britain of his friendship, Kassa wrote to Queen Victoria, "I hope you have not forgotten our aid."[24] Admitting to itself that it was a "strong measure" not to have responded to Kassa earlier the British Government hastened to express its friendship for him through a royal reply and appropriate gifts.[25] The British Government also issued an exequatur to Messrs. Henry King & Co. recognizing the Firm as Ethiopia's consul in London.

These belated British responses were unavoidable diplomatic niceties which were also partly aimed at avoiding a repetition of the costly and unhappy experience of Tewodros' time. These responses however did not signify a change in British policy towards Ethiopia. The British attitude towards that country remained cold and discouraging. Thus Emperor Yohannes was told that thereafter the Queen neither wished to receive nor send gifts. Lord Granville, the Foreign Secretary, remained convinced that "fewer the communications we have with the princes (Ethiopian chiefs) the better."[26] Nevertheless these British responses, belated and perfunctory as they were, implied Britain's recognition of Ethiopia's right to conduct external relations with the manner of the "civilized state". It was thus an Ethiopian triumph. The Ethiopians had achieved a subtle, if minor victory of great importance for the future conduct of foreign relations.

REFERENCES

1. Hansard, Third Series, Vol. CXC, p. 217.
2. F.O. 1/28. Emperor Yohannes to Queen Victoria, September 1871.
3. For an analysis of British Policy see; K.V. Ram, *The Barren Relations: Britain and Ethiopia 1805 to 1869* (Concept; New Delhi, 1985).
4. F.O. 1/29. Clarendon's Minute 10 December 1869 on the letter from the India Office to the Foreign Office of 9 December 1869.
5. F.O. 1/29. Captain Good Fellow, Acting Political Resident, Aden to the Secretary, Government of India, in the India Office to the Foreign Office, 8 July 1869.
6. F.O. 1/29. Napier's letter to the F.O. 1 January, 1870.
7. F.O. 1/29. Calrendon's Minute on the India Office to the F.O. 10 December 1869.

8. A.I.A 583 Government of India to the Secretary of State for India.
9. Erlich Hagai *A Political Biography of Ras Alula Michigan* 1982.
10. F.O. 1/29. Kassa to Napier, 10 August 1869. Encl, in the Under Secretary, Government of India, 29 October 1869.
11. London. India Office Library A.I.A./540; *Aden Residency Records*. Tekle Giorgis to Napier, 10 February, 1870.
12. A.I.A./540 Menelek to Queen Victoria, 12 June 1869. I.E.
13. F.O. 1/29. Clarendon to Yohannes, 24 December 1869.
    Clarendon to Tamale Giorgis, 24 December 1869.
    Claremont to Menelek, 4 December 1869.
14. F.O. 1/21. Stanley to Northcort, 20 September 1867.
15. F.O. 1/28. Political Resident, Aden to the Under-Secretary Government of India, 18 November, 1869.
16. F.O. 1/29. F.O. Minute, December 1869.
17. F.O. 1/29. Napier to Hammond, 1 January, 1870. Captain Good Fellow to Merrivale 18 November 1869.
18. I.E.; No. 19. A.I.A/583. Secretary to the Government of India to the Political Resident at Aden.
19. F.O. 1/28. Col. Stanton to Granville, 20 October 1870; Granville to Stanton, 3 November 1870.
20. Rubenson, Sven, *The Survival of Ethiopian Independence* (Heinemann; 1975) p. 280.
21. F.O. 1/28. Col. Stanton to Granville, 20 October 1870: Granville to Stanton, 3 November 1870.
22. F.O. 1/28. Stanton to Granville, 7 November 1870.
23. F.O. 1/28. Hammond's Minute, 12 July 1872.
24. F.O. 1/28. Yohannes to Queen Victoria, September 1871.
25. F.O. 1/28. Political Resident, Aden, 12 June 1872.
    Granville to Kassa, 30 March 1872.
    Queen Victoria to Kassa, 22 March 1872.
26. F.O. 1/29. Granville's Minute, 4 July 1872.

2

Egyptian Aggression on Ethiopia, Britain's Reluctance to Intervene, Ethiopian Triumph

Anglo-Ethiopian relations, spanning the 1870-1885 period, was marked by increased Ethiopian initiatives to involve Britain in the resolution of the regional conflicts. This again met with Britain's refusal. The major issue in these relations was Egyptian aggression upon Ethiopia. A striking element was the simplistic and innocent Ethiopian view of Britain as the New Byzantium with power and will to protect Christian interests all over the world against Moslems. This unfortunate perception misled Ethiopia into the erroneous conclusion that Christian Britain was axiomatically a friend and natural ally of Christian Ethiopia against her Moslem enemies Egypt and Turkey. This misconception hurt Ethiopia as British policy, formulated to protect British interests, transcended religious considerations and in humouring Moslem Egypt in order to serve those interests Britain ignored Ethiopian desires. Faced with Egyptian aggression and Britain's indifference Ethiopia mustered her internal strength to defend her territorial sovereignty. When Ethiopia humiliated Egypt and emerged as a powerful state in the Nile Valley in 1882 Britain was forced to reverse her policy to secure Anglo-Egyptian interests in the region.

In the 1870's Ethiopia and Egypt the two oldest African states which had lived mostly in peace since Biblical times, came into conflict when Egypt began an expansionist policy. Ismail Pasha, the Khedive of Egypt, was both a dreamer and a great achiever. Imbibing the drive and ambition of Mohammed Ali, his grandfather, Ismail strove to carve out an empire in Africa from the Mediterranean Sea to Lake regions of Central Africa and from the Sahara to the Indian Ocean. Modernizing his army with the help of European and American experts and equipping it with the latest firearms, Ismail also built a navy. As first steps to empire building in 1866 he acquired the Red Sea ports of Suakin and Massawa through a *firman* from the Porte and began to extend his authority southward along the Western shore of the Red Sea. The Khedive's African dream also included Ethiopia and in 1867 he offered military aid to the British Government against Emperor Tewodros in the hope of securing footholds in Ethiopia for the services rendered.[1] The rejection of the offer by the British did not discourage Ismail. On the contrary the British victory at Magdala and the death of Emperor Tewodros spurred his territorial ambitions in Ethiopia. Its apparently disorganized political situation and its undefined frontiers were tempting to Ismail.

Ever since the occupation of the Sudan by Mohammed Ali in 1820 friction had entered Ethiopia-Egyptian relations. No demarcated borders separated Egypt and Ethiopia. As Haggai Erlich observed "throughout Ethiopian history borders were spheres of raids rather than lines of demarcation." As no *de Jure* frontier existed the *de facto* zone between the two countries shifted as either of the contenders showed aggressive designs. There were frequent collisions between frontier chiefs on either side, from Quallabat to Kassala on the west and from Kassala to the Red Sea northward.[2] In the disputed region the people paid tribute and taxes to both governments to avoid molestation.

While the undefined frontiers between the two countries gave Egypt the needed pretexts and opportunities for invasion the changed demographic and religious factors on Ethiopia's northern frontiers presented Ethiopian with further dangers. A number of arabized autonomous Moslem communities lived along the Ethiopian border from Kassala to Massawa. These were under Ethiopia's suzerainty though they also paid tribute to Egypt to escape molestation. In the late 1860's Khedive Ismail tried to bring the border chiefs of Barya, Hamassen and Mensa under Egyptian rule and in 1869 he invaded Kunama.[3]

Egyptian expansion into northern Ethiopia was also assisted by the Swiss and French Catholic missionaries who had settled in Bogos and Akele Guzay districts since 1865. Claiming more than 30,000 Ethiopian converts to the Catholic faith and faced with the opposition of the Ethiopian Orthodox Church, the Catholic missionaries had been anxious to establish a French Protectorate in the region, but the French Government showed little interest.[4] However under the patronage of Munzinger,[5] the French Consul at Massawa who regarded himself as protector of Catholics in the region, the Catholic missionaries began to meddle in Ethiopian politics to ensure the succession of chiefs well disposed to Catholicism.

Catholic missionary aspirations and activities became matters of serious concern to Kassa in whose territory they resided. He was also being pressed by Ethiopian chiefs and Orthodox Church to act against the missionaries strongly. But he could not act against them as Munzinger, the French consul at Massawa, exerted pressure on him to ensure toleration to Catholic missionaries and accord them friendly treatment arguing that such a policy would ensure him French friendship as well as their support in resisting Egyptian aggression. Kassa tried to win over Munzinger by assuring him that he was not against Roman Catholic missionaries but their clandestine political activities. He might even consider the appointment of a Catholic Bishop in Ethiopia in future though at the time he was not strong enough to oppose the Wishes of the *Abuna* and the Orthodox Church whose support he needed to buttress his authority. In the Circumstances Kassa appealed to Munzinger to dissuade the French Roman Catholic missionaries from indulging in local politics.[6] But this approach did not deter their political intrigues.

Catholic missionaries aspirations and activities became a matter of serious concern to Kassa in whose territory they resided. Fearing the subversion of the loyalty of the Ethiopian Catholic converts who were being encouraged by the missionaries to regard themselves as French protected persons

Kassa decided to act against them. The opportunity arose soon. When Catholic missionaries Dufflot and Cavalier implicated themselves in political intrigues against him and incited the people of Akule Guzay not to pay taxes to Ethiopia, Kassa expelled the French Catholic missionaries from Akule Guzay, closed their churches and severely punished the defiant Catholic Converts.[7] This led to unfortunate consequences. Convinced that there was more religious toleration under the rule of the Khedive of Egypt, than under Emperor Yohannes, the Catholic missionaries encouraged their protégés to apply for Egyptian protection.[8] Supporting them fully, Munzinger schemed to detach the northern frontier regions from Ethiopia. After inciting the chiefs of Halhal Barya, Bogos ad Akele Guzay to declare their allegiance to Egypt. In his capacity as the Egyptian governor of Massawa, Munzinger advised Khedive Ismail not only to grant them protection but also to occupy Bogos soon to prevent its possible seizure by France under the pretext of protecting Catholic in the regions.[9]

Suspecting territorial ambitions behind Munzinger's threats and having failed to check him on his own, Yohannes tried to restrain him through the British Government.[10] Explaining the difficulties created by the French Catholic missionaries and Munzinger, who had also served as British consul at Massawa earlier, Yohannes appealed to Queen Victoria "to help him in his difficulties with his enemies".[11] Disinterested in religious matters and missionary politics the British Government refused intervention pointing out that Munzinger was no longer in its service.[12] Yohannes had to fend for himself.

Yohannes did not allow internal religious policy to affect his relations with Moslem Egypt, with which he wished to be friendly. Even before ascending the Solomonic throne he had written to Khedive Ismail seeking friendship and firearms. Moreover friendly relations with Egypt was vital to him in order to procure the Abuna from the Coptic Church of Alexandria and ensure better treatment for Ethiopian merchants and trade at Massawa. However the Khedive's territorial aspirations in Ethiopia frustrated Yohannes's hopes for cordial relations with Egypt.

After the British withdrawal from Ethiopia in 1868 Khedive Ismial schemed to use the French Roman Catholic missionaries in Ethiopia to off-set British influence there. More important, hoping to neutralize possible French opposition to his territorial expansion in Ethiopia, Ismial proposed to Paris a joint Franco-Egyptian policy—*"unpolitique d'amitie"*—which would ensure them equal influence in Ethiopia to protect the Roman Catholic and Moslem interests.[13] Though the French Government rejected the proposal it welcomed Ismail's intervention with Yohannes in favour of the missionaries and Catholics. To capitalize on French missionary support and their government's goodwill Ismial at once warned Yohannes that unless toleration was granted to the French Catholic missionaries Egypt might interfere on their behalf. This interference in Ethiopian affairs, and the Khedive's territorial pretensions in northern Ethiopia no, led to further deterioration in Ethiopian-Egyptian relations. Pleased with Munzinger's suggestions, the Khedive ordered him to occupy Bogos. Commanding a thousand wellarmed Egyptian soldiers Munzinger occupied Bogos, fortified its capital Keren and turned his attention towards Hamassen, the district bordering Adwa.[14]

The Egyptians had chosen a good time to invade Ethiopia. Yohannes had been on the throne for only six months and had not yet subjugated Menelek of Shoa and Ras Adal of Gojjam. Nor was Dejaz Warenna, the commander of the former Emperor Takla Giorgis, fully reconciled to Yohannes though he had been made governor of Begember and the adjacent territories. Even in Tigre and its vicinity local chiefs were in rebellion and the political situation across Takaze was confusing.[15] At the time of the Egyptian aggression Yohannes was in Wollo suppressing the rebellion of Ijebu Gallas which had reportedly been provoked by Munzinger.[16] On learning of the Egyptian occupation of Bogos, Yohannes moved north with 15,000 soldiers with the intention of "meeting force with force" and driving the invaders out, but gave up the idea on the advice of his chiefs.[17] It was too risky to become involved in a war with an outside power when his own hold on the empire was precarious. After stationing his soldiers all across the northern frontier Yohannes wrote to Khedive Ismial demanding immediate withdrawal of the invading troops and the restitution of the occupied territories.[18] Doubtful of the outcome however, Yohannes decided to internationalize the issue by appealing for European intervention. He dispatched General Kirkham[19] an Englishman in his service on a diplomatic mission to Europe with letters to Queen Victoria, the President of France and the Emperors of Germany, Austria and Russia.[20]

The primary concerns of Yohannes were the Egyptian aggression and the Khedive's pretensions to northern Ethiopia up to the Mareb. Pointing to the grave threat posed to Ethiopian independence and Christian faith by the intimidating Egyptian troop concentration on his northern frontier, Yohannes asked the British Government to arbitrate the Ethiopia-Egyptian frontier question either singly or with other European powers.[21] He wanted a comprehensive territorial settlement with Egypt and not just the restitution of Bogos. Another pressing matter which needed British intervention was Ethiopia's trade and communication at Massawa, the *entrepot* of northern Ethiopia, where Egypt placed exorbitant duties on Ethiopian trade and obstructed external communications. Yohannes wanted Britain to help him to acquire and to develop Amphyla as an independent Ethiopia port. He offered to make it a free port and introduce "civilizing arts" into Ethiopia. Obviously he had an understanding of Britain's commitment to free trade, reform and the suppression of the slave trade. Proposing to adopt those programmes he hoped to win for himself Britain's support and sympathy at the crucial hour.[22] Yohannes wanted a *quid pro quo* from the British Government for the help given during the British expedition to Magdala. The point was not missed by the British Government. Consulted by the Foreign Office, Lord Napier of Magdala urged Granville to meditate on the border issue in favour of Ethiopia against Moslem Egypt.

Yohannes's attempts to seek European support for Ethiopia faced a barrier difficulties to cross. This was the ignorance and disinterestedness of Christian Europe in Ethiopia and its perception of Egypt as a progressive modern state, threatened by a "savage neighbour." The sauve, shrewd and Paris educated Khedive Ismail of Egypt never missed an opportunity to reinforce those perceptions on Europe and the West in general. With his grand schemes for modernizing Egypt and his lavish entertainments on the "pleasure grounds of opulent Gezeireh palace" which was "furnished and ornamented in the highest style of Parsian art and Eastern magnificence" the Khedive easily won the admiration, friendship and support of European diplomats and their governments.[23] At the same time the suggested contrast between "civilized" Egypt and its progressive ruler and "savage Abyssinnia" and its "semi-civilized ruler" was not lost on the European representatives. Most Europeans considered Ethiopia a politically divided, socially degenerate, culturally barbarous and economically backward country and dismissed its Christian faith as syncretic and hardly worth its name.[24] Even Egyptian aggression against Ethiopia could be ignored and if necessary defended. For instance Jessamund, the German Consul-General in Egypt, told Berlin that "the territories (Ethiopian) must be brought under Egyptian rule and hence exposed to European influence."[25] To penetrate through European prejudices and the Khedival propaganda and win the hoped for European support for Ethiopia was not easy. Kirkham, Yohannes's envoy, realized this soon after he arrived in Alexandria enroute to London.

So successfully had Khedive Ismail portrayed Ethiopia as the aggressor and Egypt as the aggrieved defending power, that Edward Stanton, the British Consul-General in Egypt, almost ignored Ethiopian complaints against Egyptian aggression. Accepting the Khedive's statement that Egypt had only dispatched a few battalions to defend its southern frontier against Ethiopian incursion, Stanton had not bothered to investigate the situation on the frontier independently. It was ironic that it was not he, but the British Foreign Office which first learnt of the Egyptian aggression through London newspapers.

Responding to Granville's enquiry if there was any foundation for the London newspaper's report regarding the Egyptian invasion of Ethiopia, the British Consul-General assured him confidently that he was inclined to place more confidence in the Khedive's explanation than in the highly "improbable and sensational story published by the London correspondent based on the report of a newspaper."[26]. Strongly supporting the Khedive, Stanton advised the Foreign Secretary: that "Bogos can hardly be considered as an Abyssinian territory, many years having elapsed since its first occupation by Egyptian troops since which date as far as he was aware, the district has enjoyed some sort of semi-independence, but as the frontiers of the two countries had not been strictly defined, the renewed occupation of the country by Egyptian troops may not improbably give rise to serious complications between Egypt and Abyssinia".[27]

Stanton could not admit to himself that Bogos was an Ethiopian territory, that Ethiopia had never recognized the Egyptian pretentions to it and that Egypt had neither effectively occupied nor administered it until the aggression of 1872. He knew that Ethiopia had been collecting taxes from Bogos though he choose to describe tax collections as "incursions." Many contemporary witnesses like Mc Dye and authoritative writers like Douin regarded Bogos as Ethiopian territory.[28] As far as the British Consul-General was concerned Egypt had not aggressed upon Ethiopia; she had merely reoccupied the territory which was her own and Ethiopia had no reason to complain.

Disinclined to be drawn into Ethiopian affairs and influenced by its Consul-General's pro-Egyptian reporting, the British Government was lukewarm to Yohannes's diplomatic mission. Kirkham could not cut through the prevailing prejudices against Ethiopia nor could he, with his poor social background, commend himself to aristoctaric Granville who did not receive him at the Foreign Office. Handing over Yohannes's communications to the Queen and the British Government along with his memorandum on the objective of the mission to the British Foreign Office, Kirkham moved to other European Chancelleries to appraise their governments of the Egyptian aggression.[29]

Whatever Stanton's pro-Egyptian reporting on the Ethiopia-Egyptian border issue, there were other influences on the British Foreign Office to help Ethiopia. Lord Napier of Magdala advised Granville to negotiate in the dispute "in favour of a Christian prince and people who had rendered a valuable service."[30] Notwithstanding his earlier reluctance to become involved, Granville agreed to offer mediation in the dispute and informed the Khedive of it.[31] However, considering the prevention of further Egyptian aggression upon Ethiopia was more urgent than the resolution of the border question, the British advised the Khedive of Britain's great interest in "Christians of Abyssinia" and asked him to arrange matters with her peacefully.[32]

Obviously the British advice and interference were distasteful to Khedive Ismail. The last thing he wanted was normalisation of relations with Ethiopia, when he was planning further aggression. Rejecting the British advice the Khedive argued that Ethiopia-Egypt difficulty was not just a border problem but a complex issue which should be settled bilaterally. Accusing Ethiopia of violating Egypt's frontiers and carrying away a number of Egyptian subjects and property the Khedive threatened to occupy Hamassen district of Ethiopia as a material guarantee if Yohannes failed to comply with the demands that would be made.[33]

Obviously the Khedive did not expect strong British opposition to his proceedings and in any event he was confident of support from the British Consul-General. In this he was not mistaken. Stanton writing to the Foreign Secretary said that, 'If His Highness's statement as to the origin of the existing complications can be relied he would certainly appear to be the defending and not aggressing power". He only hoped that Yohannes would be given enough time to comply with the Khedival demands before being attacked.[34] Apparently the Consul-General was working at cross purposes with his own Foreign Secretary. However his support for the Khedive came to be neutralized from unexpected quarters.

The French diplomats at Alexandria, Istanbul and Massawa had a very different view of the Khedive's intentions and warned the French Government of his territorial ambitions in Ethiopia.[35] Having learnt of Khedive Ismail's warlike preparations and the

Egyptian troop movements near the Ethiopia" frontier' and spurred by Emperor Yohannes's appeals for intervention, the French Government decided to restrain the Khedive.

Notwithstanding its displeasure with Yohannes's anti-Catholic policies the French did not wish to see Egypt rule Ethiopia. Instead of acting unilaterally the French told the British Government of their desire "to act in concert with the British Government in matters relating to Ethiopia."[36] Apparently the French believed that Joint Anglo-French pressure on the Khedive would be more effective in achieving the result than otherwise. Perhaps they also wished to commit Britain to a firm course of action in the matter. Not wanting to sacrifice their freedom of action the British rejected the French proposal; instead they suggested that both France and Britain simultaneously warn the Khedive against "the extension of Egyptian authority at the expense of Abyssinia."[37] The French concurred and warned the Khedive not to occupy the Ethiopian territory. Expressing his great disappointment at the Khedive's belligerency Granville warned him that the British Government regarded the matter seriously and "would much regret that any hostile action should be directed against Yohannes from Egypt."[38] Advising him to settle the dispute with Ethiopia peacefully "through friendly offices of an impartial power" the British Government offered to bring about the result either singly or in concert with other powers.[39] Furthermore they pressed the Sultan of Turkey to check Egypt's military build up and restrain the Khedive's aggression upon Ethiopia recommending an impartial enquiry into the matter.[40] This was as far as the British went in responding to the Ethiopian appeal for aid. No distinction was made between the aggressor and the aggressed. Egyptian aggression was not condemned; instead Yohannes was advised to keep peace with the aggressor. Arbitration was not pressed and Yohannes's request for a port was ignored.[41] However responding to the British request the Porte advised the Khedive to abstain from violence and to settle the dispute with Ethiopia peacefully.[42]

Convincing the Porte that he had undertaken military operations against Ethiopia only to defend the sublime Porte's territories and rejecting the offer of British mediation, Khedive Ismail continued his territorial acquisitions in Ethiopia. Besides imposing his rule on Hamassen he occupied Amphyla Bay frustrating Yohannes's hopes of making it an independent Ethiopian port. Imposing a strict arms emargo at Massawa, the Khedive hoped to keep Ethiopia weak. The arms embargo was so strict that even the French consul had great difficulty in getting through Massawa a few pieces of firearms sent as gift to Yohannes by the French Government.[43]

Growing tension between Ethiopia and Egypt led to serious skirmishes and bloodshed in 1873. Yohannes was much concerned that Egypt had seized not only the northern border districts and the coastal territories but also Quallabat in the west. Though armed conflict would perhaps be the quickest and effective way to force Egypt out of Ethiopia, both domestic and diplomatic considerations did not favour the approach.[44] The continuing disloyalty of provincial chiefs made it risky to engage Egypt in a war which might also forfeit him Britain's sympathies. Friendship with Britain was the foundation of Yohannes's foreign policy. Despite the want of full support from Britain, she was the only power which had some influence with Egypt and had tried to restrain her. Still optimistic of persuading Christian European powers to mediate in the Ethio-Egyptian difficulty, Yohannes appealed for their help once again. However the focus was now on the British Government.

Yohannes repeated his earlier requests to the British Government for aid and intervention. Complaining of the Khedive's new territorial aggrandisements in Ailet, Hamassein and Amphyla he emphasized that peace could not be maintained with Egypt until she vacated the aggression.[45] Reiterating the request for Amphyla port Yohannes offered to end the slave trade in the region, declare all slaves in Ethiopia free and enter into "most liberal" treaties of commerce with European powers.[46] He was trying to make himself as agreeable as possible to the reform minded Victorian aristocracy to win its support.

Unfortunately Yohannes's strategy failed to produce the desired result. Unnoticed by the Queen and ignored by

Gladstone, Yohannes's requests failed to win the Foreign Secretary's support. There were three interrelated issues to be considered: the question of the actual frontiers between Egypt and Ethiopia and the creation of an arbitration council to determine them, the Egyptian aggression; and the Ethiopian request for a seaport. Involving opposing territorial claims and sovereignties, the Ethio-Egyptian frontier had been an explosive issue since the Egyptian occupation of the Sudan in 1820. While Emperor Yohannes claimed all the coastal territory, including Massawa, to have been Ethiopian, Turkey and Egypt rejected the claims. While Turkish claims to the coastal region could be traced to the fifteenth century, Egypt had established control over the Ethiopian coast south of Massawa in the last decade. Britain had recognized Turkey's rights to the coast by seeking permission of that power to land British troops at Annesley Bay in 1868.[47] The frontier question was a thorny and complex issue.

However Granville was reluctant to interfere with the issue preferring the disputants to settle the matter bilaterally. Advising Yohannes to do so he warned him "that foreign intervention might involve him in an embarrassment... more serious than he sought to escape.[48] Nevertheless he offered British mediation to Egypt to settle the territorial dispute with Ethiopia. Distrusting Ethiopia's ability to manage an independent port Britain excused itself by pointing to the conflicting territorial sovereignties involved in the matter. The British Government was however interested in seeing Ethiopian independence preserved and further Egyptian aggressions prevented. Expressing its "lively interest it the welfare and independence of Abyssinia," the British Government advised the Khedive not to launch an aggression against that country.[49] However Egyptian aggression was not condemned and the Khedive was not pressed to hand over the occupied territory to Ethiopia. Manifold British interests in Egypt required that the Khedive be not alienated. Nevertheless the British diplomatic intervention forced Khedive Ismail to drop for a while the planned attack on Ethiopia. This allowed time for

Yohannes to consolidate his authority internally and to check Egyptian aggression when it occurred later.

Ethiopian diplomacy had failed to secure European intervention to undo the Egyptian aggression. While the British response was half-hearted and France's lukewarm those of Germany, Australia and Russia were offending. Preoccupied with the problems of the Franco-Prussian War of 1871, France did not evince much interest in the Ethiopian difficulty other than warning the Khedive against his aggression on Ethiopia and advising Yohannes to offer toleration to Catholics. Concluding that "Egypt was more significant from the view point of German economic interest than Ethiopia" Bismarck's Germany decided to ignore Ethiopia. Yohannes's letter was not answered,[50] while Austria did the same on Bismarck's advice the Russian Government also ignored Yohannes.[51] Faced with Europe's indifference and the Khedive's aggression Yohannes strove to strengthen himself as best as he could to face the situation.

Having failed to get European support to get an independent port for Ethiopia Yohannes took certain initiatives to achieve it on his own. In 1873 he appointed Kirkham as Governor of Guinda and the adjoining coastal district including Annesley Bay, Soho and the territory up to Ailet. He was instructed to open the port of Zullah to Ethiopian trade by enlisting the support, capital and enterprise of British Indian merchants and British subjects. To encourage Kirkham in this venture Yohannes conferred on him the freehold of Guinda. Kirkham at once raised the British flag at Guinda obviously to protect himself from Egyptian attack.[52] While He obtained the promise of French protection for himself and his property his efforts to get French involved in developing Zulla into a good port failed. However he was unrealistic in his expectations, since the Egyptian had already been holding Annesley Bay with a small force and Ethiopia could not keep a port without a navy of her own. In any event the Egyptian did not miss the implications of Yohannes's moves. Before the matter could advance further they occupied Guinda and hoisted the Egyptian flag.[53] The episode is only significant in so far as it confirmed Yohannes's view that Ethiopia could not have a port without the support of a friendly European power.

Domestically Yohannes followed a policy of accommodation and compromise. He achieved firm control over northern Ethiopia and in October 1874 received the submission of Ras Adal of Gondar whom he used to neutralize Menelek of Shoa who had not only avoided to submit to Yohannes but also had been in friendly communication with Khedive Ismail of Egypt. The Khedive seemed disposed to satisfy Menelek's request for arms and ammunition only if he aligned himself with Egypt in attacking Yohannes.[54] Though the intrigues failed, Menelk's dissidence inhibited Yohannes from initiating a strong policy towards Egypt to liberate the occupied territories.

Though Khedive Ismail had suspended the invasion of Ethiopia in 1872 under Anglo-French diplomatic pressure he had not abandoned his hopes for conquests in that country. While preparing militarily to invade Ethiopia, the Khedive had also been endeavouring to isolate her diplomatically. He tried to detach Britain from Ethiopia by alleging that Ethiopia had passed under French influence; that she had been receiving French firearms and was being incited into belligerency by the French Consul at Massawa; the Khedive requested Britain to appoint a consul to neutralize the French at Massawa.[55] Holding that Yohannes's belligerency had made it impossible to maintain peace on the frontier the Khedive implied that the difficulty could only be settled militarily. That the intended result was achieved is revealed by the comment of Derby, the British Foreign Secretary, "The King of Abyssinia seems likely again to embitter relations (with Egypt). The less we have (to do) with the Abyssinian Egyptian disputes and intrigues the better. Keep absolutely clear of them in future."[56]

Convined that British symnpathies for Ethiopia were muted and that the French would be unlikely to rush to her aid even were she invaded, and confident of his own strength, Khedive Ismail decided to invade Ethiopia. Under the pretext of reinforcing Massawa against the alleged threatened Ethiopian attack the Khedive dispatched supplies and soldiers to that port.[57] While Arkil Bey and Arendrup Bey were ordered to occupy northern Ethiopia up to the Mereb, Munzinger was instructed to enter Shoa and Rauf Pasha to seize the territory from Zeila to Harar. McKillop was to occupy Somali coast.[58] While Munzinger was wiped out with his expeditionary force by the Danakils, McKillop was forced to turn back under the diplomatic pressure of the Sultan of Zanzibar. Although the Egyptian troops were well armed and led by trained European and American Commanders in the service of the Khedive Ismail they were wiped out by the Patriotic and determined Ethiopian forces. Arendrup Bey and his three thousand soldiers were engaged and destroyed by Emperor Yohannes at Gundet on 16 November 1875.[59] Eighteen soldiers alone of the invading Egyptian army escaped. Arendrup and Arkil died. The Egyptian defeat was total; 2,000 to 2,500 Remington rifles and six cannon fell into the Ethiopian hands. The Ethiopians killed and wounded were only three hundred and fifty.[60] Since they did not pursue the enemy or seize Massawa the British Consul-General at Cairo concluded that the Ethiopians were unaware of the magnitude of the victory achieved. In fact they were very much aware of it and the victorious and confident Ethiopian chiefs advised Emperor Yohannes, in the War Council held at Addua Huala on 17 November 1875, to occupy Massawa. But the Emperor rejected the advice, fearing international complications.[61]

The humiliating defeat was unacceptable to Khedive Ismail who wished to restore Egypt's prestige by inflicting a crushing defeat upon Yohannes, by occupying his capital and dictating peace. Such an achievement was thought essential "to prevent calamitous political consequences (of the defeat) in the Sudan and the frontier region."[62] The Khedive decided to invade Ethiopia. Though the British Consul-General, to whom the news was conveyed, did not restrain him, the British Government expressed its displeasure to the Khedive.[63] What bothered Britain most was not Ethiopian welfare but the plight of Egyptian finances. Predictably the planned expedition would cost much and the overburdened Egyptian Treasury would find it more burdensome. Moreover it was uncertain if the Khedive would achieve a victory of the magnitude which he had been aspiring in the light of the disastrous defeat suffered by Egypt at Gundet. Even were such achieved it would be difficult for Moslem Egypt to rule Christian Ethiopia. These ambitions only aggravated Egypt's problems. Advising the Khedive to settle the matter with Ethiopia peacefully the British Government offered to assist him diplomatically.[64]

Disregarding the British advice the Khedive argued that the planned invasion of Ethiopia was an unfortunate necessity and that the restoration of Egypt's prestige was indispensable if the rest of Egypt's African empire were to be retained. While conceding that the expedition might cost half a million sterling or more he insisted that it would be a trifle compared to the value of his African dominions. Admitting the impolicy of territorial acquisition in Ethiopia, the Khedive denied any such ambition. Much as he claimed to prefer peace, he regretted he could not make advances to Emperor Yohannes who had allegedly rejected earlier Egyptian peace overtures.[65] Obviously the Khedive had set himself on the war path; obviously he was the one who had aggressed upon Ethiopian; obviously he was seeking not only victory against Ethiopia but also vengeance. Though the British Government could not have been blind to this fact it did not press him to call off the invasion. Egypt's friendship was important to Britain. Britain ignored Egypt's planned aggression; she understood Ismail's humiliation; she probably sympathised.

Diplomatically and militarily prepared, Khedive Ismail dispatched a fully equipped military expedition of 12,000 soldiers under the command of Ratib Pasha and General Loring to occupy northern Ethiopia up to the Mareb. He ordered that "the principal object was to regain in the Sudan as well as Egypt prestige lost in the last campaign. To accomplish this it would be necessary to engage the king in a battle, even to go to his capital to bring an engagement."[66] Securing communications and building forts the Egyptian army reached Gura, in northern Ethiopia, by the end of January 1876.

Aware of Egypt's aggressive proceedings and Europe's indifference Yohannes prepared to meet the challenge by calling on his people to mobilize. Considering the Egyptian invasion as an attack of Islam on the Christian faith of Ethiopia the Ethiopian Orthodox Church urged the people to respond to Yohannes's call under the threat of ex-communication. Most of Ethiopia, except Shoa, answered the call. This was the expression of Ethiopian National spirit. As the Egyptian forces moved southward Yohannes moved north towards Gura with an army of 45,000 of whom 15,000 bore firearms. The battle was joined at Gura on 18 March. Unable to withstand the determined Ethiopian attack, inspite of their superior arms and organisation, the Egyptians succumbed. Ethiopia won a brilliant victory. Of the six thousand Egyptians who joined the battle only four hundred escaped; more than a thousand five hundred were wounded and three thousand five hundred were captured or killed; others remained unaccounted for. The Ethiopians captured thirteen pieces of artillery, five thousand Remington rifles, all the small arms of those killed, wounded and imprisoned, as well as the unexpended ammunition on the field.[67] The Egyptian army was also demoralized by the Ethiopian propaganda that prophet Mohammed had laid a curse on any Moslem who attacked the god-fearing Christian Ethiopians who once gave an asylum to his Moslems followers when they were being persecuted by the rulers of Macca.[68]

The result was devastating; the immediate future was unnerving; the Egyptian forces in Ethiopia faced the possibility of annihilation at the hands of the victorious Ethiopians. Fortunately for them Yohannes did not seek vengeance. After making a military demonstration before the Egyptian held fort of Gura he moved with his army towards his capital. Whether the peace process was initiated by the defeated and nervous Egyptians or by Yohannes is controversial. However on 12 March Yohannes wrote to Prince Hassan at the Egyptian camp suggesting immediate cession of hostilities. Regretting bloodshed he offered to receive and send accredited envoys to arrange peace.[69] Responding immediately the Egyptians proposed terms for peace; they offered free trade at Massawa, a treaty of friendship and commerce between the two countries, the release of all prisoners of war and the restitution of all firearms captured by Ethiopia in the last two wars. While agreeing to release all the Egyptian war prisoners and demanding immediate Egyptian withdrawal from Ethiopia and the restitution of all occupied territories Yohannes named Lidj Marcha as his peace delegate. Accompanied by the Egyptian delegate Ali Rubi Marcha arrived at the Egyptian camp to a reception of Egyptian brass bands where he was presented with a fully caparisoned white Arab steed as an emblem of peace by prince Hassan.[70] The Egyptians were more concerned to move their soldiers and stores to the safety of Massawa without provoking an Ethiopian attack than to seek peace. To gain time, which they needed to effect this, the Egyptians dragged on the negotiations insisting that peace could not be concluded with Ethiopia unless all captured firearms were returned by her. While voluntarily releasing all the Egyptian prisoners Emperor Yohannes refused to return the firearms. After moving their soldiers and stores to safety the Egyptians dropped the demand for the restitution of firearms. Believing that peace could be concluded without further delays Yohannes sent a signed draft treaty to Ratib Pasha, the Egyptian commander. However being anxious to avenge Yohannes the Egyptians were inciting Ethiopian chiefs Wolde Michael and Menelek to rebel against Yohannes while maintaining the facade of peace negotiations. When Wolde Michael rebelled and ravaged Hamassen with Egyptian support Yohannes called off the negotiations. Meanwhile Ratib had moved to Massawa deputing Usman Pasha to continue the negotiation.[71] Distrusting the local Egyptian negotiators Yohannes sent Gebre Exiabher as his envoy to Cairo to arrange peace with Khedive Ismail directly. Still soured by the defeats, the Khedive tried to humiliate Yohannes by incarcerating his peace envoy. After several months of detention in Cairo, with the help of the British Consul-General, the Ethiopian envoy returned to Adwa. Thus ended the peace parleys exposing the Egyptian insincerity.[72]

It was ironic that Ethiopia won the war but lost peace. The victor of Gura had all cards in his hands; obviously he did not play them well. After the battle of Gura Yohannes could have had the Egyptian forces at his mercy by depriving them of supplies through interposing his victorious army by keeping the Egyptian prisoners of war in his hands until peace was concluded he could have enforced his terms on Egypt. Soon after the battle of Gura he could have taken Massawa when the Egyptians were in no position to oppose him. By doing none of these things Yohannes lost the golden opportunity to undo the Egyptian aggression and secure advantages for Ethiopia to which the victory entitled her. Perhaps there were strong reasons for Yohannes's conduct. It would have been difficult to retain his large army on the field for long, given the difficulty of provisioning since Ethiopian soldiers carried only three days rations and would have returned home thereafter with spoils of war. An attack on Massawa might have escalated the war and invited international complications, which Yohannes was most anxious to avoid. Internal needs of Ethiopia also dictated rapprochement with Egypt. The old Abuna Salaama had been dead for long and the Ichige also died after the Egyptian war. Yohannes had to have a new Ethiopian Bishop from the Orthodox Church of Alexandria as the tradition demanded and this could not be done without Egypt's co-operation. The disloyalty of Ethiopian chiefs, especially of Menelek, who had been in correspondence with the Khedive, and the desertion of northern chiefs like Wolde Michael prevented Yohannes from pursuing an offensive policy towards Egypt. Pleased to have defeated Egypt, Yohannes set out to normalize relations with her. He choose the path of peace and moderation which was in tune with his nature. His reported statement to his warlike General Alula that "My throne is only established on prayer and peace and cautious diplomacy, not on force of arms" explains his actions.[73] However after the humiliating treatment meted out to his envoy at Cairo Yohannes decided not to take further initiatives to treat with Egypt bilaterally. Neither the humbled Egypt nor its European patrons were happy with the turn of events. Ethiopia had won brilliant victories resisting both European diplomatic and Egyptian military onslaughts against her independence. There could be neither war nor peace except on Ethiopian terms. This was unacceptable to European powers and their client Egypt as it went against the political philosophy of the times. A "savage and uncivilized African state" was expected to accept European tutelage and not to challenge. They sympathised with Egypt which was progressing and modernizing under their tutelage.

REFERENCES

1. Mc Dye, *Moslem Egypt Christian Abyssinia* first published (New York 1880). Reprint Negroe University Press 1969. p. 10-15.
2. Haggai, Erlich *Ethiopia and the Challenge of Independence* (Lynn Reiner; 1984) p. 32. DOUIN, G. *Historie da Regne du Khedive Ismail* 3 Volumes (Paris; 1939) Vol. 3, pp. 301-361.
3. Rubenson, *Survival* p. 289.
4. Gebre Selassie *Yohannes IV of Ethiopia.* Oxford 1975.
5. Munzinger was both Vice-consul and Acting Consul-General of France and Britain both before and after the British expedition to Mogdala. He was also Political Advisor to Napier during the expedition to Ethiopia in 1866. He was appointed as the Egyptian Governor of Massawa on 23 April 1871.
6. Douin, G. *Op cit. Ismail* Vol. 3, p. 361.
7. *Ibid.*
8. Mc Dye, Moslem Egypt, p. 136.
9. Rubenson *Survival,* p. 282.
10. Douin, G, *Op cit.* Vol. 3, p. 361.
11. A.I.A 573, Yohannes to Queen Victoria, 12 April 1869.
12. *Ibid,* The British Foreign Office note on the above letter.
13. Douin, *Op cit.* Vol. 3, p. 361, Tesema Ta'a "Prologue to Ethio-Sudanese Frontier p. 26-30, *Kasa and Kassa.*
14. Rubenson *Survival,* p. 296.
15. Douin *Khedive Ismail* Vol. 3, p. 325.
16. A.E.C.P.C.E Masswa de Sarzac to M.A.E. 17 January 1873 cited by Zewde Gebre Selessie, *Yohannes IV* p. 48.
17. Douin, *Op Cit.* Vol. 3, p. 34.
18. Rubenson *Survival,* p. 297.
19. F.O. 141/80. Of. footnote on Kerkhem's letter.
20. F.O. 141/80. Stanton Granville 21 September 1872.
21. Mc Dye, *Moslem Egypt* p. 11. Adheme Magistrates, *Yohannes* p. 250.
22. A.B. Wylde *'83' to '87' in the Saudan,* 2 vol. First published (London; 1830 Reprint; Negroe University Press, 1969) Vol. 2, p. 326.
23. Mc Dye, *Ibid.*

24. Bairu Taffla, *Ethiopia and Germany Cultural, Political and Economic Relations* (Weisbaden; 1980) p. 80.
25. Bairu Taffla, *Op cit.* p. 78-80.
26. F.O. 141/72. Col-Stanton to Granville 9 August 1872. F.O. 1/27. Granville to Stanton 15 August 1872.
27. F.O 141/72. Stanton to Granville 10 August 1872, 12 August 1872, A.B. Wylde, *Op cit.*
28. A.B. Wylde, '83' to '87' *in the Saudan*, Vol. 2, p. 320. Douin, *Op cit.* P. 297. Mc Dye, *Op cit.* p. 124.
29. F.O. 1/27 B, statement regarding General Kerkham's Mission from the King of Ethiopia 31 October 1872, General Kerkhem to Granville 31 October 1872.
30. F.O. 1/27 B. Napier to Granville.
31. F.O. 881/2263. Granville to Col-Stanton 7 November 1872.
32. F.O. 1/27B. Granville to Stanton 28 November 1872.
33. F.O. 881/2263 Stanton to Granville 5 December 1872.
34. *Ibid.*
35. France M.A.E. The French Ambassador to Turkey to Duc De Broghe, A.E. Rurence, 3015; De Vogue to M.A.E Therapic 24 June 1873 Cited by Gebre Selassie, *Op cit.* p. 46.
36. F.O. 881/2263, The French Consul at Suez to Remsat, 19 October 1872 communicated to the Earl Granville by N. Gorord.
37. *Ibid* Lord Lyons to Granville 15 November 1872.
38. F.O. 881/2263. Lord Lyons to Granville 26 November 1872 and 5 December 1872.
39. F.O. 881/2263. Lord Lyons to Granville, December 1872.
40. F.O. 1/27B. Granville to Stanton, 18 December 1872.
41. F.O. 1/27B. Granville to Sor. H. Elliot 18 December 1872.
42. Queen Victoria to Emperor Yohannes 18 December 1872.
43. Abdine to M.A.E. 12 January 1873 cited by Gebre Selossie, *Yohannes* p. 43.
44. Gebre Selassie, Yohannes IV *Passim.*
45. F.O. 141/80. Yohannes to Granville 15 May 1873.
46. F.O. 141/80. Kerkham to Granville 15 May 1873.
47. 141/80 copy of the memorandum communicated to Nubar Pasha, in Vivian to Granville 18 October 1873.
48. Bairu Taffla *Op cit.* p. 81, Mc Dye, *Op cit.* p. 128.
49. Mc Dye *Op cit.* p. 125-127.
50. Gebre Selassie *Yohannes IV* p. 50-260.
51. *Ibid.*
52. Gebre Selassie, *Op cit.* p. 260-271 passion.
53. *Ibid* p. 55-56.
54. Mc Dye *Op cit.* p. 58, 128.

55. F.O. 403/8. Vivian to Granville, 22 September 1873 F.O. Memo 27 June 1874.
56. F.O. 881/3058 Cookson to the Earl of Derby 11 August 1875.
F.O. 881/3058. Hunter's Memorendum in Sneider to Salisbury 27 November 1875.
Mc Dye, *Moslem Egypt* p. 147.
57. F.O. 881/3058. Government of Bombay to Lord Salisbury 27 November 1875.
58. The Bombay Government estimated the number of the Ethiopian dead as 310.
59. Mc Dye *Moslem Egypt* p. 159.
60. F.O. 881/3058. Hunter to Sneider 23 December 1875.
61. Mc Dye, *Op cit.* p. 146.
62. F.O. 881/3058. Derby to Stanton 17 December 1875 and 29 December 1875.
63. Stanton to Derby, 27 November 1875 and 18 December 1875.
64. *Ibid.*
65. Mc Dye, *Op cit.* p. 395, p. 159.
Rubenson, *Op cit.* p. 329-331.
Gebre Selassie Yohannes IV, p. 61 to 63.
66. Mc Dye, *Op cit.* p. 436.
67. Gebre Seleccie, *Op cit.* p. 76.
68. McDye. *Op cit.* p. 433-446.
69. Gebre Selassie *Yohannes IV* p. 77.
Mc Dye *Op cit.* p. 438-440.
70. Bairu Taffla, *Op cit.* p. 82.
71. Rubenson *Op cit.* p. 336.
72. Hansard III Series, CXXVII.
73. Burke to Eveylyn Ashley 8 March 1877.

3

Primacy of British Interests in the Red Sea and Egypt Determines Britain's Ethiopian Policy

Ethiopia's brilliant victories on the battlefields had placed Egypt in impossible position. Seething with humiliation of the defeats Khedive Ismail refused to make peace overtures to Ethiopia.

Much as he liked he could not avenge Ethiopia militarily in the light of the military disaster. Moreover with the burden of supporting his suzerain in the Russo-Turkish war he could not indulge in further military adventures. Instead the Khedive tried to hurt Ethiopia by blocking her external communications and taxing her trade at Massawa exorbitantly. He aborted Yohannes's diplomatic mission to Europe by imprisoning and poisoning his envoy Kirkham at Massawa.[1] European travellers bound for Ethiopia were denied entry at Massawa and those who dared were caught and punished. Even nationals of friendly Britain were not excepted. Two British nationals Haughton and Barlow were arrested and treated with violence for attempting to reach Adwa disregarding Egyptian restrictions.[2] The imprisonment and "mysterious disappearance" from Cairo of Yohannes's envoy sent to treat with the Khedive became a scandal. Each of these episodes came up for discussion in the British Parliament.

It was embrassing to the British Government to defend Egyptian Government Ethiopia's brilliant victories on the battle fields had placed Egypt in impossible position. Seething with humiliation of the defeats Khedive Ismail refused to make peace overtures to Ethiopia. Much as he liked he could not avenge Ethiopia militarily in the light of the military disastes. Moreover with the burden of supporting his suzerain in the Russo-Turkish war he could not indulge in further military adventures. Instead the Khedive tried to hurt Ethiopia by blocking her external communications and taxing her trade at Massawa exhorbitantly. He aborted Yohannes's diplomatic mission to Europe by imprisoning and poisoning envoy Kirkhan at Massawa.[3] European travellers bound for Ethiopia were denied entry at Massawa and those who dared were caught and punished. Even natinoals of friendly Britain were not excepted. Twop British nationals Haugton and Barlow were arrested and treated with violence for attempting to reach Adwa disregarding Egyptian restrictions.[3] The imprisonment and "mysteriuos disappearnace" from Cairo of Yohannes's envoy sent to treat with the Khedive became a scandal. Each of these episodes came up for discussion in British parliament and it was embrassing to the British Government to defend the Egyptian government.[4]

The British were unhappy with Egypt's interference with Ethiopian commerce and communications at Massawa and warned the Khedive that the interruption of communications with Ethiopia could not be maintained indefinitely since he had not declared a war on that country formally, and advised him, "in his own interest", to conclude an agreement with Ethiopia regarding access to sea and customs and commerce.[5] When no action was forthcoming the British pressed the Khedive to send an European in his service to treat with Ethiopia.[6] Concurring reluctantly the Khedive appointed General Gordon to treat with Emperor Yohannes.

The informal Egyptian initiatives to normalize relations with Ethiopia between 1877 and 1879 were not serious attempts. Neither his dictatorial temperament nor unsympathetic disposition towards Ethiopia qualified Gordon to undertake sensitive and explosive frontier problem with Ethiopia. After arriving at Massawa in April 1877 and not finding Emperor Yohannes or his General Alula in the neighbourhood of Adwa, Gordon sent off a letter to Emperor Yohannes offering terms for peace with Egypt. These included free trade at Massawa, a limited import of firearms and ammunition for Yohannes's personal use, and a traditional frontier which left much of the occupied Ethiopian territory to Egypt. Without meeting Yohannes or discussing peace terms with him and concluding that they would be accepted Gordon hastened to assure the Khedive that the Ethiopian question was settled.[7] Though Yohannes rejected the proposals his courteous reply to the "Englishman and Christian," Gordon paved the way for further contacts. By 1879 as Ethiopian pressure on the frontier increased and Wolde Michale, the dissident Ethiopian chief in Egypt's pay submitted to Emperor Yohannes, Gordon despatched Winstanley to Adwa to conclude an agreement with Yohannes.

Arriving at Adwa in April 1879 Winstanley established good personal rapport with Yohannes but no agreement could be reached since Gordon maintained that Egypt would not return the occupied Ethiopian territories. His offer to return late Emperor Tewodros's crown to Ethiopia and allow her to appoint a consul at Massawa did not impress Yohannes.[8] Declaring that he did not want a consul at Massawa but Massawa itself, Yohannes swore to occupy the disputed territories first before treating with Egypt. While stating that he neither liked nor trusted foreigners he nevertheless expressed his warm feelings for the British. Though confident of his ability to reconquer the lost Ethiopian territories from Egypt Yohannes still hoped for a peaceful resolution of the matter through British mediation. He informed Queen Victoria: "I am able to take my country back, but I do not like to do it without asking Your Majesty's advice."[9] Britain could not ignore the situation and allow it to drift into a war though the issue was not urgent to her.

While Ethiopia was struggling to defend her territorial integrity, ignoring her appeals for aid Britain virtually acquiesced in the Egyptian aggression. Strategic and financial interests in the region dictated her to be friendly with Egypt. For instance a large amount of British capital had been invested in Egyptian railways and the Suez Canal Company. According to one estimate British financiers had provided nearly 45 per cent of all Egyptian loans. Equally important were strategical considerations. A year after the British expedition to Magdala in 1868, the Suez canal was opened connecting the Mediterranean and the Red Seas making it the most direct and shortest route to India and the East. Within a short time thereafter nearly 82 per cent of all trade passing through the Suez Canal was British.[10] As the controlling power of the Canal region Egypt became strategically and politically more important to Britain than ever before.

Besides the Suez Canal there was the question of the Egyptian role in protecting British imperial interests in the Red Sea region. In fact it can be argued that this consideration dictated Britain's Ethiopian policy from 1870 to 1890. A comprehensive view of British interests on the Somali Coast, and how Britain moved to convert Egypt, a potential rival, to a "watch dog" will help to understand British responses to Ethiopia.

Ever since the establishment of a British Naval base in Aden in 1839 Britain had come to regard the Red Sea as a "British lake" and she was opposed to the establishment of rival European bases or colonies on either side of the Red Sea shore. While not wishing to occupy or administer the coastal region herself, Britain tried to frustrate the designs of other European powers from so doing by opposing to them Turkey's prior rights. That policy succeeded only so long as other European powers were not aggressive in seeking bases in the region and Turkey remained closely tied to Britain.

In the 1870's the situation however changed drastically. Not only had France and Italy been evincing keen interest in the Red Sea region but also Egypt, hitherto unsuspected of territorial ambitions, had begun to challenge Britain by her expansion into the Somali coast. Khedive Ismail tried to establish Egyptian administration under Turkish Suzerainty in all the Red Sea ports from Suakin to Berbera as a part of his grand strategy to carve out an African Empire for himself. The first reaction of Britain to the Egyptian venture was hostile.

Two overriding British concerns in the Red Sea region were ensuring British primacy on either shore of the Red Sea and guaranteeing uninterrupted food supplies to Aden from the Somali ports. Aden was the seat of British Residency, an important naval station and "the Gateway to India." Determined to keep the Red Sea shores free from rival European influences the British Residency closely watched happenings in the region. Strategically sensitive and commercially prosperous Aden's importance had increased since 1839, especially after the opening of the Suez Canal. With a resident population of 25,000 Aden was an important refreshment and refuelling station to ships plying between Europe and the East and in 1875 alone 855 ships of several nations called on Aden, excluding those of the Royal Navy.[11]

Aden however was arid and survived on meat, cereals, fodder, ghee, coffee and other victuals imported from the Somali ports of Zeila, Bulhar and Berbera. In 1884 alone Aden's imports from Zeila and Tadjurah amounted to £=100,000 sterling while the exports were of equal value. Only thirty two miles of sea separated Aden from the port of Berbera on the opposite African coast. Keeping the Somali ports open and free for British trade and securing uninterrupted communication between those ports and Aden were important British interests. These the British had secured through the treaties concluded with the chiefs of Berbera, Tadjurah and Zeila in 1827, 1840 and 1867 respectively. The treaties had bound the Somali chiefs to keep open their ports for ships flying British flag, to receive and respect visiting British officials, to accept their advice on matters of mutual interest and to suppress the slave trade. The Somali chiefs of Tadjurah and Zeila had also been bound not to alienate their territories to any other power or to enter with them into bonds and agreements prejudicial to British interests without British consent. Supporting Somali's independence Britain informally controlled the Somali coast.[12] With East Indiaman and ships of Royal Navy patrolling the ports, with the treaties in force and Aden Residency supervising matters Britain exercised informal influence on the Somali Coast rejecting Turkish claims of suzerainty over the coast. There never was a serious challenge to her position though there were anxious moments when French men of war stowed in the Red Sea waters scouting for footholds. All this changed when the unexpected competitor, Khedive Ismail of Egypt, came to claim and possess the Somali Coast in the 1870's.

Khedive Ismail's ambition was not only to acquire mainland territories up to the Lake regions of Central Africa but also the Coastal regions from the Suez in the north to Kismayu on the Indian Ocean in the south. The Khedive had acquired in 1867, through a *firman* from the Porte, Red Sea ports of Suakin and Massawa with their dependencies. Soon after the opening of the Suez Canal, appreciating the strategic significance of the region, the Khedive decided to occupy the Somali Coast claiming it as a part of the territorial grant made by the Porte.[13] The Khedive's effective occupation of the Somali ports was indeed thorough.

Appointing an Egyptian Governor for his coastal territories Ismail instructed him to occupy and administer the new region effectively. Commanding Egyptian warships Djemil Bey and later Radhwan Pasha landed soldiers and guns at Berbera, Zeila, Bulhar and Tadjura imposed Egyptian authority on the Somali chiefs through threats, intimidation, persuasion and money grants. It was not just a military occupation. With his characteristic thoroughness the Khedive established peace and order, opened trade routes into the interior, built aqueducts, laid water pipes, constructed piers and encouraged merchants to move into Berbera to settle and trade under Egyptian protection.[14] Within a short span of three years from 1870 the effective Egyptian occupation of the Somali coast was a *fait accompli*. Legitimacy of the Khedival right to the territory was doubtful and contestable; but the reality of effective occupation was visible and undeniable.

The first official communication from the Egyptian Government of its rights to the Somali coast based on the *porte's firman* of 1867, and its rejection of British claims to the Somali coast based on British treaties with the Somali chiefs reached the British foreign office through its Consul-General in Cairo in June 1870. The British reaction to the Egyptian occupation of the Somali coast was hostile though the views of the India Office and the foreign office differed on how Egypt was to be neutralized to protect British interests in the region. The British Residency at Aden and the Governor-General of India feared that the Egyptian occupation of the Somali coast would weaken the loyalty of its chiefs to Britain, interrupt free trade between the Somali coast and Aden and endanger Aden's security[15]. They advised the British Government to end the Egyptian occupation of the Somali coast at once and maintain the *status quo*.[16] When formal protests to Cairo was seen to be ineffective, the British Resident of Aden requested the Governor-General of India to send a warship to the Somali port of Berbera to drive Egypt from the port[17]. With the intention of avoiding diplomatic complications with Egypt and Turkey though the Governor-General of India refused to despatch a warship he advised Duke of Argyle, the Secretary of State for India, to act expeditiously to check Egypt.[18]

The British foreign office viewed the situation differently. While the Indian Government and the India office saw the issue "locally". The Foreign Secretary considered the issue diplomatically and legally in a larger context. Duke of Malmesbury, the Foreign Secretary Wryly commented "It may be convenient to Aden that Turks should not hold sway over Berbera but it would be scarcely the ground for disrupting their rights to do so."[19] It was not a matter of gunboat diplomacy. Moreover both Egypt and Turkey were Britain's friends and had roles to play in Britain's imperial strategy. The matter had to be considered in the context of Turco-Egyptian claims to sovereignty over the region.[20] At the same time the British diplomats in Turkey and Egypt who perceived greater threats to British interests in the Red Sea region from European rivals than from Egypt and Turkey urged the British Government to conclude a friendly settlement with the latter. Elliot, favoured the recognition of the Turco-Egyptian rights to the whole of the Red Sea region and the gulf of Aden. A dynamic and friendly Egypt might be even very friendly to Britain in preempting the possible occupation of the region by France and Italy.[21] Though Britain had consistently rejected

Turkish sovereignty over the Somali coast maintaining that the chiefs of Berbara, Bulhar and Tadjurah were independent, in fact they were tributaries of the pashallic of Jeddah over which Turkish suzerainty could not be disputed. Britain's treaties with those Somali chiefs supporting British interests like non-alienation of their territories without prior British consent could not be legitimate given the prior sovereign rights of Turkey. The very basis of Britain's informal control over the Somali coast had been shaken by the Egyptian intervention. More important, in any event, the Somali chiefs like those of Bulhar and Berbera had passed order Egypt's *defacto* rule and were no longer free to enforce their treaties with Britain. Egypt would not withdraw from the Somali coast unless forced out militarily. The Foreign Secretary ruled out this option given Britain's diplomatic and strategic needs for friendly relations with Egypt. It was essential to reach an agreement with her regarding their territorial claims, free trade, Britain rights to maintain consulate in the Somali ports and suppression of the slave trade. Even the usually anti-Egyptian British Resident of Aden and the Government of India thought it prudent to recognize Egyptian territorial rights to the Somali coast up to cape Guardafui; an important consideration behind this move was to prevent the possible occupation of ports of the Somali coast by France and Italy "There was less likelihood of those powers obtaining a footing under Egyptian rule than while it was under a number of 'barbarous' tribes."[22] The British Government offered to recognize the Khedive's rights to the Somali coast up to cape Guardafui if he agreed to make all Somali ports free, accepted a British Consul at Berbera with freedom to interact with Somali chiefs, suppressed the slave trade and agreed not to alienate the recognized territories without Britain's consent. Lord Salisbury considered the last provision was of great importance for retaining "permanently" British influence on the Somali coast.[23] The Khedive however refused to sign the convent unless Britain agreed to recognize Egyptian territorial rights to the coastal region up to Kismayu.[24] This the British Government refused. The Khedive complained that he saw no reason to sign a convention at all with Britain without any corresponding advantage to Egypt.[25]

Infuriated with the Khedive's pressure tactics the British Government warned him that if he continued with his reluctance to accept the proposed Anglo-Egyptian convention Britain would not recognize his rights to the Somali Coast by a diplomatic instrument and keep to itself the right of dealing with the Somali chiefs independently.[26] Shocked by the strong British reaction and realizing the importance of British support to protect his Red Sea Somali coast position from possible French and Italian incursions the Khedive agreed to sign the convention with Britain in September 1874.[27]

In the Somali Coast Convention which was signed on 7 September 1874 the British Government recognized Khedival jurisdiction over the Somali coast up to Ras Haufun, under the suzerainty of the Sultan of Turkey. The Khedive undertook not to alienate any territory under his jurisdiction and recognized Britain's right to appoint consular agents in all Somali ports with the usual privileges, exemptions and immunities; he agreed to declare Berbera and Bulhar as free ports and not to levy more than 5 per cent duty on imports in other ports. Undertaking to suppress the slave trade in the territories under his jurisdiction he conferred on the British the rights of search, interception and trials on all ships carrying or suspected of carrying slaves in the region. The agreement was to become fully operational soon after formal assent of the Sultan of Turkey was received.[28]

Without any cost to herself Britain had ensured the continuation of her informal influence in the Somali Coast and blocked the establishment of rival European bases in the region and also had buttressed anti-slavery operations in the Red Sea region. As British opposition to the Egyptian occupation of the Red Sea region disappeared and Egypt came to be seen as British policeman in the region, British policy towards Ethiopia tilted in Egypt's favour. A rival and competitor on the Somali coast, Egypt, had been converted into Britain's watch-dog and partner. To keep that power satisfied was an important British interest. Naturally Ethiopia's complaints against that power could not be supported.

While British policy towards Ethiopia until 1880 was influenced by the concern to keep Egypt in good humour thereafter it became highly responsive to the changing fortunes of that client state. So long as Egypt was strong enough to pursue its imperial ambitions and act as Britain's watch-dog in the Red Sea region Britain refused to intervene in the conflict between Ethiopia and Egypt ignoring the justness of Ethiopian cause and Yohannes's appeals. However with the breakdown of Egyptian finances and the creation of the Commission of Public Debt in 1876 Britain became increasingly concerned about the disastrous financial consequences to her client state of another war with Ethiopia. Egyptian collapse would surely hurt British interest as Wylde, the British Consul at Jeddha pointed to Salisbury, it was a British interest to prevent hostilities between Egypt and Abyssinia because the war could only tend to impoverish Egypt and would end in further disaster to her arms; and in a country where so many British interests were at stake disaster to Egypt must mean difficulties to Britain.[29]

In fact a military confrontation between the two states did not appear remote as a strenghtened Ethiopia began to demonstrate her military might on the Egypt-Ethiopia border. Commanding a large Ethiopian army of 30,000 soldiers Ras Alula had overrun and collected taxes from Bogos, Marya and Mensa regions without facing Egyptian resistance and had threatened to seize Massawa.[30] As Gordon warned the Khedive Ethiopia was in a position to take Bogos whenever she decided and she could not be stopped by Egypt given her military and financial weakness. The retrenchment in the Sudan army and the rebellion in the Sudan had so wakened Egypt that war with Ethiopia could only bring her "disaster".[31] Weak as Egypt was she might be drawn into a war with Ethiopia; border skirmishes might degenerate into a war. In the circumstance Britain felt impelled to act to protect Anglo-Egyptian interests. Giving up her disengagement policy she chose to be an interventionist. The first step was to prevent a possible war; besides warning Emperor Yohannes that "she would view with extreme concern" any act which might provoke a frontier war with

Egypt, Britain advised the Khedive "to end the existing state of war with Abyssinia" and to send an European envoy to treat with her.[32]

The British intervention was timely. Cairo was willing to listen. The deposition of Khedive Ismail, the architect of aggression upon Ethiopia, had removed the psychological barrier for normalizing relations with Ethiopia. With a worsening revolt in the Sudan peace was a military necessity to Egypt. Aware of this Tewfik Pasha, the new Khedive, decided to treat with Ethiopia and commissioned General Gordon to conduct a mission to Ethiopia.

In spite of Tewfik's expressed wish for peace with Ethiopia and his courteous letter to its Emperor the Gordon mission was doomed to failure. The peace terms offered by Tewfik belied his assurance to Britain of giving "satisfaction to just claims of Abyssinia." Britain had warned him of the "impossibility" of establishing friendly relations with Ethiopia unless better communication facilities were offered to her at Massawa.[33] Ignoring the advice the Khedive proposed limited importation of arms for personal use of Yohannes, facility for the passage of Abuna and fair trade at Massawa. He made no mention of retrocession of the occupied Ethiopian territories which was the bone of contention. Yohannes was annoyed as well as offended. No agreement could be reached.

Disappointing as Tewfik's terms were insufferable was his envoy. Gordon was unsuited for peace making. Arrogant and domineering he ignored Ethiopian nuances and sensitivities. He knew perfectly that the Egyptian proposals were inadequate and would be rejected by Ethiopia. As he put it in common parlance "King John wanted twenty shillings for his pound" and the Khedive was short changing. But Gordon could have produced better results by capitalising what he had and which Yohannes appreciated much; his English nationality and Christian faith; with shocking shortsightedness which he mistook for frankness Gordon threw away the personal advantage he had as a peace envoy. By insisting from the start that he be considered first and foremost an Egyptian and a Moslem rather than an Englishman and Christian Gordon antagonized Yohannes; his intemperate language ruined whatever slim chance of success the mission had. Recounting the ferocity of Gordon's speech Yohannes wrote to Queen Victoria, "The ambassador said to me a speech which never was never was!"[34] Furious with Egypt and annoyed with Gordon Yohannes upstaged his demand. Declaring that no peace could be concluded unless Egypt returned Bogos, Gallabat, the Red Sea ports of Massawa Zula and a war indemnity of a million sterling he dismissed the Gordon mission. Closing the door against bilateral negotiations with Egypt Yohannes wrote to Tewfik curtly: "Your father made a clandestine war with me; you want to make a clandestine peace with me; I cannot allow that; if peace is made between us it must be witnessed by eight kings."[35] Egypt lost another opportunity to make peace with Ethiopia. Tewfik had shown himself a shortsighted ruler.

After the failure of the Gordon mission Emperor Yohannes renewed his diplomatic efforts to secure European intervention to resolve the Egyptian difficulty. Notwithstanding his awareness of Egypt's weakness and his military strength Yohannes did not use force to reoccupy the territories seized by Egypt. As one who regarded himself as a responsible member of community of Christian rulers he thought it indispensable to have the sanction of European Christian monarchs for any proceedings against Egypt. Preferably he wanted an European solution to his difficulty. Certainly he wanted a European guarantee for any agreement with Egypt as he had lost faith in her in the light of his experience with the Khedive and the failed peace missions. He wrote to Emperor Wilhelm of Germany that he wanted an agreement concluded with Egypt "with the full knowledge of European powers."[36]

Equally pressing on Yohannes was the need of an independent sea port for Ethiopia. His appeals to Britain and France to help him procure one having failed he hoped to achieve this through German intervention. He appealed to Emperor Wilhelm to help him procure Zulla or Annesley Bey. Explaining the difficulties with Egypt and the failure of the Gordon mission he also solicited Germany to mediate in the frontier question with Egypt. The German Emperor's reply, sent with Gerhard Rholfs in 1881, though evasive in most respects was appreciative of the Ethiopian need for a sea port. Though German mediation was not offered to resolve the territorial dispute with Egypt the contrary impression seems to have been made on Yohannes either by Rholfs himself or by the Ethiopian translators of Wilhelm's letter.[37] Sincerely believing that Germany would mediate Emperor Yohannes authorized Gerhard Rholfs to negotiate an agreement for Ethiopia with Egypt. After appraising the German Emperor of the former limits of the Ethiopian Empire and reiterating the request for a sea port he requested him to permit Rholfs to undertake the mission for Ethiopia. Likewise he appealed to Bismarck.[38]

Inspite of his apathy for Ethiopia Bismarck would appear to have initially favoured Rholf's proposed mission to Cairo. Informing the British Government of the Ethiopian Emperor's request for mediation he sought Britain's reaction to the proposed mission of Rholfs.

Expressing Germany's goodwill for Britain Bismarck assured Granville of his "desire" to act "in a most agreeable manner". He also conveyed Yohannes's strong desire to acquire and develop Amphyla port with the assistance of the British. Speaking at length Munster, the German Ambassador, emphasized that this was a matter in which Germany had no ulterior motives except promoting peace and that Bismarck would not approve any measure disagreeable to the British government.[39]

British response to Rholf's mission was actually determined by Edward Malet, the British Consul-General at Cairo. Consulted by Granville the anti-Ethiopian Malet, strong defender of Egypt, feared that Ethiopia would use the port to acquire firearms and its "semi-savage" emperor might appear at Cairo leading an army with the help of "low class European adventurers" and destroy Egypt. Fearing that "The Egyptians could not stand before the Abyssinians," he advised against Ethiopia being given a sea port. He suggested that Rholfs might be asked to arrange peace between Egypt and Ethiopia providing for free commercial intercourse between them and the restitution of some of the Egyptian occupied territories to Ethiopia.[40] Agreeing Granville communicated this view to Berlin emphasizing that "peaceful development of Abyssinia would be ensured if she did not have a port."[41] The myopia of British diplomats and British Government defied reason and ignored reality of the situation. Disregarding the fact that Egypt was the aggressor and that it was Ethiopia which had been acting with great restraint by not using force to recover her territories Britain saw Ethiopia as a threat to Egypt. Britain was determined, no less than Egypt, to keep Ethiopia weak. Surprisingly there was no further move by Berlin. Bismarck would appear to have lost interest in the matter. Neither was Rholfs authorized to negotiate for Ethiopia nor was a reply sent to Emperor Yohannes. Yohannes was disappointed by Emperor Wilhelm whom he had complemented as a person of "Clear conscience and enlightened mind."[42]

Though Rholf's mission did not materialize, Britain could not fail to see that Emperor Yohannes was becoming disillusioned with her and would use any other interested European power to resolve the frontier problem with Egypt. In fact Yohannes had complained to the French Consul at Massawa that Britain had "taken him up and dropped down." It was not in British interest to see him pass under rival European influence and the British Vice-Consul at Jeddha had warned his Government "not to let cards fall into other hands."[43]

Apart from diplomatic considerations the financial burden of the dispute with Ethiopia on Egypt was causing concern to the British. Ethiopia's increasing military strength and military movements in the disputed frontier regions was forcing the Egyptian Government to spend more money in strengthening her own border defences. As Egypt edged towards financial bankruptcy the cost of running feud with Ethiopia was becoming unbearable. For instance in October 1880 agitated by Ethiopian troop movement in the neighbourhood of Massawa Cairo despatched two additional Egyptian battalions to defend that port from the suspected Ethiopian attack.[44] The request for supplementary charge to defray the expenses induced Auckland Collins, the worried Auditor-General of Egypt, to enquire whether it would not be desirable for Egypt to give up the whole of the Red Sea coast and end the feud with Ethiopia which was draining the Egyptian Treasury. In addition to the normal budgeted defence expenditure on Massawa and Harar, in 1880 alone, Egypt had spent an additional sum of £51,000 sterling in sending four more batallions to Massawa's defence and £33,000 sterling on Harar. The planned increase in Massawa's defence in 1881 would cost an additional sum of £22,000 sterling. The total amount of £106,000 sterling, "outside the normal budget of Egyptian expenditure as presented and accepted by the Commission of Liquidation", was a serious matter. Given the financial drain the question, was it "imperatively necessary to retain its possession at Massawa and Harar country"?[45].The Auditor-General could not help pointing "the grave danger to Egypt in continuing in remote districts of Africa a policy which opens out an unlimited horizon of military and political complications." He recommended the abandonment of even Zeila and Berbera ports.[46]

Auckland Collin's suggestion was indeed most sensible and it would be implemented five years later. But in 1880 the advice looked preposterous to strategically oriented British policy makers. First priority was Britain's imperial interest; then only Egypt's financial health. The British Consul-General was more concerned with the fate of the abandoned territory, if Egypt were prevailed to act on Collin's suggestion, than with the health of Egyptian finances. Fearing that Ethiopia would occupy Massawa and other Somali ports and imperil the security of both Egypt and Britain he shunned the suggestion.[47] Concluding that British interests would be gravely affected if Egypt abandoned the territories, the British Government advised Collin's not to revive the question.[48] Nevertheless it was obvious that the state of war between Egypt and Ethiopia must be ended to save Egypt. A more effective British intervention would be required to achieve that.

Inspite of the pressing need for peace with Ethiopia the explosive political development in Egypt during the next two years forced the issue to the background. The collapse of the Anglo-French dual control, the seizure of political power by Arabi Pasha, his overthrow and the British occupation of Egypt in 1882 followed in quick succession. Even before Britain could settle down to establish law and order in Egypt she had to turn her attention to the deteriorating political situation in the Sudan which was slipping away from the Egyptian control.

Speraheading the Sudan revolt and declaring himself al-Mahdi Muhammed Ibn Abdullah inflicted humiliating defeats on the Egypt army at Gedir in July 1882 and at El-Obeid in November 1883. While an Egyptian force of 10,000 under General Hicks was destroyed by the Mahdists on 5 November another Egyptian force was annihilated by Usman Digna the same month at Taka in the eastern Sudan. From west and east disaster overwhelmed Egyptian arms simultaneously. In fact Egypt lost effective control over much of the Sudan. It was this military rout of the client Egypt which impelled the British protector to open negotiations with Ethiopia to salvage her client's interests.[49]

One of the pressing matters which Britain faced was how to rescue the besiezed Egyptian garrisons from their isolated positions in Kassala, Keren and Bogos in the Sudan. Caught between a fanatical Mahdi and enemical Ethiopia they could not withdraw. There was a distinct possibility of their annihilation at the hands of the Mahdi unless moved to safety with Ethiopian co-operation. This could not be done unless a friendly settlement was concluded with Ethiopia. An equally compelling necessity for concluding peace with Ethiopia had arisen from Egypt's military vulnerability. Even before the Sudan revolt Egypt did not have adequate forces to defend her southern frontier. Retrenchments forced by budget cuts had slimmed Egyptian army to 18,000 soldiers. As early as 1879 Grodon, the Governor-General of the Sudan, had warned the Khedive that he could not resist an attack by Ethiopia. Moreover during the Mahdists attacks some Egyptian soldiers had been moved from the southern frontier to El-Obeid and Khartoum leaving Egypt's border with Ethiopia more vulnerable than ever.[50] Egypt feared that Ethiopia might take advantage of the difficulty in the Sudan to attack her.

Compelled by political and military necessities the Egyptian Government requested Britain to help arrange peace with Ethiopia.[51] Britain consented.

Naming Rear Admiral Hewett, Commander of the British Fleet at the Red Sea, as Head of the British Mission to negotiate with Emperor Yohannes the British Government advised Egypt to offer terms "likely to satisfy Abyssinia". While agreeing to return Bogos, which had been the bone of contention, and offering light duties on Ethiopian trade at Massawa Egypt refused either to cede a port to Ethiopia or lift the arms Embargo.[52] This was bound to raise difficulties as Yohannes had been demanding either a port or strip of coastal territory for Ethiopia. Yohannes was genuinely interested in promoting Ethiopians trade with outside world. He wanted to open roads, develop commerce and enrich his country. He was keen on sending embassies to Europe to express his friendship to "foreigners" and seek "higher civilisation".[53] Egyptians had been frustrating Yohannes by taxing Ethiopian goods at Massawa exorbitantly, attacking Ethiopian trade caravans in the coastal region and, pillaging the goods for which reparation was denied. They were even stopping Yohannes's letters and presents to Europe. As the British Vice-Consul to Jeddha Wylde observed, anything more insane or childish than the behaviour of the Egyptian officials could not be imagined and yet all blame was thrown on King John.[54] Emperor Yohannes had high expectation that the British would free Ethiopian trade and communication from the Egyptian clutches by complying with his request for a free port. The British occupation of Egypt had raised his hopes for its realization and he had specifically requested Queen Victoria: "Ismail Pasha had wronged me... Now that Moslem Kingdom has perished and is in Christian hands I request that you will arrange that my land may be restored to me. My wish is... the frontier I require may be sufficient for articles to pass through".[55]

Britain's Influential Policy advisers supported Ethiopia's request for a sea port. Lord Napaier urged on Granville that the transfer of Massawa to Ethiopia would be the "just solution." If this could not be done she might at least be given a coastal strip where a new port might be established. Consul Baker shared the view qualifying however that such a port should be British protected.[56] The anti-Slavery Society, some British Newspapers and even the anti-Ethiopian Gordon urged the British Government to seize the opportunity to give Ethiopia a sea port.[57] Going further, Evelyn Baring recommended that in the event of Egypt's relinquishment of the Sudan "the best policy would be to give Abyssinia not only Massawa but also as much territory inland as King John could govern thus establishing a Christian and anti-slavery power to act as a counter-weight against the Mahdi.[58] Combining "real-Politik" and justice this was the best suggestion that the Foreign Office received and could easily have been implemetred. But the suggestion had bitter influential critics. For instance that pro-Egyptian Edward Malet had been urging Granville that independent sea port for Ethiopia would udermine Egyptian interests and should not be advocated unless British policy of protection towards Egypt changed into one of hostility. Lord Granville was more inclined to the view of Malet than Baring.[59]

Determined to keep her land-locked and dependent Egypt too strongly opposed a sea port for Ethiopia lamely arguing that the coastal territory, which was under Turkey's suzerainty, could not be alienated. Britain was unconvinced. If Egypt could give some inland territory to Ethiopia without Turkey's consent she could as well cede her some coastal territory also. However all these arguments were facetious. Britain was occupying Egypt and it was in her power to do what she pleased. A Foreign Office official said as much bluntly that "It remains for HMG to determine what they will allow King John to have as the sea coast is being protected by us."[60] Granville knew this; the Khedive knew this; Ethiopia knew this; However the British Government did not favour giving a sea port to Ethiopia doubting her ability to manage one and suspecting that it would eventually pass into the hands of a rival European power. Ironically it was destined to fall into the hands of an

European power, not preferably agreeable, causing endless problems to Britain in her relations with Ethiopia.

However the pressure was increasing for the safe withdrawal of the besiezed Egyptian garrisons from the Sudan. "If the Khartoum garrison should return by way of Kassala and Massawa the friendship of Abyssinia would be essential."[61] To secure this Britain would make minimum concessions to Ethiopia and not what was "justifiable." She was no more generous to Ethiopia than Egypt. The British Government instructed Hewett to conclude an agreement with Ethiopia by offering her Bogos, free trade at Massawa and safe passage to Abuna in return for her undertaking to effect safe withdrawal of the Egyptian garrison from the Sudan.[62] As the terms fell far short of Yohannes's expectation, worried about the success of the mission Hewett requested a better offer. Seizing the opportunity Baring advised the Foreign Secretary to give a strip of the coastal territory to Ethiopia.[63] Rejecting the suggestion Granville advised that if "absolutely necessary" a little more inland territory, for instance Quallabat, might be given to Ethiopia. She could also be offered free transit through Massawa of all goods including arms "under British protection".[64] However a sea port was denied; another opportunity was thrown away to right the wrong.

Accompanied by Mason Bay, the Egyptian delegate, and other members of the mission Hewett reached Asmara in northern Ethiopia to a warm welcome by Ras Alula, the Governor of Tige and confidant of Emperor Yohannes. Even the hostile Egyptian envoy told the Khedive that "the reception was most cordial and magnificent.[65] After substantive discussions with Alula on terms of the proposed treaty the mission met Emperor Yohannes at Adwa. The Emperor accepted the terms proposed by the British with some reservations. While pleased with the restitution of Bogos Yohannes demanded Kassala as well. On being told that it was not included in the concession he expressed his determination to take it if it fell into the hands of the Mahdists. Obviously he hoped that Britain would not oppose. Though he demanded some coastal territory, unfortunately, he did not exert enough pressure on the British to make the concession. Had he done he could surely have got it as the British could not have risked a break-down of the negotiations by rejecting the demand. The British had anticipated the demand. Forseeing the situation a Foreign Office official had minuted, "If he presses for a sea port give him one—Anfila." However Hewett persuaded Yohannes to withdraw the demand arguing that since the British would guarantee Ethiopia unhampered communications and free importation of goods including arms at Massawa and also share with him the port revenues he should not burden himself with the problem of managing a port. Hewett warned that "he would not be a gainer by having ports of his own". Yohannes agreed hoping credulously that "all would be well under British protection." He undertook to evacuate the Egyptian troops from the Sudan.[66]

The Hewett Treaty which was signed on 3 June 1884 consisted of seven articles. Article I promised Ethiopia free transit at Massawa, under British protection, for all Ethiopian goods including arms. Article II restored Bogos to Ethiopia. In Article III Yohannes undertook to evacuate the Egyptian troops from Kassala, Amadid and Senheit. In Article IV Egypt bound itself to facilitate the passage of the Abuna from Egypt to Ethiopia. In Article V Egypt and Ethiopia agreed to mutual extradition of criminals. Article VI bound Ethiopia to refer to the British Government all differences with Egypt arising out of the Hewett Treaty.[67] By signing the Hewett Treaty Yohannes exchanged a weak enemy Egypt for two strong ones; Italy and the Mehdit Sudan. Britian made use of Yohannes as long as he was of some service to her and let him down to the mercy of Italy which she installed in Massaswa and allowed her to break all promise made to him in the treaty. The Hewett Mission returned to the coast soon afterwards and Captain Speedy was appointed as British representative at Massawa to supervise the execution of the treaty and oversea the evacuation of the Egyptian garrisons from the Sudan.

The Hewett Treaty ended the longstanding dispute between Ethiopia and Egypt. Not only had Ethiopia acquired some of the Egyptian conquered territory but also forced that power to recognize Ethiopian rights to free communication and arms import. However Ethiopia's victory was only partial. Britain had seen to it that the paper guarantees given to Ethiopia regarding arms import at Massawa could only have substance if she willed it. In fact Britain had managed through the Hewett Treaty to acquire control over Ethiopia's trade and communication. She had replaced Egypt.

Seeing the Hewett Treaty in a historical context one is inclined to conclude that Ethiopia ended up accepting much less than she was entitled to by her misplaced confidence in Britain. The curious behaviour of the Ethiopian Government during these crucial events can hardly pass unnoticed. What must be considered is the lack of Emperor Yohannes's action during a period when it became obvious that Egyptian hegemony was collapsing in the Sudan along the Red Sea and indeed in the homeland itself. No other power, not even Britain, was in such a favourable position to take advantage of new international circumstances as Ethiopia. Only four years earlier, in 1875-76, Ethiopia had demonstrated her military superiority over and invading Egyptian army. Thus Ethiopian inaction can hardly be described as military inadequacy or inability. Egyptian forces had been reduced in the southern frontier while those along the Red Sea had been cut off by the success of the Mahdist forces in the Sudan. No support could be expected from Cairo which was in a turmoil. The sudden British concern for Ethiopia arose simply because they took for granted that Emperor Yohannes would move to rectify the frontier and seize the Red Sea ports which he had claimed he wanted since first coming to power. Yet the Emperor allowed the critical months to pass, allowed the British install themselves in Egypt, allowed the international situation to stabilize and then wrote to Queen Victoria that his historic lands and sea port be handed over to him.

It has often been noticed that Ethiopia continued to see international diplomacy through the eyes of the Crusaders where Christian powers naturally stood together against Moslems. In the years 1875-1883 Ethiopian diplomacy seems to suggest that the Emperor looked upon Britain as the New

Rome or New Byzantium. The changes in the international order must of necessity have her approval; or that Ethiopia and other European nations were subject to Pax Britaanica. Yohannes was firm in demanding the return of his historic lands and the right of passage which Egypt had seized thereby violating the Pax of the New Byzantium. But he was less insistent on a sea port which he seemed to see as a change in the international pax. For that he must beg. Many British policy makers assumed that given the balance of power which had tilted far so much in Ethiopia's favour the Emperor would tolerate nothing else. The Egyptians understood better. They recommended returning Bogos, limited import of arms and the passage of the Abuna. The British doubted that this would be enough, but the Egyptian were correct in their assessment. If the phrase "historic lands" was stretched far enough it would include the Red Sea coast. However Ethiopia seemed to accept the changing populations and circumstances of the coast and did not look upon the coast as being within the country's 'historic right', though she consistently demanded a sea port which was indispensable to her. For more than half a millennium at least the historic lands involved the interior mountainous stronghold. Consequently the twin concepts of a stronghold to be vigorously defended and Britain, the New Byzantium, who must approve and even facilitate any changes in historic boundaries guided Yohannes in his approach to international relations. Seen in the light Hewett Treaty was satisfactory to Yohannes. He did not want to dare Britain asking more. What probably meant most to Ethiopia was that the treaty was a climax of series of momentous events which signalled the collapse of Egypt, the most dynamic of Moslem powers. Christendon had triumphed. Ethiopia was pleased.

REFERENCES

India Office Records Aden,

1. A.I.A/725, Taazer to Sneider, in Sneider, to the Resident of Aden, 1 March 1876.

2. F.O. 403/8. Vivian to Derby March 1876.
3. F.O. 403/8. Vivian to Derby 8 March 1876.
4. Hansard 3rd Series, Vol. CCXXXII, Evelyn Ashle to Forster 15 March 1876, Drummond Wolff to the Minister in British House of Commons. Hansard 3rd Series, Vol CCLXVI, 17 July 1876 Bourke to Wolff 17 July 1876.
5. F.O. 403/B. Vivian to Derby 18 December 1876.
6. F.O. 403/B. Vivian to Derby March 1877.
7. Anthony Nutting, *Cordon Martyr and Misfit* (London 1966) pp. 137; 168-169.
8. Winstanley, *A Visit to Abyssinia* (London; 1881) Reprint, (Negroe University Press; New York) pp. 242-244.
9. Gebreselassie, *Yohannes IV* of Ethiopia (Oxford; 1975) p. 111.
10. Keith Wilson (ed.) *Imperialism and Nationalism on the Middle East* (London 1985) p. XI.
    Ronald Robinson and John Gallagher with Alice Denry *Africa and the Victorians* (London 1986) pp. 85-109.
11. F.O. 403/8. Brigadier Sneider to Stanton 18 March 1875.
12. F.O 403/8. Russell to Djemali Bey 17 April 1870 incl. 4 in Stanton to Clarendon 3 June 1870 Aitcheson to Gonne 8 June 1870 also incl. 1 in No. 33 Hamilton to Tenteraden 7 August 1979.
13. *Ibid.*
14. F.O. 403/8. Sneider to Stanton 22 February 1870, incl. in Stanton to Derby March 1875; incl. 18 in the Resident at Aden to the Governor-General of India 4 March 1870.
    Sneider to Gonne, 2 September 1973 in Grant Duff to Duke of Argyll 8 October 1873; Capt. Hunter to Sneider 9 October 1873; Frideaux to Sneider 1873.
15. F.O. 403/8. Merivale to Hammand 5 August 1870.
16. F.O. 403/8. Hammand to Merivale 8 August 1870. Mayo, Governor-General of India to the Duke of Argyll 5 August 1870.
17. F.O. 403/8. Captain Prideanx to Brigadier General Sneider 2 November 1873; Capt Hunter to Sneider 9 October 1873 in Grant Duff to Tenterdon 17 June 1874.
18. F.O. 403/8. Tenterdon to Merivale 9 February 1874.
19. F.O. 403/8. Hammand to Merivale 8 August 1870.
20. F.O. 403/8. Tenterden to Merivale 8 Febraury 1874.
21. F.O. 403/8. Elliot to Granville 13 November 1873.
22. F.O. 403/8. Temenheer's Memorandum 14 July 1874. Bertlefrere's Report 27 June 1874; Prideaux to Sneider 20 November 1873 Governor General of India to the Secretary of State for India 18 September 1874.
23. F.O. 403/8. Malet to Tenterden 23 March 1875. Tenterden to Hamelton 25 Febraury 1876. Stanton to Derby 18 October 1876.

24. F.O. 403/8. Malet to Tenterden, *Ibid.*
25. F.O. 403/8. Stanton to Derby 7 April 1876.
    Cookson to Derby 15 October 1876.
26. F.O. 403/8 Vivian to Derby 18 October 1876. Malet to Tenterden 13 November 1876. Vivian to Derby 2 December 1876.
27. F.O. 403/8, Vivian to Derby 21 February 1877. Draft Somali Coast Convention 7 September 1877.
28. F.O. 403/8. Vivian to Derby 7 September 1877.
29. F.O. 403/8. Wylde to F.O.
30. Rubenson, *Survival* p. 342.
31. F.O. 881/4082 Lascelles to Salisbury 26 August 1879.
32. A.I.A/777 Vivian to F.O. 26 December 1879.
33. F.O. 881/4082. Salisbury to Loscelles 29 October 1879.
34. F.O. 407/14. Mallet to Salisbury 26 January 1880.
35. F.O. 407/14. Mallet to Salisbury 15 December 1879.
36. Gebre Sellassie *Yohannes IV* pp. 111 to 120.
37. Bairu Tafla, *Op cit.* p. 83.
38. *Ibid.* p. 87. Adhane Mengista ab "Yohannes IV and Keren" p. 250 *Kasa and Kasa*
39. F.O. 407/14 Granville to Walsham 27 June 1881.
40. F.O. 407/8113. Edward Mallet to Granville 1st July 1881.
41. F.O. 40/81B. Granville to Walsham 19 July 1881.
42. Bairu Tafla, *Op cit.* p. 87.
43. F.O. 881/408. Wylde to Salisbury 16 September 1879.
44. F.O. 403/81. Cookson to Granville 7 October 1880.
45. F.O. 403/81. *Ibid.*
46. F.O. 403/81. Colvin's Memorandum in Mallet to Granville 7 December 1880.
47. F.O. 403/81. Mallet to Granville 8 December 1880.
48. F.O. 403/81. Granville to Mallet 20 December 1880.
49. A.B. Theobold *The Mahdiya* (London; 1949).
    P.M. Holt. *A Modern History of the Sudan* (N.Y. 1961).
50. F.O. 881/4082 Gordon to Lascelles 17 August 1879 in Lascelles to Salisbury 29 August 1879.
51. F.O. 1/30 Mallet to Granville 1 May 1882.
52. F.O. 1/30 Baring to Granville 28 November 1883, 12 December 1883.
53. F.O. 1/30 Yohannes to Queen Victoria 10 December 1883. This was the real ambition of Yohannes since his accession to the throne of Ethiopia as Emperor. See Munzinger's Report to the French Ministry of Foreign Affairs. A.E. Massawa. Munzinger a Minister des affaire's Etrenger 27 March 1870. also Douin, *Op cit.* pp. 312-313.
54. Wylde, *Op cit.*
55. F.O. 1/30. Baring to Granville, 5 January 1884.
56. F.O. 1/30. Napier to Granville 9 January 1884.

57. F.O. 1/30. The Anti-Slavery Society to Granville 10 April 1884.
58. F.O. 1/30. Baring to Granville 10 January 1884 and the F.O. Minute on Baring's Letter of 10 January 1884.
59. F.O. 1/30. Granville to Baring 6 June 1884.
60. F.O. 1/30. Baring's Letter to Granville 6 June 1884.
    F.O. Minute the above 7 March 1884.
61. Granville to Baring, 8 March 1884.
62. F.O. 1/31. *Ibid.*
63. F.O. 1/31. Baring to Granville 8 March 1884.
64. F.O. 1/31. Hewett to Granville.
65. F.O. 1/31. Hewett to Granville 9 June 1884.
    Mason Bey to Nuber Pasha 7 May 1884.
66. F.O. 1/31 Hewett to Granville; 15 June 1884, 9 June.
67. *Ibid*; Wylde, *Op cit*. p. 38 Adhane *Op cit.*

4

Watch-Dogs and Victims

If British policy towards Ethiopia changed in the 1880's from disengagement to partial engagement the catalyst was Egypt. It was Britain's direct involvement in Egypt and the need to preserve and protect Egyptian and British interests on the Red Sea shore of Ethiopia which forced Britain to deal with Ethiopia. British Government considered that British interests were gravely concerned in the maintenance of Egyptian jurisdiction wherever it had been acknowledged under the *fireman* and convention of 1868 and 1877. This carefully built British strategy to protect her interests in the Red Sea region based on the Anglo-Egyptian Convention on the Somali coast however collapsed in less than a decade after it was devised. Egypt was the linchpin of the strategy and its effectiveness depended on her continued strength and co-operation. However Egypt herself soon became the problem child of Britain.

The financial breakdown of Egypt in 1879 and the British occupation of the country three years later forced the British Government to reconsider the situation. With 60 per cent of Egypt's revenues reserved to service the European creditors very little money was available to Egyptian Government for administration. In the circumstances Egypt could not maintain her African empire which could not pay its own administrative costs. At the same time in the light of successful Mahdist revolution in the Sudan which by 1883 nearly ended Egyptian rule there, the British Government advised the Egyptian Government to abandon the Sudan and offered to assist in maintaining order in Egypt proper as well as the ports of the Red Sea.[1] The Egyptian Government agreed and requested the British Government to relieve it of all costs for the administration of the Red Sea ports. Since Britain did not want to assume the burden of administering the region herself arrangement was to be made soon to fill the vacuum, that would be caused by Egypt's withdrawal from the ports. A reversion to the position which existed before the Egyptian occupation of the cost was not possible because the circumstances had altered considerably.[2] It was important that a power friendly to Britain should occupy the ports lest the security of the British settlement at Aden and the sea route to India be threatened. The logical and easiest solution to the difficulty was to invite Turkey, the suzerain of the ports, to occupy them. Turkey was advised that unless she provided men and money to administer Massawa and other Red Sea ports Egypt would withdraw from them.[3] Burdened by a public debt of over two hundred million sterling and deterred by severe financial constraints Turkey declined to assume responsibility for the Red Sea ports, while insisting on her nominal suzerainty and territorial integrity.

Turkey's bankrupt policy did not help Britain. Notwithstanding Turko-Egyptian opposition Italy officially took over Assab Bay in 1884 and was aspiring to expand farther.[4] Having occupied Obock France was reportedly waiting to take over Massawa soon after the Egyptian withdrawal.[5] France's opposition to Britain had been growing since the British occupation of Egypt. The growing French activity in the Red Sea region was causing great concern to the British Residency at Aden, which feared that the French had lately pushed their territorial claim to the neighbourhood of Tajurah and if Egypt withdrew from that port France would occupy it.[6] She might also seize Amphyla south of Massawa, if a power vacuum arose in those Red Sea ports, their occupation by interested European powers could not be stopped either by unenforced Turkish rights or by feeble local chiefs. It was becoming apparent that Turkey could no longer be trusted to act as a scarecrow to keep the Red Sea secure for Britain. Since

1878 Britain's diplomatic influence with the Porte had been declining and if Turkey could not be relied upon to do what Britain wished, then other expedients had to be tried.[7] Britain began the search for a new watch-dog to replace Egypt.

British policy-makers became concerned with the future of the Red Sea ports soon after the British occupation of Egypt in 1882. Immediately there were doubts whether Turkey would agree to take over the administration of the Red Sea ports from Egypt and different solutions were considered.[8] Northbrook, the Secretary of Admiralty, saw "no insuperable difficulty" in settling the future of the Red Sea ports. Since Berbera and Zeila were indispensable for provisioning Aden Britain might take them. Because Emperor Yohannes of Ethiopia had been asking for a sea port he might be given one while Egypt might keep Suakin and Massawa.[9] He even considered handing over Massawa to Ethiopia though some way would have to be found to guard the nominal sovereignty of the Porte.[10] Evelyn Baring, the British Consul-General in Cairo, agreed with Northbrook that Ethiopia might be given "a bit of sea coast,"[11] and with an English Governor at Massawa, Northbrook assured, that "no difficulties would arise." In fact he suggested the appointment of English or European Governor to all Red Sea ports. At Assab and Obock the Italians and the French were already lodged and they could not be interfered.[12] Major Hunter, the acting British Resident at Aden recommended the cession of ports of Zeila and Berbera to King Menelek of Shoa on such conditions as would protect British interests. This would, he hoped, stifle French ambitions in southern Ethiopia and help consolidate British position there.[13] Even Gladstone, the British Prime Minister, categorically stated in Parliament, in November 1882, that British Government would assist Ethiopia to get a port on the western Red Sea shore.[14] Of course that was the time when the British Government was most anxious to seek Ethiopia's help in securing the evacuation of the beseized Egyptian garrisons in the Sudan to safety.

During these early considerations Italy was no where in the view as a possible watch-dog of Britain in the Red Sea. On the contrary there was a great deal of antagonism to Italian territorial aspirations there. The War Office warned the British Government that from the British point of view the creation of an Italian settlement on the shores of the Red Sea was "distinctively objectionable."[14] Until 1882 both Conservative and Liberal Governments in London had been uncompromisingly opposed to Italy's territorial ambitions in the Red Sea. When General Gordon advised the Khedive to cede Zulla on the western Red Sea shore to Italy. Salisbury warned Egypt "that any cession by Egypt would be absolutely opposed by Her Majesty's Government."[15] When Italy occupied Assab Bay the British warned the Italian Government that it was a part of the Ottoman dominion within the Khedivate of Egypt and Britain would not recognize the occupation.[16] Granville was no less emphatic about the Turko-Egyptian rights to Assab though, under extreme Italian pressure, he allowed himself to be persuaded that Britain should intervene diplomatically with Egypt and Turkey to relieve the Italian Government from the embarrassment at Assab Bay. Like Salisbury, Granville was sure that from the point of Indian interest it was undesirable that any foreign power should acquire by purchase or otherwise any territory along the western Red Sea shore from local *Sheiks*.[17] However Britain's needs in Egypt soon brought about a radical change in her attitude towards Italy as a political surrogate.

A late entrant into modern imperial ventures Italy was anxious to build a colonial empire. She had her eye both on the Mediterranean and Red Sea shores of Africa believing that the "key to the Mediterranean was in the Red Sea." Lately she had bought the Red Sea port of Assab from the Rabbatino company and was anxious to occupy neighbouring territories as quickly as possible.[18] In the context of the European diplomatic alliances this did not seem impossible. Faced with France's continuous opposition to her colonial objections Italy had come to regard British support as essential for the realization of her territorial aspirations. Given the raging Anglo-French rivalry and her membership in the anti-French Triple Alliance Italy hoped to succeed. A grand opportunity to accomplish this opened up for Italy in 1876 when the International Commission for Egyptian Debt was created with

Britain, France, Germany, Australia and Italy as members. Facing strong French opposition and uncertain German support, the British came to lean on Italian backing to push through financial reforms in Egypt. No one could better appreciate the value of Italian support than Evelyn Baring, the British Consul-General in Cairo.

However Italian support carried a price. During the crisis which followed the Italian occupation of Raheita in the Assab Bay, seeking British support Rome told London: After faithful support which Italy had given for two years to Her Majesty's Government in every question which affected England, either slightly or closely, the Italian Government on this occasion counted upon an act of reciprocity, from Britian and they would feel their disappointment all the more keenly if their expectations were unrealized.[19]

In fact there was no need for Italy to feel disappointed. As early as 1882, on the eve of British naval demonstration against the Arabi Government at Alexandria, the British Government had invited Italy to join it in the forthcoming operations, holding out good hopes for future.[20] Though Bismarck's disapproval then prevented Italy from joining Britain, Italy had decided not to miss future opportunities. So was Britain determined to keep Italy in good humour to ensure her continued co-operation in Egypt and Granville expressed his "desire on this, as in all other circumstances to act in as conciliatory manner as possible," the Italians were not slow to exploit the situation.[21] In October 1884 the Italian Government requested British concurrence to their planned acquisition of Beilul port, north of Assab. Considering the Italian Government's wish of proceeding in harmony with the English cabinet in everything connected with the Egyptian question, Mancini, the Italian Foreign Minister, hoped that "England would look without jealousy a moderate extension of the colony of Assab".[22] Impressed with the Italian aid in Egypt Gladstone was all for giving "friendly support to Italy."[23] No wonder Granville was generously assuring Italy that the British Government not only felt no jealousy over the extension of Italian influence in that part of the Red Sea coast but also would "welcome it".[24] This was a decisive turning point in British policy towards Italian ambitions in the Red Sea region. The Liberal Government of Galdstone which had earlier opposed the Italian acquisition of Raheita, south of the Assab, was now welcoming Italy as a partner in the Red Sea. Within a short time of less than two years since 1882 the Egyptian situation had forced the British Government to support Italy to fill the vacuum that would be created by Egypt's withdrawal from Massawa.

Having effectively occupied Raheita and Beilul by November 1888. Italy had set her eyes on Massawa and Zulla. She knew that Egypt had been advised to relinquish much of the Sudan and the Red Sea ports and Britain herself was disinclined to keep them. Turkey had failed to move in. Italy feared that France might occupy Massawa. Encouraged by earliest friendly British responses the Italian Government offered its intervention in Massawa if details and conditions were satisfactorily worked out.[25] Granville was receptive.[26]

Evelyln Baring had concluded by November 1883 that it was Egypt's interest to withdraw from Massawa and other ports without further delay. Concerned about the financial burdens which the depleted Egyptian Treasury had been bearing in administering the Red Sea ports. Baring was pressing London to act soon.[27] Administering Massawa cost £ 29,735 sterling annually, while its revenue was £ 21,689. It had become a "serious embarrassment".[28] The situation was likely to worsen as the revenue, which primarily derived from the duties levied on Ethiopian trade at the port, was about to dry up since Egypt had committed herself in the Hewett Treaty to exempt all Ethiopian imports and exports from duties.[29] If Egypt retained the port increased grants would be necessary to administer them. However if Egypt withdrew from Massawa who should step in was the question, when neither Turkey nor Britain seemed willing to assume direct administration of the port. Though Baring at first considered the cession of Massawa to Ethiopia, he retracted fearing "Abyssinia's administrative incompetence" to utilize a port and the probability of the traffic of such "degenerating into protective monopoly in the hands of some European rivals.[30] He preferred a European power at Massawa; that was to be Italy. Dropping a hint to the Italians, Baring worked out a strategy to entice them into Massawa without formally committing the British Government. He confided to Granville that he had casually mentioned to De Martino the Italian Consul-General in Cairo that a letter had gone to the Porte and that if the Turks did not go to Massawa, and Britain had no intention of going there, all that was required would be done. The Italians would draw their own inferences and do whatever please them.[31] Becoming impatient about the delay over the Massawa question "on the score of expenses", Baring advised London to act quickly.

The British Government considered Baring's recommendations very sympathetically. Certainly it did not like to see either Italy or France entrenched on the Red Sea shore. The ideal solution for Britain would have been the reoccupation of the ports by Turkey. But Turkey did not want to occupy them; Egypt could not keep them; Ethiopia was not trusted; possession by the local chiefs was feared. By process of elimination there remained Italy. Without doubt that was the best option in the circumstances.[32] Impressed by the unswerving Italian co-operation in Egypt Gladstone had advised Granville, as early as October 1884, that if the Porte did not occupy Massawa Italy might be allowed to take it and "friendly support might be given to her in Constantinople to overcome Turkey's opposition".[33] European diplomatic considerations also impelled the Prime Minister to support Italy as it would please Bismarck; Germany's goodwill would help overcome French opposition. Moreover as the least powerful European nation, dependent on Britain's naval support in the Mediterranean against France, Italy could pose no serious threat to British interests in the Red Sea and seemed to be manouverable. Italy thus pre-eminently suited to fill the vacuum at Massawa. By favouring the Italian occupation of Massawa Britain would also ensure herself continued Italian support in Egypt. No wonder Gladstone advised Granville to give up Massawa to Italy to make a friend of her.[34] Italy was soon assured that the British Government would raise no objection to the Italian occupation of Zulla, Beilul or Massawa subject to Britain's existing treaty arrangements with Ethiopia as regards the latter port. While the British Government was desirous of showing its friendly feelings to Italy in all possible ways it was entirely up to her to settle the matter with Turkey which was the suzerain of the ports.[35]

Fully assured of Britain's support Italy prepared to occupy Massawa. Between 22 December 1884 when Granville offered Britain's "no objection certificate" to the contemplated Italian occupation of Massawa and on 5 February 1885, when Italy occupied the port, London and Rome worked closely together. The British Government endeavoured to smoothen the path for Italy in the Red Sea in every possible way. When rumours regarding Italy's intended occupation and Britain's collusion reached Turkey, the Porte made known its concern to the British Government. Regretting that Turkey had allowed such a situation to develop by failing to occupy the ports of the Red Sea the British Government advised that the Italian occupation of Massawa was least injurious to Turkey's interests than by any other European power. Granville told Masrus Pasha, the Turkish Ambassador, "that if other friendly powers wished to acquire ports on the Red Sea it was a matter of agreement between such powers and the Porte."[36] Severely ensconced in Egypt, and her new surrogate in the Red Sea, Britain was rapidly abandoning the Turkish cloak of Responsibility.

Although the British Government had made its position clear to the Porte, still there was the question of Turkey's legal sovereignty to the coast which could not be ignored. Egypt had held the Red Sea ports in Turkey's name and legally they reverted to the ports automatically as soon as Egypt vacated.[37] Unless Italy negotiated a settlement with the Porte any Italian occupation of Massawa and Zulla would be illegal. Though the British Government had suggested to Italy's seeking the Porte's approval to occupy Massawa the prospects for obtaining it seemed bleak. Moreover if Italy waited for legal formalities before occupation there was a possibility of its pre-emption by France. Such a prospects was unwelcome. Britain rejected the idea. Italy feared it. In the circumstances

Baring masterminded the plan for the Italian occupation of Massawa.

Emphasizing prudence and patience, Baring advised Italy not to act "too precipitously and to delay the occupation" of Massawa until Egypt's notification of her intended withdrawal from the Red Sea ports and request for Turkey's reoccupation had reached the Porte. After the landing of the Italian troops at Massawa the Ottoman flag should be left flying and Egypt should not be pressed to withdraw her garrisons or administration from Massawa immediately. The Porte should be confronted with a *fait accompli.* After notifying the Porte of the landing of the Italian troops at Massawa Italy should try to secure its recognition. Italy was to repeat what Britain had done while occupying Zeila.[38] The British Government approved Baring's proposal which was followed by the Italian Government literally.[39] Rarely a surrogate had been tutored so carefully!

There was one last manoevre to facilitate the Italian occupation of Massawa. Though the Egyptian Government had acquiesced in the British advice that Italy be allowed to occupy Massawa, it could not officially instruct the Egyptian Government of Massawa to surrender the port to the Italians. First of all Egypt could not cede to Italy what belonged to the Porte. Secondly it did not wish to compromise its position in the eyes of Turkey by appearing to be in league with Italy. In the circumstances Cromer, the British Consul-General, sent private confidential instructions to Chermside, the Egyptian Governor of Massawa, to facilitate the Italian occupation of that port. The instructions demonstrated clearly the depth of British intrigue in planting Italy at Massawa and needs to be quoted fully.

"The attitude of the English Government is that the Egyptian Government cannot stay at Massawa and if they retire, the place should return to the Porte, who was invited some months ago to occupy the port on the Red Sea. If the Porte takes no action and the Italians decide to go to Massawa the English Government offer no objection, and indeed would prefer them to others... When the Italians arrive, your position as Egyptian official, will be one of some difficulty. Nuber Pasha can scarcely give you any official instructions at present. But I tell you privately what course you had better adopt". Nuber Pasha approves the following instructions: "There can be of course no question of armed resistance to the Italians. The action of Italy will not be unfriendly either to England or Egypt. You need therefore have no hesitation in getting on very friendly terms with them, and giving them whatever information they require... Unless they use force, which they will not do, you cannot consent to withdraw the Egyptian garrison or lower the Egyptian flag without authority to do so. If they land troops, or haul down the Egyptian flag, you should put into the hands of the commander of the party a protest, couched in distinct but courteous terms, on behalf of the Egyptian Government".[40]

The Commander of the British Navy in the Red Sea was also confidentially informed of the expected Italian occupation of Massawa and instructed not to oppose or act in a way embarrassing to the Italians.[41] A pretext was invented to justify the landing of the Italian troops at Massawa, after enquiring and being told by the Egyptians, that in the circumstances, no guarantee could be given for the lives or property of Europeans at Massawa. Italy would then land troops to maintain order. The Italians kept the British fully informed about their moves.[42] On 5 February 1885 Italian troops occupied Massawa under Egyptian protest, but without resistance and hoisted the Italian flag besides those of Egypt and Turkey: "both sides showed a conciliatory spirit".[43] However the Italians did not show the same restraint elsewhere. They occupied Beilul after forcefully disarming the Egyptian garrison.[44] Protesting strongly to the British Government about the Italian occupation of Massawa, Turkey urged Granville to prevent Italy from making any moves contrary to the principles of international law as it would encourage other countries to do the same.[45] Turkey also expressed its horror at the reported secret understanding between the British and the Italian Governments regarding the arrangements. Disclaiming any responsibility for the Italian occupation of Massawa the British Government blamed the Porte for ignoring its advice to occupy the Red Sea ports when

Egypt requested, reiterating its view that Italian occupation was less injurious to Turkey's interest than by any other power.[46] When Turkey threatened war if Italy did not withdraw from Massawa the British warned that "the Italians were ready and determined to oppose any measures to dislodge them forcibly."[47] Turkey was weak and had no real intention of asserting her rights to Massawa militarily. She admitted that her threat was a bluff, but the Porte was "much more vexed with Britain than with Italy."[48]

Upset with Britain, and ill-equipped to fight Italy, Turkey appealed to European powers to uphold her territorial integrity. France was sympathetic to Turkey. Moreover annoyed with Italy for occupying Beilul and Massawa after denying any such intention even a week previous to the incident, Jules Ferry urged both Russia and Germany to check Italy and protect Turkey's integrity.[49] While the unenthusiastic Russian Government preferred to await the reactions of other countries before acting, Bismarck was clearly unhelpful. He told Courcel the French Ambassador that the matter was to be considered in a wider context of repeated violations of Turkey's sovereignty and frequent acts of belligerency in the Red Sea by the big powers.[50] It was a clear condemnation of both France and Britain and there was not much to be expected from the Chancellor who did not want to displease his Italian ally. London could not be and was not of any help to France in the matter. British Government informed the French that it would not oppose Italy.[51] Since delayed protest might mean acquiescence, France advised Russia to act at once against the Italian occupation of the Red Sea ports.[52] Simultaneously the French Ambassadors in London, Berlin and St. Petersburg were instructed to have serious exchange of views on the Italian aggression with respective Governments.[53] No further measures were forthcoming from France and it was not comforting to Turkey. Turkey's direct approach to Berlin was no more productive. Bismarck advised her to settle the matter with Italy directly.[54] The disillusioned and hapless Porte instructed the Khedive not to accept the Italian occupation of Massawa tacitly by withdrawing the Egyptian administration from the port.[55]

The British Government nevertheless maintained the charade of Turkey's sovereignty over the Red Sea ports by advising Italy that no formal recognition would be given to her occupation of Massawa until the matter had been settled with Turkey.[56] When the Conservatives replaced the Liberal Government of Britain in June 1885, fearing their hostility, the nervous Italians sought Salisbury's view on the matter. He assured Italy that if there were no considerations connected with Turkey's rights, there was no other power which he would see more willingly established along the coast of the Red Sea than Italy, Salisbury calmed that power.[57] While withholding formal recognition he helped Italy to overcome difficulties with the Egyptian administration at Massawa which had not been withdrawn even after the convention of 1887.[58] Britain also effected a safe withdrawal of the Egyptian garrisons from Harar and restored that famed town to Abdullah Muhammud of the local royal family. In 1887 King Menelek defeated Abdullah Muhammud and occupied Harar, thus pre-empting possible European occupation of that city. The British accepted the *fait accompli*.[59] Britain's myopia was evident here too. They might as well have given Harar to Ethiopia voluntarily and earned her goodwill as Consul Baker had suggested earlier.

In endeavouring to secure her interests in the Red Sea region Britain had violated the Hewett Treaty, betrayed Ethiopia and endangered her security. General Gordon had foreseen that the planting of Italy on the Red Sea shore would soon lead to conflict between her and Ethiopia. The nature of an imperial power is to expand and Italy was aspiring to be an imperial power. Coveting northern Ethiopia and eastern Sudan Italy was determined not to limit herself to Massawa which was seen as a base for expansion into the interior.[60] Within six weeks after occupying Massawa the Italian Government expressed to Britain its need to occupy "healthy grounds of Bogos" on the pretext to establish sanitary stations for the scorched Italian troops at Massawa, although she was fully aware that by the Hewett Treaty the territory belonged to Ethiopia.[61] Britain advised Italy to arrange with Ethiopia before moving into any part of Bogos. Having occupied the port of

Massawa disregarding the Turkish sovereignty Italy was in no mood to worry about Ethiopian rights to the territory which she desired. Italy soon occupied Sahathi and Uva on the Highlands and the coastal territory up to "the edge of the salt plains" which was Ethiopian.[62]

While expanding into the Ethiopian Highlands Italy also endeavoured to enter into treaty relations with Emperor Yohannes hoping to secure from him trade and territorial concessions. Forseeing Italy's territorial designs on Ethiopia Yohannes rejected her approaches.

Disappointed and vindictive Italy stopped the passage of arms and ammunition to Yohannes at Massawa violating the Hewett Treaty.[63] She hindered Ethiopian trade; planned aggression on her disregarding Britain. The surrogate was becoming uncontrollable. These developments affected Ethiopia adversely. Emperor Yohannes was indignant and felt cheated. Expressing his disappointment to the British Government he contrasted Ethiopia's candid conduct with Britain's duplicity. While Ethiopia had fully and sincerely discharged her treaty obligations towards Britain and Egypt by relieving the beseized Egyptian garrisons from Bogos, Amadib and Kassala at great cost to herself, even incurring further hostility of the Mahdists, Britain had ignored her obligations to Ethiopia. An year after signing the Hewett Treaty Ethiopian trade at Massawa was still being taxed, and worse, Italy had been allowed to possess Massawa. Fully trusting Britain's assurances regarding free transit of arms into Ethiopia and duty free trade at Massawa Ethiopia had dropped the demand for Massawa. She had been misled into believing that she might be allowed to take Massawa after the Egyptian withdrawal.[64] Britain had failed to keep faith with Yohannes and had broken the Hewett Treaty. Writing to Queen Victoria Yohannes lamented, "I wished to be the faithful son of Queen Victoria forever, but before a year the treaty I made is broken."[65] Fearing that a permanent Italian occupation of Massawa would endanger Ethiopia's security and independence and hoping to reverse the situation, he appealed to the Queen, "I wish you to give me Massawa and I will hold it against any foreigner."[66]

Protection of imperial interests was more important to Britain than upholding a treaty with an African ruler. Having herself planted Italy at Massawa Britain had no convincing explanation to offer. She tried to calm Yohannes with friendly assurances and decorations. A sword of honour was presented "as an acknowledgment for the distinguished and friendly assistance rendered... in the relief of the Egyptian garrison at Gallabat." It was evident however that Yohannes could not be mollified.

A complete violation of the Hewett Treaty would lead to serious troubles with Ethiopia besides sullying Britain's image. It could also enhance Ethiopian pressure for an independent sea port. Britain did not like the prospects. Moreover Britain's primary interest was the Red Sea shore and she did not want a change in the *status quo*. The best solution was to keep Ethiopia quiescent by ensuring unhindered importation of arms at Massawa as agreed in the Hewett Treaty. Undoubtedly that would make Ethiopia strong militarily, something Britain had resisted when it seemed a threat to Egypt's security. But now peace established and frontiers settled between Ethiopia and Egypt and the latter under British control Ethiopia was no longer a threat. On the contrary a strong Christian Ethiopia might even be a preferable counter-weight to the hostile Mahadist Sudan. A friendly Ethiopia in the interior and a friendly Italy on the coast could equally serve Britain's strategic and imperial interests. Thus it was a British interest to see that both Ethiopia and Italy co-operated and British influence with both remained in tact. While such a strategy was conceptually attractive it was bound to fail functionally unless Britain could halt Italian expansion into northern Ethiopia.

Salisbury reminded the Italian Government of its obligations to Britain to execute the provisions of the Hewett Treaty towards Ethiopia and advised it "to arrange for the execution of this stipulation in a manner satisfactory to King John."[67] Certainly it was not in Italy's interest to see Ethiopia strengthened with free import of arms given her determined opposition to the Italian presence at Massawa and their planned expansion into the interior. So Salisbury's advice was ignored and Italy attempted to strengthen Emperor Yohannes's rivals by supplying them arms while insisting that the assumed obligations towards Ethiopia were being executed.[68]

As to the territorial acquisitors, Italy admitted occupying Mancullo, Arifalle Sahati and Viabut while denying that these had been ceded to Ethiopia in the Hewett Treaty.[69] Having earlier advised Italy not to occupy any territory in Bogos without Ethiopia's prior consent, the British did nothing to check further Italian expansion into Ethiopia. Confident of Britain's diplomatic support and her own military might Italy persisted in her forward policy while assuring Britain that her objective in Ethiopia was the same as Britain's; "Trade and civilization."[70] Italy had become belligerent and was in no mood to do the British bidding. Rapidly Britain's surrogate had become her rival threatening the headwaters of the Nile and the Sudan. In the early 1880's events had moved too fast for the sluggish imperial mind in London.

Though Yohannes suspected Britain's role in planting Italy at Massawa, given Ethiopia's diplomatic isolation he was unprepared to alienate himself from the London authorities. He expected them to restrain Italy. While protesting against the Italian behaviour Yohannes prepared himself for a possible conflict with Italy.

Convinced that Italy had come to Massawa "because of ambition to aggrandize" he supported his Governor Ras Alula's strong opposition towards the Italians at Massawa. Alula questioned Italy's right to Massawa and resented her arms embargo on Ethiopia. He hoped to overcome her arms embargo on Ethiopia and to neutralize Italy by encouraging the French to occupy Zula. Soumagne, the French Consul at Massawa visited Asmara and concluded a draft treaty with Alula which was to be confirmed by Yohannes later. Alula expected the French to support Yohannes in resisting Italy's violation of Ethiopia's territorial sovereignty. However before the matter progressed, the Italo-Ethiopian relations deteriorated and France cancelled further negotiations with Ethiopia.[71] The Ethiopian strategy of neutralizing one European colonial power with the aid of other did not materialize.

The Italian occupation of Sahathi was galling to Ethiopia. Determined to drive them out Yohannes assigned the task to Alula, his general. An ultimatum was issued to Italy to evacuate Sahathi and Zulla. Disregarding this when Italy tried to reinforce Sahathi with a column of five hundred soldiers, Alula attacked and wiped out the entire force in January 1886. None survived.[72] Certainly Yohannes had not sanctioned the unfortunate bloodshed and it bothered his conscience.[73] Nevertheless he did not disown Alula his most loyal general and great patriot. The happening shocked Europe. Gaining notoriety as "the massacre of Dogali", it stunned Italy and the public clamoured for vengeance. Hoping to chastise Yohannes and vindicate Italy's honour, the Italian Government despatched 20,000 soldiers to Massawa.[74] The Italian Governor of Massawa publicly announced a state of war against Ethiopia and prohibited all commercial communications with that country. A naval blockade was imposed to ruin Ethiopia's trade and to stifle her. The British Government fully supported the Italian blockade by permitting the Italian navy to police the entire Red Sea region up to Ras Kassar ignoring the advice of both Cromer and Kitchener.[75]

Despite co-operating with Italy Britain was unhappy with the developments in north-east Africa. The British Ambassador in Rome confessed to a feeling of uneasiness about the Italian proceedings in Ethiopia.[76] The British did not want to see "the massacre of Dogali" degenerate into a war between Ethiopia and Italy, both of which had their assigned, if unspoken, roles in Britain's imperial strategy. A war with Italy could only enfeeble Ethiopia which would only serve the purpose of the rebel, fundamentalist Muslim al-Mahdi of the Sudan. In the circumstances the British Government favoured a peaceful solution to the Italo-Ethiopian difficulty and offered mediation to Italy since such would also please Bismarck who wanted Italy assisted.[77] Declining mediation the Italians requested Britain's good offices to open talks with Ethiopia. The British Government agreed assuring Italy "that it would not take any step in the matter without a clear understanding and compliance with the Italian."[78]

Unfortunately allowing itself to be guided by Italy Britain fully identified with the Italian position in the dispute. Neither did Britain consider Ethiopia's grievances against Italy nor contain Italy's threat to Ethiopian independence; neither did she admit her complicity in the Italian occupation of Massawa nor offer amends for the non-implementation of the Hewett Treaty. Instead Britain blamed Yohannes for "disputing with the Italians" and not treating them in a friendly way. After repeating the Italian version of the difficulty she blamed Ethiopia for attacking them at Dogali "unjustly." After conveying Italy's determination to seek reparation from Ethiopia for the Dogali "massacre", Britain warned Yohannes that Italy was a "powerful nation" determined to "pursue war'. Finally she offered to assist Ethiopia if she wished to seek peace with Italy.[79]

Yohannes was furious. The communication confirmed his doubt that Britain was now a partisan of Italy. Certainly Britain had misled him while negotiating the Hewett Treaty. While, in fact, planning to substitute Italy for Egypt at Massawa Britain mislead him to think otherwise.[80] More specifically, Britain, with her liege Egypt, was responsible for the current dispute with Italy over Sahathi. Sahathi had been an Ethiopian territory and this had been acknowledged both by Britain and Egypt even before the Italian occupation of Massawa. Had these two powers kept faith with Ethiopia certainly they could have averted the events which culminated in the "Dogali massacre". Colonel Chermside who was the Governor of Massawa, when the Hewett Treaty was negotiated, told Portal: As regards the occupation of Sahati I fear the Italians are technically in the wrong. Sometime ago the occupation of Sahati by Egypt so incensed the Abyssinians that they attacked and annihilated the post. In recent times it was a neutral territory... During Admiral Hewett's Mission Sahati was temporarily occupied, on the strength of an understanding with Abyssinians: but on the return of the Mission its evacuation was demanded. This Egypt was not prepared for at once, as, having the right of way through Abyssinian for her retiring garrisons, the post became important as a depot. I received numerous communications on the subject, and one or more overt threats, recalling the past destruction of the post and warning me that it would be repeated... The question of Sahati was, however, never lost sight of by Abyssinian, and the Massawa Government distinctly undertook to abandon the post as soon as it was no longer required as a depot for the retiring garrison... In the spring of 1885, as a responsible governor... I asked leave to give up the post. This was not approved. This evacuation was recommended earlier than had been intended, from fear that the Italians might advance claims to the position. I repeated my views to Her Majesty's Consul at Suakin and Bubar Pasha. Finally orders were received, to give over the post... to the Italians. These orders were executed.[81]

Deliberately Ethiopia had been cheated of her territory. She could not have done otherwise than to retake it. Certainly the British Government was wrong in accusing Ethiopia of "unjustly" attacking the Italians and supporting their demand for reputations.

Notwithstanding his frustrations Yohannes decided to use Britain's good offices to settle the dispute with Italy. Preferring arbitration to negotiation he offered to send Ethiopian delegates to London or Cairo to explain Ethiopian views if Italy would do likewise.[82] In view of the expected confrontation with the Mahdists Yohannes wished to avoid a simultaneous military engagement with Italy though he knew of her sinister designs "to make Abyssinian a tributary of Rome." But he was determined to frustrate the Italian ambitions, to defend Ethiopia and not to acquiesce in Italy's unjust demands. Lord Salisbury had been forewarned that "Yohannes would never consent, without fighting, to permanent occupation by Italy, of Sahati and Wara (Via?) to which places he considered himself to have a just claim strengthened by the promises of Egypt."[83] The Italian Government, under crispy, too was in a bellicose mood. Having secured a special vote of £ 800,000 sterling from the Italian Parliament to raise an African corps of 20,000 soldiers to extract a quick "satisfaction" from Ethiopia for the "massacre of Dogali". Clearly a war between Italy and Ethiopia seemed unavoidable.

The Italian adventure in Ethiopia and the threatening war there caused deep concern to Bismarck who had blessed Italy's "passion for acquisition" in the hope of "countering the scheme of conquest by other powers." While he wished Italy to succeed in her colonial venture he did not want her to be overburdened financially and militarily least she become too weak to be a useful ally in the Triplice.[84] He wanted to protect Italy from a possible military upset by preventing a war between her and Ethiopia. Bismarch exerted pressure on British to intervene and mediate between Italy and Emperor Yohannes. He told Salisbury that it was their "common interest" to bail out Italy.[85] Moreover close relations between Britain and Italy was important to Bismarck as "Italy's military significance would become much more important (to Triplice) if she were allied with England".[86] Salisbury obliged immediately since good relations with Germany was important to keep France and Russia in line. He would also appear to have shared to some extent Bismarck's view that "the Mediterranean alliance involved supporting Italy in Africa" so long as it was not opposed to British interests.[87]

Informing Bismarck that the British Government would mediate he proposed to the Chancellor the points which might form the basis for future negotiations with the Emperor of Ethiopia. These were the surrender by Ethiopia of Sahathi and via to Italy in return for the latter's commitment to abstain from further territorial demands and consent to conclude a favourable commercial treaty with her.[88] Emphasizing the importance of moderate demands for achieving successful results, Salisbury requested Bismarck to let him know soon Rome's reactions and minimum expectations. It is significant that though *pourparlers* had been going on between London and Rome on the subject the proposed terms were routed through Berlin. Obviously Salisbury wanted to satisfy Bismarck's *amour-propre*. Satisfied by Britain's attentions and wanting to ensure that Italy toed the proper line Bismarck called on the Italian Ambassador at Berlin inspite of "parliamentary exigencies" and advised Rome to arrange matters on the basis of Salisbury's proposals. He assured that he would stand "shoulder to shoulder with" Italy in maintaining general peace.[89] Bismarck's message to Italy was clear. She must seek peace. Highly impressed by the "Bon Volunte" of the Chancellor, De Launay, the Italian Ambassador, assured Crispi that proper route to London was through Berlin where Italy would be fully supported.

Though Berlin, like London, had advised peace and moderation to Rome Crispi was in a belligerent mood to consider it. A "hero of Resorgimento... a lonely authoritarian with a peculiar (sense of) responsibility as the custodian of Italy," Crispi considered Italy a great nation, a heir to ancient Rome.[90] Committed to upholding Italy's greatness he did not count costs of a war with Ethiopia. Admonishing his tormentors in Italian Chambers Crispi had once declared: Gentlemen in public affairs benefits are not counted in lires and cents... Great nations have the need to assert themselves in various parts of the world for the protection of the commerce and for the performance of that civilizing mission in whose triumph we are obliged to participate... There is something greater, if the dignity of the Fatherland and the interests of civilization.[91]

Thirsting for retributive justice Crispi was determined to extract both reparations and an apology from Emperor Yohannes for the "Dogali Massacre." Conveying his terms for peace with Ethiopia Crispi told the British Government "Italian non-cerca pace...disposte dignitaele legittimo interesse."[92] The highly emotional and bellicose Crispi was the very opposite of the cool headed and calm Salisbury. They could not easily transact any business together. Least enthusiastic about the assumed mediation Salisbury suggested to Rome that the Italo-Ethiopian difficulty might be referred to the arbitration of the Emperor of Austria-Hungary.[93] Rejecting the proposed arbitration and the offered mediation Crispi only availed Britain's "good offices." Determined to have his way Crispi dictated not only the terms for peace but also the content of the Queen's letter to Emperor Yohannes and the mode of its expression.[94]

The Italian Government wanted not only Sahathi and via but also more Ethiopian territory. Salisbury's advice "for utmost

utmost moderation" In framing their demands was ignored.[95] She demanded an apology from Emperor Yohannes "for the unjust attack made on the Italians" at Dogali, an end to his opposition to the Italian occupation of Ailet, Sahati and via and recognition of an Italian protectorate over Assorta and Habab. The Italian Government also demanded Sanheit in Bogos from Yohannes and his consent to a treaty of peace and amity with Italy.[96]

Some of these Italian demands were embarrassing even to Britain. She found it difficult to advice Ethiopia to cede Bogos having lately assisted her to reacquire it from Egypt.[97] Though the Italian Government finally dropped the demand the prospects for a peaceful settlement looked bleak. What Crispi did was to make Britain to deliver an ultimatum to Emperor Yohannes either to fully comply with the Italian terms or to face war. The British Government consented and deputed Gerladld Portal, Secretary at the British Residency, Cairo, to conduct a mission to Emperor Yohannes. Identifying itself with the Italian position and ignoring British intelligence that Emperor Yohannes would neither yield to Italy nor seek peace with her, the British Government allowed itself to be guided by the Bellicose Crispi.[98] It is indeed surprising that, disregarding his own inclinations, Lord Salisbury did not press Italy to moderate her demands. Corti, the Italian Ambassador in London, warned Crispi of the repeatedly expressed misgivings of Baring regrading the proposed British mission to Ethiopia.[99] This was of no avail. Crispi remained belligerent.

The British had blundered again. Through mediation they had been given an opportunity to reign in their surrogate. Clearly they failed to comprehend their original mistake or understand that the client state was now controlling them. Given the absolute attention to legal niceties which had governed the British policy thus far, it is difficult not to conclude that there were two or three codes of international behaviour, one for Europeans, one for Moslems and finally one for Africans in which legality could be totally ignored.

Given her apparent partisanship with Italy Britain was a suspect in Ethiopia. The British had lost influence with

Yohannes and the Portal Mission had a cool and almost hostile reception. Ras Alula, the influential adviser of Yohannes on foreign affairs, criticized Britain for "pretending" to be a friend of Ethiopia and giving away Massawa to Italy. Protesting that Portal had been sent to plead for the Italians and not to mediate in good faith, he declared that the sea was the natural frontier of Ethiopia and the Italians should come to Sahati only if he could go as Governor to Rome.[100] As Ethiopia rightly surmised Portal had not been sent "to mediate in a real sense" but to obtain Yohannes's consent to the humiliating Italian demands. While Portal had been authorized "to use the name of England" generally in urging peace he was to abstain from promising "expressly or by implication" that the British Government "would secure the performance of any terms of peace."[101]

The British Government did not agree that the disputed Sahati and Via were Ethiopian territories. Maintaining that they had been under the administration of Egypt it proposed that the misunderstandings which had arisen should be discussed. This, as noted earlier, belied the fact.[102] There were fundamental and irreconcilable differences on territorial issue itself between the negotiators. The Portal Mission, like that of Gordon's in 1879, was doomed to failure by the very nature of its mandate.

In view of the tough Ethiopian attitude towards Italy and indignation at Britain's duplicity, Portal did not advance all the Italian demands. He was most anxious "to avoid any expressions that was galling to the Abyssinian national pride."[103] Omitting all references to the Italian demand for Emperor Yohannes's apology and Italian claims to protectorate over Ailet, Portal urged Yohannes to avoid the calamity of war with Italy by accepting her claims to Sahati and Via and a joint Anglo-Italian Protectorate over Bogos. He assured the Emperor that in return for these concessions Italy would sign a treaty of peace and amity with Ethiopia and abstain from further territorial demands. Portal concluded that Queen Victoria "earnestly hoped and confidently trusted that King John would without delay signify the acceptance of the terms."[104]

Protesting that Sahati and Via were still regarded as Egyptian territories, Yohannes insisted that by the Hewett

Treaty that all territories evacuated by Egypt belonged to Ethiopia and that he would not conclude any agreement with Italy "which did not confirm this. He refused to give up even" an inch of territory" and rejected the Italian terms. Declaring that even Massawa was his by right and cirticizing Britain for giving it a way to Italy, he defended Ras Alula's action at Dogali and saw no reason to make amends to Italy. He fulminated that if the Italians could not do without Sahati, then they should return to Italy. As to Britain, implicit threat about Italy's military might, Yohannes assured Portal that he was also strong, "that the right was on the side of Abyssinia and the issue of war was in the hands of God." Furious with Britain, Yohannes hoped that she should not interfere any more in the Italo-Ethiopian dispute and leave him alone to face Italy.[105] This was the strongest statement that he had ever made to Britain and it was a clear indictment of British Policy in Ethiopia. He questioned Queen Victoria:

> How can you say that I shall hand over to them (the Italians) the country which Jesus Christ gave. That would be as a command to me, unjust on your part... If your wish was to make peace between us it should be when they are in their country and I in mine. But now on both sides the horses are bridled and the swords are drawn; my soldiers in numbers like sand are ready with their spears; the Italians desire war, but the strength is in Jesus Christ; let them do as they will; so long as I live I will not hide from them in a hole...[106]

The dismal result of the Portal mediation was increased Ethiopian irritation both with Britain and Italy and Ethiopia's strengthened resolve not to yield to external pressures. The Portal Mission symbolized the Nadir of British influence in Ethiopia. Concluding wrongly that Ethiopia "was bent on fighting" the Italians and there was nothing to be done until the disputant resolved the matter militarily, Britain abandoned any idea of mediation and withdrew from Ethiopia without striving to regain the lost influence.[107] As an imperials power

Britain could not appreciate the courageous stand of an African state in defence of her independence and territorial integrity. It was Britain which had sponsored and planted Italy on the Ethiopian frontier; it was Britain which had misled and let down Ethiopia; it was Britain which had created problem for Ethiopia. It did not matter to Britain what happened to Ethiopia so long as the *status quo* was left undisturbed in the Nile Valley and the Red Sea region.

By 1888 a major war between Ethiopia and Italy seemed inevitable. Before that happened Emperor Yohannes wanted to ensure that all his chiefs would be with him in this national effort. The most important of these was Menelek whose friendly relations with the Italians was disturbing. Even while the Portal Mission was in Ethiopia the Emperor had despatched messengers to Menelek with Queen Victoria's letter expressing his disappointment with the British and resolve not to allow them to interfere in Ethiopian affairs. Pointing at the same the danger posed by the Italians Yohannes had urged Menelek to join him at once in resisting them.[108] Having entered into treaty relations with Italy, and the Italian representatives still at his court, Menelek did not want to be dragged into a war against Italy; as usual he dodged with excuses.[109] Reporting these happening, Antonelli, the Italian Representative, advised Rome that the time was propitious to start military operations against Emperor Yohannes and to invite Menelek to join Italy. Assuring Crispi of Menelek's neutrality even were he to refuse a military alliance against Yohannes, Antonelli advised him to send a large gift of firm arms to the Shoan monarch.[110] Hoping to prevent a war between Ethiopia and Italy Menelek offered his mediation to Rome to reconcile with Yohannes. But Crispi rejected the offer.[111]

In the mean time the Italians had reinforced their defences at Sahati, Via and Ailet with a resolve to hold on to them. Much of Ethiopia was aroused and was up in arms against Italy. The momentum could not be sustained longer and engagement against the Italians seemed unavoidable. Emperor Yohannes approached Sahati with a large army with the intention of driving the Italians out, but held back. He was in a dilemma.

The Mahdists had attacked western Ethiopia and raided Gondar where the King had appealed for Yohannes's help. Thus Yohannes was simultaneously facing two external threats to Ethiopian independence: the religious imperialism of the Mahdists and the territorial imperialism of the Italians. Both were dangerous. Believing that Italy posed an immediate and greater threat to Ethiopia than the Mahdists, he preferred to fight and dislodge her first could he be sure that the Mahdists would not take advantage of his military engagement with the Italians. He tried to arrange a detente with the Mahdists. Disdainfully rejecting the overture and declaring a Jihad they invaded Ethiopia.[112] In the circumstances Yohannes decided to crush the Mahdists first and to deal with the Italians later. Re-evaluating his strategy and reversing his policy Yohannes decided to seek peace with Italy.

Making peace overtures to Italy Yohannes offered them Sahati and Via for a pledge to confine themselves to Massawa and desist from further territorial aggression on Ethiopia. Ignoring the demand for reparations for the "Dogali Massacres", Yohannes offered to disown Ras Alula who had been the target of the Italian wrath. Promising safety to Italians visiting Ethiopia Yohannes promised a public promulgation ordering his chiefs and people to protect them. Importantly he proposed to Italy "united action" against the Moslem Mahdists who were a menace to both Christian powers. Yohannes proposed to discuss other matters with Italy after the Mahadist menace had been overcome.[113] This was an unexpected reversal of policy towards the Italians. It was a superb move on Yohannes's part designed to hold the Italians neutral while warring with the Mahdists and scorching the suspected intrigue of Menelek with Italy.

Obviously the Italian Government was very pleased by this fortuitous turn of the affairs. After the failure of the Portal Mission Italy had not been left with any dignified alternative to save her face than to go to war with Ethiopia. But war would be expensive both in money and blood and public support could not be counted with its declining clamour for retributive justice against Ethiopia for the Dogali massacre. More important Germany was pressing Italy against any military adventure for European reasons. In February 1888 Bismarck had conveyed to Crispi German military's grave doubts about Italy's military situation and his own "dread" of Italy's military involvement in the Ethiopian interior. The Chancellor feared that, even with artillery, the Italian position on the Ethiopian highlands could not be defended forever against repeated attacks of the Ethiopians who had numerical superiority. Sahati and Via, the disputed territorial possessions were, in German opinion, unimportant economically and disadvantageous militarily. Discouraging military operations Bismarck had recommended to Crispi a naval blockade of Ethiopia which might eventually force that country to seek peace. "Preoccupied with the question solely with the desire that Crispi's politics should succeed" Bismarck had tendered the advice.[114]

Given the developments the Italian Government seized the opportunity to start peace negotiations with Ethiopia. Crispi instructed the Italian Governor of Massawa to respond to Yohannes's overtures positively, but to try to secure the concessions demanded through Portal.[115] The news of Crispi's peaceful overtone pleased Bismarck. Convinced that the time was opportune to establish durable peace with Ethiopia, as it offered the opportunity to "safeguard the dignity and prestige of Italian arms", Bismarck advised Crispi to hasten the negotiations with Yohannes. In the German Chancellor's opinion a peaceful resolution of the Italian difficulty was "highly desirable" for European political considerations.[116] Conveying the news to London Crispi sought once again British aid in smoothening the matters. Salisbury was cautious in his response and wise in his advice. Considering the peace overture of Emperor Yohannes as "an evident satisfaction to the military honour of Italy," Salisbury warned Crispi "that satisfaction will not be essentially enhanced by insisting on a few more kilometers of territory": it was a clear warning to Italy not to get too hungry territorially and ruin peace. As to the expected mediation he felt that it would be better to wait for the right time to "render it highly useful."[117] Before further moves could be made to achieve peace the Ethiopian situation changed dramatically. The Mahadist had attacked western Ethiopia and were threatening Ethiopian independence. They had to be stopped immediately. Moving away from Sahati to meet the Mahadist army, Yohannes died fighting them at Matemma on 9 March 1889. This changed the political situation in Ethiopia drastically.

Yohannes was a great patriot and a farsighted statesman. Though a great soldier he was never impetuous and shunned bloodshed to assert his rights unless it became unavoidable. He was fully aware of the need for independent sea port for Ethiopia to ensure for her uninterrupted communication, trade and import of arms. He told the British negotiator Portal in 1884 that he did not wish to have Consul at Massawa but the port of Massawa itself. Yohannes undoubtedly blundered. He failed to grasp the significance of the collapse of Egypt. He did not see as Italy clearly did that Britain desperately needed a new surrogate state to do her bidding. If ever, his emissaries should have been knocking on British doors in Aden, Cairo and London, it was in the early 1880's. Surely Yohannes had not enough experience with European duplicity. He should have never allowed the hostage Egyptian garrison to escape his control until his troops had occupied Massawa. Incredibly he failed to see that whoever occupied Massawa would probably become Ethiopia's major rival and could not be trusted to permit free import of arms to his kingdom. Finally he held a trump card in that in the early 1880, what would have been advantageous to him would also have been to Britain. By his blunder he unintentionally aided let loose an avaricious imperialist on his shore. By the time the Emperor was complaining to Britain that power had lost the initiative.

As an imperial power Britain underestimated Ethiopia's strength and failed to appreciate Yohannes's courage and determination to defend the territorial integrity and independence of his country. Violating the letter and spirit of the Hewit Treaty it was Britain which planted Italy on the Ethiopian frontier; it was Britain which misled Ethiopia and created problems for her. It did not matter to Britain what had happened to Ethiopia so long as British interests on the Red Sea shore and the Nile Valley had been protected. Nevertheless Britain had made a serious error in diplomatic judgment. Quickly it became evident. Her chosen surrogate state rapidly escaped control. Had Britain eased Ethiopia into Massawa she could have insisted on special treatment for her merchants and adherence to international treaties. The cherished *status quo* of "British Lake" might have been maintained. By sponsoring Italy Britain set in motion a train of events which would not fully play itself out until the 1940's.

International diplomacy seeks predictability. Britain's policy fundamentals were clear. She wanted to guarantee the safety of the sea route to India and expansion of British commerce without expenses to herself. The first priority was to operate under the umbrella of Turkish hegemony. In a Muslim dominated region it was prudent that a Christian power should seek its ambition under Islamic cloak. Fortunately the Turks were weak, therefore pliable to British will. Unfortunately they were too weak to act as active surrogate to implement policies favourable to their own and British interests. Nevertheless the Ottoman could not be abandoned because they provided that cloak of respectability for economic ambitions of a Christian power. Promoting their own expansion under the Ottoman cloak of respectability the Egyptians had become for Britain the second surrogate.

The diplomacy of great powers is frequently driven by the fear, real or imagined, of another great power. In the Red Sea France filled that role. Even the slightest move by the French caused a flow of warnings from British officials, great or not so great. Hence the British search for surrogate was driven by the objective of keeping them out of the grip of France. Whether stated or not, most British diplomatic manoeuvres were carefully checked with considerations for the regulations of the French. All else was subordinated to this. Thus far predictability prevailed.

Predictability was shattered in the 1880's. The first was the collapse of a powerful surrogate. The financial bankruptcy of Egypt left her empire and sphere of influence along the Red

Sea and in the Sudan along the Nile in a power Vacuum. Inevitably imperial greed became stimulated. Presumably some one must benefit. Appetites were whetted. The second disaster from an imperial, point of view was the rise of an Islamic revolutionary movement unwilling to participate in diplomacy according to European designed rules. The Islamic Mahadist movement which took over in Khartoum was not the type of Government which either Muslim or Christian powers were prepared to accommodate. The question was who would overthrow it and thereby inherit the Upper Nile. The third problem for the British involved the choice of a new surrogate. Italy candidate chosen held ambitions which went far beyond the best interests of the British. They lost control. The collapse of one surrogate, the exaggerated objectives of another and revolutionary fundamentalist Islam, taken together produced a mix which challenged British policy makers. Ethiopia became a pawn in British diplomacy and she was sacrificed to suit British interests.

REFERENCES

1. F.O. 403/8. Granville to Mallet, 20 December 1880.
2. F.O. 403/82. Hunter, Acting Resident of Aden to Kimberly, 5 June 1884.
3. F.O. 78/3727. Cromer to Granville, Confidential, 3 November 1884.
4. F.O. 402/814. Major Ardagh's Memorandum, February 1883.
5. F.O. 403/84. Lumley to Granville, 2 January 1885.
6. F.O. 403/82. Acting Political Resident, Aden to Kimberley, 5 June 1884.
7. For instance Turkey refused to recognize the Anglo-Somali Convention of 1877. She refused to play the British Game.
8. F.O. 633/4. Northbrook to Baring, 4 January 1884.
9. F.O. 633/4. Northbrook to Baring,.26 December 1883
10. F.O. 603/4. Baring to Northbrook, 28 January 1884.
11. P.R.O. Cab 37/12. Northbrook to the Cabinet Committee, 8 February 1884.
12. Major Hunter to Kimberley in Godley to Pauncefote, 24 June 1884.
13. P.R.O. Cab 37/12; Hansard, Third Series, CC1XVII: House of Commons Debate; Gladstone to Sumers; 17 November 1882.
14. F.O. 403/81A. Memorandum by Major Ardagh.

15. F.O. 81/4082. Salisbury to Mallet, 20 December 1879.
16. F.O. 403/81A. Salisbury to Paget, 7 February 1880.
17. F.O. 403/81B, 81/C. Granville to Manabrea, 28 February 1882.
18. F.O. 403/813. Granville to Macdonell, 3 September 1881; Christopher Holis, *Italy in Africa* (London: 1941) p. 53.
19. Granville to Paget 29 July 1882; Granville to Manabrea July 1882; Paget to Granville to Manabrea, 29 July 1882, in Fransesco Crispi, *Memoirs of Fransesco Crispi.* 3 Volumes (London; 1912). Vol. 2, pp. 127-132. Carlo Giglio, *Impresa di Massawa* (Rome 1955) pp. 27-132.
20. *Ibid*: Carlo Giglio, pp. 25, 27.
21. F.O. 403/81B. Earl Granville to Macdonell. 3 September 1881.
22. F.O. 403/813. Mancini's Memorandum, in Mancini to Count Nigra, 29 October 1884. Carlo Giglio, *Op cit.* p. 27.
23. Gladston to Granville, 17 October 1884, Agatha Ramm, *Political Correspondence of Gladstone.* 2 Volumes (Oxford; 1962) Vol. 2, pp. 279-280.
24. F.O. 45/498. Granville to Lumley, 5 November 1884.
    Italy. M.A.I. 1/55-38, Nigra to Mancini, 13 November 1845;
25. F.O. 45/498. Granville to Lumley, 13 November 1883.
26. *Ibid.*
27. F.O. 78/3227. Baring to Granville, 3 November 1883.
28. F.O. 141/195. Chermiside's Memorandum on Massawa, 1 December 1884, in Cromer to Granville, 7 December 1884.
29. F.O. 1/31. Mason Bey to Nuber Pasha, 7 May 1884.
30. F.O. 141/195. Cromer to Granville, 7 December 1884.
31. Carlo Giglio, *L'Imprea di Massua. Op cit.* pp. 20-22.
32. P.R.O. 30/29/128. Gladstone to Granville, 17 October 1884.
    Agatha Ramm, *Political Correspondence* of Gladstone, Vol. 2, pp. 279-280,
33. Gladstone to Granville, 10 January 1884. Agatha Ramm, *Political Correspondence.* Vol. 2, p. 146.
34. F.O. 45/498. Granville's Conversation with Nigra, the Italian Ambassador, in Granville to Lumley, 22 December 1884. Rome, 23 December 1884 Giglio, *L'Impresa,* pp. 43-44.
35. F.O. 78/1855 Granville to Wyndham, January 1855.
36. F.O. 44/498. Lumley to Granville, 22 December 1884.
37. F.O. 403/83. Baring to Granville, 30 December 1884, 6 January 1885.
    Italy ASMAi, Pos. 2-1/1 De Martino to Mancini, 30 December 1884.
38. F.O. 403/83. Granville to Baring, 17 January 1885. Baring to Granville, 30 January 1885, Granville to Lumley, 3 February 1885.
39. F.O. 404/83. Baring to Consul Baker, 30 December 1885.
40. F.O. 403/83. Granville to Baring, 7 February 1885.
41. F.O. 404/83. Baring to Granville, 30 January 1885.
42. F.O. 403/83. Baring to Granville, 8 February 1885.

43. F.O. 403/83. Moleneux to the Secretary Admiralty, 2 February 1885.
44. F.O. 403/83. Granville to Lumley, 3 February 1885.
45. F.O. 78/1885. Granville to Wyndham, 2 January 1885.
46. F.O. 403/83. Granville to Wyndham, 10 January 1885.
47. F.O. 403/83. Wyndham to Granville, 5 February 1885; Giglio *Op cit.* 93.
48. France D.D.F. Series 2, Tome V. No. 549. Decrais to Jules Ferry, 31 January 1885,
    France D.D.F. Series 2, Tome V. No. 568. Jules Ferry to Courcel, 7 February 1885.
49. France D.D.F. Series 2 Tome. V. No. 571. Courcel to Jules Ferry, 8 February 1885.
50. France D.D.F. Series 2, Tome V. No. 547. Jules Ferry to De Wisme, 30 January 1885.
51. France D.D.F Series 2, Tome V. No. 568. Jules Ferry to Courcel. 7 February 1885.
52. France D.D.F. Series 2, Tome V. No. 593. Jules Ferry to the Diplomatic Representatives of France in London. Berlin. St. Petersburg, Cairo, Feb 1885.
53. F.O. 78/3871. Mallet to Salisbury, 21 January 1886.
54. F.O. 408/89. Baring to Grenville, 3 February 1885, with the enclosure of Granville to the Khedive.
55. F.O. 45/524. Lumley to Salisbury, 23 October 1885.
56. F.O. 78/3860. Salisbury to Lumley, 30 July 1885.
57. F.O. 403/285, Salisbury to Lumley, 12 November 1885.
    F.O. 141/195 Hunter to Salisbury, in Cromer to Grianville, 7 December 1884.
58. F.O. 401/83, Pauncefote to Godley, 3 February 1885.
    F.O. 403/90, Salisbury to Kennedy 20 July 1877. For a comprehensive account of these sevenths see I.M. Lewis, *The Modern History of the Somaliland* (London; 1965) pp. 40-62.
    F.O. 403/89. 7367. King Menelek to Consul Hunter, 8 January 1887: Hunter to the King of Shoa, 10 February 1887, enclosure in Baring to Salisbury, 23 February 1887.
59. F.O. 78/3859. Mancini to Nigra, 20 March 1885.
60. *Ibid.*
61. F.O. 403/84. The King of Ethiopia to Queen Victoria in Egerton to Salisbury, 10 November 1884 (No. 35 Treaty).
62. *Ibid,* F.O. 403/84. Lumley to Robilant 16 December 1885, No. 250
63. *Ibid.*
64. *Ibid.*
65. *Ibid.*
66. F.O. 403/84. Salisbury to Lumley, 10 December 1885.
67. F.O. 403/84. Count Robilant to Lumley, 18 December 1885 in Lumley to Salisbury. 20 December 1885.
68. *Ibid.*

69. F.O. 141/24. Kennedy to Salisbury, 5 May 1885; F.O. 403/85. Count Robillant to Lumley, 16 December 1885, in Lumley to Salisbury, 20 December 1885.
70. Haggai Erlich, *A Political Biography of Ras Alula,* pp. 92-111.
71. F.O. 141/24. Kennedy to Salisbury, 5 May 1885.
72. Erlich, *Op cit.* p. 106
73. F.O. 11/24. Kennedy to Salisbury, 5 May 1887.
74. F.O. 403/90. Kitchener to Saletta, 5 July 1887, Saletta to Kitchener, 20 July 1887}.
75. Same as foot note 78.
76. F.O. 403/90. Saville to Salisbury, 2 November 1887. F.O. 84. Salisbury to Kenndey, 20 July 1887.
77. F.O. 403/90. Salisbury to Kennedy, 20 July 1887.
78. F.O. 403/90. Queen Victoria to King John, 11 August 1887.
79. F.O. 403/90.93. Portal to Salisbury, 27 August 1887.
80. F.O. 403/90. Colonel Chermicide to Portal, 22 August 1888 in Portal to Salisbury, 27 August 1877.
81. F.O. 403/9. King John to Queen Victoria, 20 October 1887. enclosure, Baring to Salisbury. 7 December 1887.
82. F.O. 403/90. Portal to Salisbury, 27 August 1887.
83. Bismarck to Hatzfeldt, 3 Febuary 1887. Vol. 1, p. 288 in E.T.S. Dugdale (Selected and Translated) *German Diplomatic Documents 1871 to 1914.* 4 Volumes (London; 1927).
84. Italy *Documenti Diplomatici L'Italiani,* Second Series, No. 212, Crispi to Castalani, 10 October 1887.
85. *German Diplomatic Documents,* Vol. 1, Bismarck's Memorandum, 27 October 1887.
86. C.J. Lowe and F. Marzari, *Italian Foreign Policy.* 1870-1940. (London; 1975).P.
87. D.D.I. Series 2, No. 215. De Launay to Crispi, 11 October 1897.
88. *Ibid.*
89. Lewis and Marzari, Italian Foreign Policy, p. 47.
90. Shepard G. Clough and Salvatore Saladino, *A History of Modern Italy. Documents, Readings and Commentary.* (Columbia University; 1968) p. 210.
91. Italy D.D.I. Series 2. No. 27 Crispi to Catalani, 9 August 1887, No. 26: Catalani to Crispi, 10 August 1887.
92. Italy D.D.I. Series 2. No. 212 Copy of Promemoria given by the Italian Ambassador to Lord Salisbury, in Corti to Crispi, 25 October 1887.
93. D.D.I. Series 2. No. 27. Crispi to Catalani, 9 August 1887, No. 26; Catalani to Crispi, 10 August 1887.
94. F.O. 408/90. British Ambassador to Rome to the F.O. August 1887. F.O. 403/996. Salisbury to Baring, 21 October 1887.
95. F.O. 403/90. Salisbury to Baring, 31 October 1887.

96. F.O. 403/90. Baring to Salisbury, 1 November 1887.
97. D.D.I. Series 2. No. 161. Catalani to Crispi, 19 September 1887.
98. D.D.I. Series 2. No. 249. Corti to Crispi, 25 October 1887.
99. F.O. 403/90. Portal to Baring, 1 January 1887.
100. F.O. 403/90. Salisbury to Baring, 23 October 1887.
101. F.O. 403/91. Queen Victoria to the King of Abyssinia, 12 October 1887.
102. F.O. 403/91. Portal to Baring, 1 January 1888.
103. F.O. 403/91. Documents conveyed by Portal to the Emperor Yohannes, 8 December 1887, in Baring to Salisbury, 1 January 1888.
104. F.O. 403/91. Portal to Baring, 1 January 1888.
105. F.O. 403/91. King John to Victoria, December 1888.
106. F.O. 403/91. Baring to Salisbury, 1 January 1888.
107. Italy D.D.I. Series 2, Vol. XXI. No. 443. Benfield, Italian Consul in Aden to Crispi, 20 December 1887.
108. *Ibid.*
109. *Ibid.*
110. Italy D.D.I. Series 2. Vol. XX1. No. 339 Crispi to Bertole Viale, 110.
112. Italy D.D.I. Series 2. Vol. XX1. No. 717. Crispi to De Launay, 30 March 1888.
113. Italy D.D.I. Series 2. Vol. XX1. No. 631. Bismarck to Salms, 27 February 1888.
114. Italy D.D.I. Series 2. Vol. XX1. No. 71. Crispi to De Launay, 30 March 1888.
115. Italy D.D.I. Series 2. Vol. XX1. No. 723. De Launay to Crispi. 23 April 1888.
116. Tadesse Bayene Richard Pankhurst (Editors) *Kassa and Kassa* (Addis Ababa University 890) Zwede Gebre Selassie, Tessema Ta's "Prologue to the Ethiopia-Sudanese Frontier", pp. 273-74.
    CRO. Mahdia I/55/12, Abdullahi to Yohannes, February 1889, *Mulatu & Yohannes Abate, Ethiopia Transition and Development in the Horn of Africa,* (Westview Press, Colarado), p. 13.
    Zwede Gebre Selassie, *Yohannes IV of Ethiopia Political Biography* (Oxford 1955) *Passim.*
117. Richard Caulk, "The Mhdista and the Colonial Partition of East Africa", *Trans African Journal of History,* Vol. I. pp. 352-55.
    CRO. Mahdia I/55/16, Yohannes to Abu Anza 25 December 1888, Abu Anza to Yohannes February 1889.
    Declining Yohannes, appeal for friendly Co-operation in opposing European imperialists the fanatic Mhadist Abu Anzu replied". As far your asking for peace with us whereas you are still infidel I say this is an impossibility. You are a fool to ask for peace with us. Before you enter the religion of our God (Islam). You shall know therefore we are determined to fight. There can be nothing between us except sword unless you believe in God (Allah) alone.

5

Opportunist Britain and the Subdued Surrogate

The death of Emperor Yohannes suddenly changed the situation in Ethiopia. It removed restraints on Italy's westward expansion into northern Ethiopia from Massawa and placed the Solomonic throne within the reach of Menelek who had been impatiently waiting to seize it since Emperor Theodore's death in 1868. Menelek declared himself Emperor of Ethiopia but given the history of succession in that country, it was almost a forgone conclusion that he would be challenged by other aspirants, certainly by Ras Mangacia, the illegitimate son of Yohannes. Menelek turned to Italy for support having been in friendly relations with her since 1885. Italy had been grooming Menelek as an ally by providing him arms and ammunition in the hope of enlisting his support for her struggles against Emperor Yohannes. She gave her support to Menelek in return for extensive territorial concessions. The Italian agent Antonelli who was then in Shoa proposed a draft treaty between Ethiopia and Italy which was signed at Ucciali on 2 May 1889. In return for the Italian recognition of his right to the throne, Menelek gave Italy territorial concessions in northern Ethiopia which included not only the Italian occupied posts of Sahati, Via and Ailet but also Bogos and the coastal territory south of Massawa as far as Arafali.

Menelek's cession was indeed unfortunate. Though in later years Menelek turned out to be an adept in the game of international diplomacy and an uncompromising champion of Ethiopian independence in his dealings with Italy he demonstrated a good deal of the old Shoan isolationism. The arms he amassed from Italy were designed for his own ascendancy.

The most unfortunate part of the Treaty of Ucciali was Menelek's cession of the northern coastal and hinterland territories for which the late emperor Yohannes had fought although his life. Yohannes knew how vital was the coastal territory for Ethiopia's independent survival. Without a sea port Ethiopia could at best be ignored in regional politics, at worst could be cut off from armaments which ensured her survival. By the stroke of pen Menelek wrote off a region which even when it was returned to Ethiopia after World War II would resist incorporation. When Menelek signed the treaty with Italy not only the northern port of Massawa but also the southern ports of Assab and Tajurah bordering Shoa were in the Italian and the French hands. The only hope of an independent outlet for Ethiopia was the northern coastal territory. Its alienation in the Ucciali Treaty ensured that Ethiopia would remain land-locked. Moreover in Article XVII of the Treaty Menelek agreed to use the Italian Government to conduct his external relations.[1] However this was to be at his pleasure and as the Amharic version of the treaty clearly showed it never involved Ethiopia's freedom or sovereign right to conduct her international relations.[2] But being anxious to clamp its protectorate on Ethiopia Italy misinterpreted it to mean that Menelek had surrendered his sovereign right to her to conduct Ethiopia's external relations and notified the signatory powers of the General Act of Berlin of its African protectorate.[3] Inspite of their initial scepticism of Italy's "so called protectorate over Ethiopia" the British recognized it.[4]

Italy further consolidated her hold on the newly acquired territories in northern Ethiopia through the Italo-Ethiopian Convention of October 1889. Exploiting the stipulation that the boundary between the Italian Colony of Eritrea and Ethiopia was to be demarcated on the basis of "the actual possession" Italy soon extended her control to the territory beyond the frontier defined by the Ucciali Treaty. By January

1890 Italy acquired control over the territory from the western Red Sea shore, between Massawa and Arafali, to the neighbourhood of Kassala in the Sudan. With the claimed protectorate over Ethiopia and a colony in proximity to Kassala and Khartoum Italy had suddenly become not just a neighbour of the British but a possible rival and a dangerous competitor for the Nile Valley. This new reality made a profound impression on Britain's policy-makers.

In planting Italy at Massawa the British Government had seriously underestimated Italian aspirations in the Sudan. Italy was desirous of securing territory in the Sudan which appeared to be slipping out of Egypt's rule. Given Britain's need for Italy's diplomatic support in Egypt, Italy hoped to realize her territorial ambition in the Sudan through British support. Italy, however, did not wish to intervene in the Sudan alone risking financial and military burdens as well as likely British opposition. Instead she planned to enter the Sudan as an ally and military partner of Britain in the expectation of receiving territorial rewards for the services rendered. Soon after the death of General Gordon at Khartoum, Mancini, the Italian Prime Minister, offered Italian military support to the British Government for the settlement of the Sudan, "without self interest... to show her (Italy's) friendship for England and to contribute to the work of humanity."[5] One can imagine this must have raised little more than ironic smile in London. The surrogate brought to do the British bidding had developed a big appetite. Determined to keep Italy out of the Sudan she was told curtly that "Britain had the necessary strength to cope with the difficulty".

Notwithstanding Italy's territorial appetite in the eastern Sudan Britain did not perceive any significant Italian threat to British interests in the Nile Valley. In view of Emperor Yohannes's determined opposition to Italian expansion west of Massawa it appeared unlikely that Italy could move into the Sudan. But Yohannes's death in 1889, Menelek's succession to the throne and the Ucciali Treaty changed the political situation drastically. What seemed most unlikely two years earlier had now become possible. In the guise of supporting their ally Menelek the Italians occupied the Eritrean Highlands and established themselves at Keren near the Sudan border by 1889.

The advance of the Italians to Keren and their plan to enter into treaty relations with the chiefs of Kassala "precipitated the matters."[6] Since the occupation of Egypt in 1882, the British Government had been greatly concerned for the security of the Nile Valley. The Nile waters were the source of Egypt's existence and prosperity. It was feared that if a hostile technological power gained control over the river it could divert the Nile waters and hold Egypt to ransom and threaten Britain's controlling position. Hence it was a cardinal principle of British policy not to allow any European power, even a friendly one, to establish itself in the Nile Valley. The doctrine of the indivisibility of British control over the Nile River and its affluents from the Lake Albert Nyanza to the Mediterranean assumed the sanctity of a "Holy Writ' in the eye of British policy" makers. Italy's progress towards Kassala disturbed the British Government very much.

Evelyn Baring, the British Consul-General in Egypt, who had earlier supported the Italian occupation of Massawa became very apprehensive of the Italian movement towards Kassala as it would endanger the security of Atbara, a tributary of the Nile. He suspected the possibility of an Italian thrust towards Khartoum at the convergence of the White and the Blue Niles. Baring was convinced that permitting Italy near the Nile or its affluents would be a great price to pay for Italian support and even a dereliction of duty towards Egypt as it would Jeopardise Britain's hold on the head waters of the Nile. He advised the British Government to warn Italy not to move towards Kassala and come to an early agreement with the Italian Government regarding its territorial limits in the neighbourhood of the Sudan.[7] Appreciating Baring's view Salisbury advised Baring to have informal exchanges with the Italians on the issue.[8]

As the Anglo-German negotiations progressed for a settlement of the British and German spheres of influence in Africa, the Italian Government became anxious to reach a similar understanding with Britain. Signor Crispi, the Italian Prime Minister, approached the British Government in March 1890, for a delimitation of Anglo-Egyptian and Italian spheres in north-east Africa. But the Italian Government wanted a provision in the treaty permitting its military commanders to cross the borders in case of operational necessity. This was clearly an Italian strategy to extend their sphere of influence in the Sudan through back door. Seeing through this, Baring warned Salisbury that the Italian Government would belie all experience of all other nations if they did not extend their territory in the direction of the Sudan where their real or imaginary interests are presumed to be.[9] Salisbury not only shared Baring views but he was also determined not to satisfy the "misplaced and suicidal aspirations of Italy in the Sudan".[10] Anglo-Italian negotiations for a settlement of their spheres of influence and possessions suffered set backs and disruptions from the start. It was primarily due to their diametrically opposite view and positions on the Sudan. While the British held that the whole Sudan was an Anglo-Egyptian territory notwithstanding the withdrawal of Egypt from there and the establishment of the Mahdist State, the Italians held that the Egyptian rights to the Sudan had lapsed for good with her defeat by the Mahdists. Italy argued that the Sudan was "open for acquisition" and refused to be excluded from the possession of the adjacent territories to Eritrea.[11] While Britain claimed sole and indivisible right to waters of the Nile river and its affluents Italy opposed it asserting her claim to use waters of the Atbera, an affluent of the Nile, which was much needed for the well-being of Eritrea.[12] While Italy was keen on acquiring a frontier to the west of River Atbara, Britain was determined to keep it to the east of that affluent.[13] Likewise Britain strongly opposed Italy's moves to acquire the Sudanese territory of Kassala. Crispi the Italian Prime Minister was unyielding on the issue. When the talks were breaking down Baring feared that a displeased Italy might incline towards France. Worried about the ill effects of such a diplomatic shift on the British position in Egypt, "where until then Britain's counted" persistently on Italian friendship and support, Baring tried to save the situation by offering Italy the right of temporary occupation of Kassala and Atbara under military necessity without abrogating the territorial sovereignty of Egypt.[14] Salisbury approved on the condition that Italy clearly recognized Egyptian rights of reoccupation.[15] The militant Crispi refused to endorse the Egyptian rights though he might allow Egyptian claims and threatened not to sign an agreement at all than give a distinct undertaking to evacuate any territory which Italy might find necessary to occupy.[16]

The British stood firm on the doctrine of the indivisibility of Anglo-Egyptian rights to the Nile and its affluents. However to win Italy Salisbury considered to give her some more territory on the Red Sea shore as it would not hurt Egyptian interests. Salisbury told Baring, "I think you also agreed that we have no such well defined and imperative interests to safeguard in the Red Sea shore."[17] The British proposed a new four article draft agreement for Italy's consideration. The essential features were the limiting of the Italian sphere east of the Atbara, preventing Italy from acquiring permanent sovereign rights or protectorates beyond the proposed boundary and engaging her not to build any constructions near the Atbara or other streams which might hinder the free flow of waters to the Nile. Italy was to be allowed the right of temporary occupation of Kassala and the adjoining territory to the east bank of the Atbara without prejudice to Egypt's territorial rights.[18] Italy declined to give the pledge of evacuation of any territory which she might occupy in the Sudan. Talks failed. Baring returned to Ciaro.

By logic and precedents of international relations the British held on an untenable position. Egypt had been defeated in the Sudan and her forces withdrawn under humiliating circumstances. The revolutionary Mahdist state held firm control. No European state had recognized the Mahdists, but then no African nation, including Ethiopia, enjoyed formal recognition which presumably permitted them to be attacked and carved up without legal aggression to have occurred. Furthermore it permitted representatives of two European powers to sit down in Naples and decide their future without the least reference to the African State concerned. All this was logical and legal within the rules of international relations as they had evolved within the European State system. What had no precedent or legality was the British claim that Egypt had first claim to the Sudan. Creating a colony in the Sudan required someone to establish it by force of arms. This is what Britain intended to do when it suited her and she was determined to deny the same right to Italy.

What Crispi could not get at the conference he tried to get by pressure tactics. Raising the cry of "Dervish Menace" to the Italian colony of Eritre he asked British to join Italy in repelling the Mahdists. If the British could not join, Italy alone would march against them and occupy Kassala.[19] Salisbury suspected the tactical move of Crispi to seize Kassala and face the British with a *fait accompli*. Since no agreement had been signed committing Italy to withdraw from Kassala she might stay there unless evicted. Furious with Crispi's devious ways Salisbury warned Rome that such a step would do her no good, perhaps might cause injury. He chided "that if a threat from the Dervishes at Kassala was to justify Italy in seizing that place a further threat would assuredly be coming to justify the occupation of Khartoum."[20] He decided not to discuss the frontier question with Italy so long as Crispi was in power. His attitude towards Italy *vis-à-vis* the Nile Valley certainly underwent a significant transformation after the Naples negotiations. Until then he had not admitted to himself the seriousness of the Italian challenge to British interests in the Sudan. But by late November 1890 he had changed indicating to Baring: "Ever since Italy has put forward this doctrine to justify her claims to Kassala I have felt that we must reconsider our enmities and friendships so far as Egypt is concerned. It is evident that Italy is the most formidable enemy that Egypt has at present to fear. If this is so the Dervishes are rendering us a service by keeping Italy out".[21]

Salisbury appraisal of the situation in the Nile Valley was correct. The Dervish advance in June 1891 which threatened *Agordat* in Eritrea effectively checked Italian expansion towards the Atbara. Consequently the British felt less urgency to reach an agreement with Italy. Salisbury's irritation with Italy caused concern to Germany which advised Rome that Britain's support to her in the Mediterranean and Europe was worth more than territorial acquisition in the former Egyptian province. Berlin feared that Anglo-Italian rift would only serve purposes of France.[22] The fall of Crispi paved the way for a comprehensive settlement of the British and Italian spheres in East Africa. De Rudini, the new Italian Premier, was unenthusiastic about Italy's colonial ventures. He attached great importance to improve friendly relations with Britain whose support he needed in the Mediterranean. Indicating his readiness to meet Salisbury's wishes he requested a quick and comprehensive settlement of Anglo-Italian spheres of influence in Africa.[23] Salisbury authorized the talks. Rudini and Lord Dufferin were able to conclude an agreement relating to the British and Italian spheres from the River Juba to the Blue Nile on 24 March 1891.[24] The British Government managed to keep the important port of Kismayu in its sphere while leaving Kaffa, in Ethiopia, to Italy. On the same day Rudini conveyed his wish to conclude an agreement on their spheres between the Red Sea and the Blue Nile and "his readiness to accept the delimitation proposals made by Baring in October 1890."[25] The talks began. Rudini went much further than the British had hoped in satisfying their wishes by proposing to sign a secret protocol providing for the retrocession of Keren and the Ethiopian plateau to Egypt in the event of Italy's permanent withdrawal from the region.[26] An agreement delimiting Anglo-Italian spheres from the Red Sea to the Blue Nile was signed on 28 March 1891. The Anglo-Italian protocol demarcated the British and Italian spheres of influence on the north and west of Ethiopia.[27]

Through the Anglo-Italian protocols Britain asserted the "indivisible Anglo-Egyptian rights" not only to the Nile Valley but also to the Nile affluents. More importantly she smothered Italian ambitions in the Sudan. An irritating competitor to the Sudan, Italy, had been converted into a friendly watch-dog to protect Anglo-Egyptian interests in the Nile Valley. The East flank of the Nile had been sealed off from European rivals. To secure these interests Britain had signed away Ethiopian independence disdainfully by recognizing Ethiopia as within the Italian sphere of influence. The British Government had re-endorsed the Italian claims to a protectorate over Ethiopia without pausing to consider Menelek's loud protests that Ethiopia was not an Italian protectorate but an independent country. Even the legal facade which Britain had maintained while handing over Massawa to Italy that no *dejure* recognition would be given her until the Italians had first settled the matter with the suzerain Porte was disregarded in dealing with Ethiopia. Apparently in the existing imperial ideology of Europe no African State was permitted the basic right to independence unless it dared to uphold it with might. This was a short-sighted policy as events would prove. Britain had lost an excellent opportunity to regain her influence in Ethiopia by failing to consider Emperor Menelek.

Even as King of Shoa Menelek had shown keen interest in seeking friendly relations with Britain. Now as Emperor of Ethiopia he was keener to forge diplomatic links with her. Such seemed vital also given the challenge of the Islamic fundamentalist al-Mahdi of the Sudan to Christian Ethiopia's independence. Menelek had no reason to believe that Mahdist's hostility towards him could be less intense than it had been towards the late Emperor Yohannes. They might renew the attack on Ethiopia as soon as they felt able to do so. To safeguard Ethiopian interest Menelek hoped to organize a coalition of Christian Ethiopia, Britain and Italy against the Mahdist Sudan. Given those Christian nation's hostility towards the Mahdists such a coalition seemed natural and possible. Like Theodore and Yohannes Menelek also saw international politics in the medieval context of Christianity versus Islam. Fearing that "the Mahdists would continue unchecked unless the Christian kings unite to prevent it," Menelek expressed to Queen Victoria his desire "to see an agreement concluded between England, Italy and Ethiopia with the object of adopting measures to arrest the progress of the Dervishes"[28] It was a shrewd move since such a coalition, if it ever materialized, would not only strengthen Ethiopia against the Mahdist Sudan but also open doors for close relations on equal diplomatic status to Ethiopia with European powers which had always been the object of Ethiopian emperors.

By the time Menelek's communication reached London in November 1889. Italy had already notified Britain of an Italian protectorate over Ethiopia on the basis of the Article XVII of the Treaty of Ucciali. The British were about to recognize the Italian protectorate though France, Russia and Beljium had rejected it.[29] Without alluding to this sensitive issue of the British recognition of Italian protectorate over Ethiopia the British acknowledged Menelek's request. It would be impolitic to decline Menelek's offer as his aid might be useful in the future. Assuring Menelek of its "resolve to secure the peace and well-being of the region in question" Britain hoped to "concert measures as far as it may be possible" when the time arrived.[30] Encouraged by the response Menelek requested Britain to end arms embargo against Ethiopia. Protesting against "the unjust and inequitable agreement among European powers" which were enforcing the embargo he requested the British Government to help him overcome the difficulty. Menelek offered to send his envoys to London to arrive at an agreement on all matters of mutual interests and to strengthen relations.[31] It is important to remember that this communication was sent by Menelek within six months after the signing of the Treaty of Ucciali when his relations with Italy were warm and he had no doubts then either about his sovereignty or independence of Ethiopia. This belied the Italian claim that he had accepted their protection.

Obviously Menelek's communication put the British in some difficulty. Having recognized an Italian protectorate over Ethiopia they were bound not to communicate with him directly. However Menelek himself did not seem to be a dependent ruler having suggested an independent embassy to London. But the Italian watch dog was to be upheld. The British Government had the Queen convey to Menelek the bitter message of Britain's recognition of the Italian protectorate over Ethiopia. She informed him: "We note further Your

Majesty's intention to send some one to us hereafter to discuss matters of common interest to our kingdoms. In as much, however, the Italian Government have notified to us that, by a treaty concluded on 2 May last between Italy and Ethiopia, it is provided that the King of Ethiopia consents to avail himself of the Government of His Majesty the King of Italy for the conduct of all matters which he may have with other powers or Governments, we shall communicate to the Government of our friend, His Majesty the King of Italy, copies of your Majesty's letter and of this our reply.[32]

At the same time to neutralize his possible bitter reaction towards British Government informed Menelek that the arms embargo against Ethiopia was no longer in force at the British Somali ports.[33] In any event the Italians, who were still friendly with Menelek had been supplying arms and the French had promised to do the same. For the British to have done otherwise would have been very impolitic.

As a prelude to the partition of Africa European powers had agreed not to sell arms to African States. This agreement was designed to smoothen the path for European conquest. Given the difficulties of enforcing the ban it was remarkably successful. However the greatest attention fell upon the areas where it failed. As Africans awoke to what was happening to their continent the demands for arms rose significantly and European merchants everywhere around the coast were anxious to enhance their profits. The temptations were particularly strong where for example several European powers were interested in the same region. This was especially so along the Red Sea shore where British, French and Italian colonial enclaves were situated. Besides European merchants in the region there were also Arab, Egyptian and Indian traders anxious to sell arms. In the interior were located two of the most powerful of all African States, Ethiopia and the Mahdist Sudan. While in diplomacy Menelek had fallen into the same blunder like other African rulers by getting into European imperial net, he did realize what many others failed to understand that in the final analysis that Ethiopia would only survive by the strength of her military force.

Under modern condition survival meant arms. It is possible to determine all of Menelek's external relations was to satisfy his addiction to modern armaments. For instance to secure his signature on the Treaty of Uccilai the Italians had to supply him arms. Not only did Menelek play one arms supplier against the other but he had a second major card. Knowing that the Europeans were reluctant to break their own arms embargo Menelek could emphasize that, the arms he wanted were to hold off the threat from the Mahadists who were at war with all Christians. The Christians nations and their merchants could agree that any action to undermine the fanatical Dervishes of Khartoum were in their interest. By comparison Menelek was even "civilized". Thus in persistent approach to Britain Menelek was precisely interested in securing a new arms supplier. Since Italy had emerged as his great potential enemy it was unthinkable that his supply of arms should depend entirely upon that nation.

While it could not be publicly stated, yet Britain was possibly the only nation which secretly looked upon the Mahdi as temporarily useful. Salisbury had admitted to Baring this fact. Consequently the British warned both Italy and France that their arms policy towards Menelek would lead to disaster. However after those nations ignored the warning Britain lifted arms embargo against Ethiopia though she did not want that state to become very strong given its geographical position in relation to the British possessions in the region.

Menelek had already been uneasy about Italy, his pretended ally, having learnt through un-official French sources of the Italian pretensions to a protectorate over Ethiopia. The first official confirmation of this from Queen Victoria at once woke him up to the grave threat posed to Ethiopia's independence. Immediately he endeavoured to expose Italy's trickery. Attempting to disabuse the British Government of its belief that Ethiopia was an Italian protectorate he explained to the Queen:

"since I do not have representatives in Europe and since I have had good friendly relations with Italy for a long time, I decided to use the Italian Government, whenever I wished, with a view to get quick replies, from friendly powers in Europe. I am not obliged to conduct all (foreign) relations through them."[34]

Besides Britain Menelek had also written to France, Germany, Austria, and Russian rulers informing them that Ethiopia was an independent sovereign state which was keen to establish close friendship with our side world, and that she was not an Italian protectorate as Italy was claiming falsely; this did not produce the desired results. While expressing satisfaction with Menellek's desire to establish close friendship with Germany Emperor Wilhelm advised him that friendship should be exercised "indirectly" through Italy. Austria under Bismarck's advise ignored Menelek's request. While France and Russia refused to accept the Italian claim of a protectorate over Ethiopia they did not do more. In the circumstances Menelek attempted to sortout the matter peacefully with Italy. Pointing out the difference between the Amharic text of the Ucciali Treaty and its Italian translation, especially of Article XVII on which Italy was claiming a protectorate over Ethiopia, Menelek requested Italy to provide correct, translation of the Treaty to all European powers to enlighten them about the matter. Responding, the King of Italy sent Antonelli with a new draft treaty and a gift of 5,000 rifles to Ethiopia with instruction to persuade Menelek to sign it. The Italians were bent on enforcing their claim for a protectorate. They had changed the original draft in inserting "obligation" in place of "option" requiring Ethiopia to conduct her foreign relations through Italy. Italy's aim was to control Ethiopia's foreign relations. As Sven Rubenson aptly states Italy's role had been changed from "postman" to "Foreign Policy Advisor", while Menelek was uncertain as to how to overcome the Italian intrigue, empress Taitu, who had been an uncompromising opponent of Italy since its occupation of Massawa, influenced Menelek to oppose Italy. Many important Ethiopian chiefs supported her advising Menelek to fight Italy.

The Ucciali Treaty had been drawn both in Amharic, the official language of Ethiopia, and Italian, but the former was to prevail if any disagreement arose between the signatories.

The Amharic version confirmed Menelek. The Italians had not only misinterpreted Article XVII of the Treaty but changed the wording in the Italian version to support their claims.[35] But the British supported the Italians; ignored Menelek. Wishing to avoid further discussion on the matter the British Government did not acknowledge his communication.[36]

By the time Menelek wrote to Queen Victoria in 1890 the scramble for Africa was well underway. The Chancelleries of Europe had probably decided that every piece of Africa would soon fall to one or other of the scrambling powers. A set of rules had been drawn as to how they might be done without precipitating a major international war. Final recognition had to involve "effective occupation," but the first step was a treaty with an African power. The important provision of such a treaty was the imperial power responsible for the external relations of the African signatories. Generally African Kings welcomed the provision because they were hampered in their foreign relations with Europeans by the lack of ambassadorial relations. Furthermore treaties provided that the European powers would come to the aid of the African State should it be attacked. Equally the African King was bound to support the European power, its traders, officials and diplomats should it or they fall into trouble. Thus to the African leaders, treaties were agreements signed between equals. Usually Europeans sought to inject ownership of land into the agreement. But there is no instance where an African leader willingly or knowingly agreed to this. Diplomats trying to get African signatures on such treaties could only do so by stressing the equal nature of the treaty, by insisting that it was an alliance and often by an outright deception which was easy enough if the treaty appeared in European language only. Some African Kings insisted upon an Arabic translation only thereby making it the official version. Menelek negotiated long and heard that the Amharic version would be the official one. Hundreds of such treaties from the late nineteenth century African heads-of-state probably represent the largest body of purposeful deception in modern history.

Another problem surrounded the word protectorate. It had the advantage that it could be interpreted in many ways. No one dared to translate it as "colony" although clearly that is how European thought of it. Every Africans language could translate "colony", an unacceptable concept. But protectorate could be presented to African as "natural protection". In Europe it was widely known that the treaties had been achieved by massive deception and by consent they were accepted as legal because they assisted in the process of partitioning Africa without a major war. Finally the treaties could operate for a limited time as a military alliance. The Europeans supplied guns and their African allies the manpower to conquer the neighbouring states forcefully, secure new treaties by intimidating and achieve that final stage, "effective occupation". Whether he knew it or not Menelek was up against a solid wall of European conspiracy. If any imperial power exposed the Italian deception it left itself open to its own wrong doings paraded before the world. Consequently Menelek became a threat to the whole conduct of European deception. He and others like him had to be silenced by conquest. While many African Kings could only say that the treaty had been mistranslated to them, they could be dismissed as liars. But Menelek had the evidence in writing of Rome's deception. Chancelleries in Europe could translate the Amharic and compare it directly with the version Italy had circulated. For most Europeans the Italians sinned only because they had been caught. The quicker they silenced Menelek by conquest the better it would be for the preservation of the code of international behaviour. The fiction must be maintained. The stakes were high. War could result. Naturally London was unwavering in its diplomatic support to Italy and choose to remain unconvinced about Menelek's appeals for fair play and moral support against Italy. Equally important she was Britain's surrogate who must be helped. Within the British officialdom itself however there was no unanimity of opinion on Britain's Ethiopian policy.

British Indian authorities disagreed with the home government's view of the matter. British officials in Zeila and Berbera were keen to promote close commercial and political links with Menelek's Ethiopia. Frequent frontier incidents across the undefined border between the British Somaliland and Ethiopia also necessitated direct political contact with the Ethiopian Governor of the neighbouring Harar province. British Indian officials were also more in sympathy with Menelek's aspirations than with Italy's. Obviously the attitude of British officials in the Red Sea region was more influenced by an Indian rather than European perspective. In January 1891 Emperor Menelek requested the British Government to give him control over the Zeila-Harar caravan route so that he may promote commerce. More important he proposed the establishment of "regular relations between the Ethiopian Governor of Harar province and the British Resident at Aden and Zeila."[37] This was a very shrewd move on Menelek's part. Given Britain's local needs at Aden and the Somali Coast, Menelek's proposal was attractive to the British. But its acceptance by the British Government would certainly make a mockery of Italy's pretension to a protectorate over Ethiopia. This would appear to have been a more important goal of Menelek than the mere promotion of trade. Lord Salisbury did not miss the implication. He noted that "the matter is one on which the Italian Government would feel more keenly." Nevertheless he appreciated the need for having direct official links with Ethiopia but the difficulty was to device a *modus operandi* "to relieve the Italian Government of any apprehension of an intention to interfere with the Italian protectorate over King Menelek."[38] The British kept the Italians informed of Menelek's proposals. Clearly having great difficulty with Menelek about its claims to a protectorate, the Italian Government begged the British not to establish direct official relations with Ethiopia but to communicate through the Italian delegate at Harar.[39] Salisbury sympathized. But Viscount Cross, the Secretary of State for India, had reservations about the *bonafide* position of the Italian delegate. He thought that the "Italian delegate at Harar could only be regarded by the Indian authorities in that capacity if he was duly acknowledged by the ruler of Ethiopia as an Italian agent."[40] It is evident that Viscount Cross had no sympathy with the Italian pretension to a protectorate over Ethiopia. He advised Salisbury: "if however King Menelek repudiated the construction which is placed by Italy on this Article (Article XVII) of the Treaty (Ucciali) it seems to Lord Cross that Her Majesty's Government must resume direct dealings with the Ethiopian State".[41]

Though Salisbury clearly realized "that the Italian Government no longer exercised any influence on King Menelek or his Governor" he rejected Lord Cross's advice. The Foreign Secretary saw British support to Italy in Ethiopia in the wider context of European diplomatic alignments and Britain's strategy for the defence of the Nile. Moreover Britain had concluded the Mediterranean Agreement with Italy with the ploddings of Bismarck and Anglo-Ethiopian co-operation could not be weakened because of the Ethiopian considerations.

The Earl of Rosebery, who succeeded Lord Salisbury, as Britain's Foreign Secretary, supported Italy even more enthusiastically than his predecessor. This was indeed a testing time for Italy whose diplomatic efforts to induce Menelek to withdraw his opposition to the protectorate had failed. In February 1893 Emperor Menelek notified European Governments of his intention not to renew the Treaty of Ucciali when it came up for revision in the following year declaring that "the Ethiopian empire was of sufficient importance to exist independently and would not accept any protectorate."[42] While even the German Government, a friend and ally of Italy in the Triple Alliance, just choose to be silent on Menelek's notification, Rosebery assured the Italian Government that "Menelek had no right to denounce the Treaty with Italy" and that he was most anxious to do "whatever was most agreeable to the Italian Government."[43] Ignoring Menelek's explanation for the denunciation of the Treaty and appeals for Britain's equity and fair play in the dispute with Italy the British told Menelek: that they did not think that Article XVII of the Treaty entitled the parties to the Treaty to give notice of its termination, but only to any modifications which they may consider advisable to introduce in it.[44]

Furthermore the Queen advised Menelek to carefully consider any observations on the point which "her good friend" the King of Italy may make.[45] When Ras Mangacia, the illegitimate son of Emperor Yohannes, sought British support for his political pretensions he was advised that "he could not give better proof of his friendship to Her Majesty's Government" than by remaining faithful to "Italy the loyal friend of her country."[46] Rosebery's energetic support for Italy sprang from his over concern for the defence of Anglo-Egyptian interests in the Nile Valley. Believing that he had "scorched both the Congolese and French thrusts from the west by bribing the one to block the other" he was anxious to safeguard the eastern flank of the Nile by supporting the Italian hold on Ethiopia. If the eastern flank gave way the entire British strategy for its defence would collapse and such possibility could occur if Menelek, with French aid, escaped the Italian imperial net.

Britain's strong support to Italy and total disregard for Ethiopian independence hurt Menelek. Like Yohannes, realizing the hollowness of Britain's friendship, he told Britain that he had sufficient courage and power to defend his country's independence and to preserve its ancestral heritage. Denouncing the Ucciali Treaty and rejecting Italian protectorate Menelek prepared himself to fight Italy.

As Italy's relations with Ethiopia degenerated into a military confrontation Anglo-Italian relations came under strain. The Italian Government expected greater British support for its colonial policy both in Ethiopia and the Sudan. Italy was nervous that taking advantage of her military involvement in Ethiopia the Mahdist might attack Eritrea. She requested the British to mount military operations in the Sudan "to show that they are on the side of Italy."[47] She also asked to be allowed to occupy the British controlled Somali port of Zeila to make it a base to open a second front against Ethiopia if war broke out. An Italian attack on Shoa in southern Ethiopia would relieve the Ethiopian pressure on the Italian invasionary forces in the north and ensure quick victory. In fact Germany had advised Italy against preferring such a request fearing that it would only strain Anglo-Italian friendship.[48] While supporting Italy diplomatically on the Ethiopian question and stopping the flow of arms to Ethiopia,[49] the British Government refused to give her any military aid. Apart from her dislike for Italy's military adventures Britain was under French and Turkish diplomatic pressure to disallow landing of the Italian troops at Zeila to launch attack on Harar and Southern Ethiopia.[50] The French warned that British compliance with the Italian request for Zeila would be a violation of the Anglo-French convention on Harar and would affect the friendly relations between them seriously.[51] Britain told Italy, even out of friendship she could neither cede Zeila to her nor allow its use to avoid difficulties with France.[52] In view of reports about the possible attack of Eritrea by the Mahadists when Italy was facing Ethiopian army, Italy's requests for British military demonstration against the Mahadist at Kassala was rejected by Salisbury who was unforgiving. He told Cromer, "I doubt if we are justified in risking these contingencies for a nominal advantage. We have no great interests in the occupation of Kassala by Italy who went there without consulting us rather against our wish".[53] He was ready to see the Italian to stew in their own Juice.

So long as Italy kept out of the Nile Britain wanted her established in Ethiopia, but on her own. As a surrogate State Italy was both naive and brazen. She had been manipulated into the region by the master imperialist. Italy then failed to understand the implications of the assistance and first turned against the British in the Sudan. This touched upon British interests and it took some time for Italian officials to realize that either they followed the path of expansion laid down by the master imperialist or remained wrapped in the Red Sea. Ethiopia was the objective. But as a good surrogate they were expected to move unprompted. With their demand for the joint control of Zeila and British military moves against the Mahadists Italy, as a surrogate, was demanding more from the master imperialist than she was giving. The idea of Italian flag at Zeila must have raised eyebrows in London. Surely that was naive. The British stopped the flow of arms at Aden into Menelek's Ethiopia but beyond that they were hardly expected to go. One moment the surrogate Brazenly challenged Britain in the Sudan, the next humbly begged for help. Once Rome behaved like a great power, the next as a dependent client. By this behaviour she exasperated Britain. While Italy was a legal asset to British as a co-signatory of the Anglo-Italian protocols of 1891, militarily she was a weak watch-dog.

By September 1895 all hopes for a peaceful settlement between Italy and Ethiopia disappeared and both powers were moving towards a military show down. The Italians had a fully equipped army of 20,000 soldiers in Eritrea half of whom were Italians and the rest Ethiopians from Eritrea. They had also 52 cannon. But Italy's efforts to entice even the disaffected Ethiopian chiefs, against Emperor Menelek, failed including the rebel Ras Mangacia, the illegitimate son of the Late Emperor Yohannes, who had challenged Menelek's accession to the throne. Almost all chiefs of Ethiopia including Mangacia, Ras Michael of Wollo and the Gallas joined Menelek in fighting the Italians. A large number of irate Eritrean peasantry who had been dispossessed of their land by the Italian colonialists, joined the Emperor's army in a bid to drive the Italian away.[54] Menelek commanded 100,000 soldiers of whom at least 80,000 had been equipped with modern firearms like the Remington's and breechloaders; ironically much of this had been supplied to Menelek in the halcion days of friendship by the Italians.[55] Ethiopians had also 20 cannon which they had captured from the Egyptians during the battles of Gundet and Gura. The battle was joined at Adwa on 1 March 1896. Ethiopia triumphed. Inspired by patriotism the Ethiopians fought with Italians valiantly. The Italian defeat was total; seven thousand Italian soldiers died on the battlefield, 1500 were wounded and 3000 were taken prisoners. The Ethiopian dead were six thousand and 8,000 wounded. The invading Italian force was wiped out on the battlefield of Adwa whereas Menelek had intact under his command a fighting force of more than sixty thousand soldiers.[56] However instead of humiliating the Italians further by occupying Eritrea he accepted the Italian request for peace. The Ethiopian victory reverberated through-out the world, while it shocked Europe that a black African State could inflict such a massive defeat on a European power, it held a beacon light of independence to the enslaved and oppressed Africans everywhere. A major result of Adwa was a rush of European powers to Menelek's capital to extend recognition to the Ethiopian State. This was the first ever formal diplomatic recognition of an African kingdom. It was a fulfillment of the age long objective of Ethiopian emperors.

In the decade between 1887 and 1897 the British failed dismally in their Ethiopian policy. The Portal Mission of 1887 and the Rodd Mission of 1897 stand as monuments to British bungling. Both were dismal failures. In its maoepic pursuit of strategic interests, ignoring Ethiopia, Britain had brought Italy as a surrogate to checkmate France on the western Red Sea shore and the Nile Valley. But the surrogate had turned into a challenger of British rights to the Sudan and the Nile affluents besides endangering British interests in the Nile Valley by her military collapse at Adwa. Britain's refusal to aid Rome's efforts in Ethiopia had only turned that power into a disgruntled and critical ally in the Nile Valley. Britain's alignment with Italy only hurt her in Ethiopia by driving the latter into the French orbit. From the vantageous and influential position of being a most trusted friendly power Britain had become almost a *persona non grata* in Ethiopia by 1897, facing a new threat to the Nile from that African State which had emerged as a strong power in the Nile Valley.

REFERENCES

1. Sven Rubenson "The Protectorate Paragraph of the Ucciali Treaty", *Journal of African History*. Vol. XL, 1964, pp. 244-283.
2. This will be discussed later in the chapter.
3. F.O. 403/124. Catalini to Salisbury, 12 October 1889.
4. F.O. 403/120. Queen Victoria to Menelek, 20 February 1890.
5. F.O. 45/521. Granville to Lumley, 13 Febuary 1885.
6. F.O. 148/121. Situation Report on the Sudan.
7. F.O. 141/128. Baring to Salisbury, 15 December 1889.
8. F.O. 141/274. Salisbury to Baring, 14 March 1890.
9. F.O. 170/432/219. Vol. 2, p. 168. Baring to Salisbury, 15 March, 1890. Quoted by E.J. Lowe, *The Reluctant Imperialists*, 2 Volumes (London, 1967). Vol. 2, p. 168.

9. F.O. 170/432/219. Vol. 2, p. 168. Baring to Salisbury, 15 March, 1890. Quoted by E.J. Lowe, *The Reluctant Imperialists,* 2 Volumes (London, 1967). Vol. 2, p. 168.
10. F.O. 78/4243. Salisbury to Baring, 19 November 1889. Also Robinsin and Gallagher. *African and Victorians,* p. 284. and G.N. Sanderson, *England, Europe and the Nile,* pp. 60-62.
11. F.O. 141/277B. Baring to Salisbury, 3 October 1890.
12. *Ibid*
13. F.O. 141/227B. Baring to Salisbury, 30 September, 6 and 30 October 1890.
14. F.O. 141/277B. Salisbury to Baring, 8 October 1890.
15. *Ibid*
16. F.O. 141/277B. Baring to Salisbury, 30 September 1890.
17. Vol. 2, p. 61. Salisbury to Baring, 31 August 1890. Cesil IV. 330-31. Quoted by Lewis. S. *Reluctant Imperialists*. Vol. 2, p. 61.
18. F.O. 141/277B. Baring's Proposal to Italy.
19. F.O. 403/126. Salisbury to Dufferin, 12 November 1890.
20. F.O. 45/648. Salisbury to Dufferin, 12 November 1890.
21. Salisbury to Baring, 21 November, 1890. Lowe, *Reluctant Imperialists.* Vol. 2, p. 69, Salisbury told the Italian Ambassador, " The Occupation of Massawa by Italy had been favoured by the Government of Great Britain at that time, but her Majesty's advisor had little idea then that it would ever lead to doubts being entertained as to the possibilities of the difficulties thereby being created in the Valley of the Nile.
22. Chancellor Caprivi to Count Solms, 3 April, 1890. E.W. Dugdale (Selected & Translated), *German Diplomatic Documents* 4 Volumes (London, 1928).Vol. 2, p. 155.
23. F.O. 45/667. Dufferin to Salisbury, 14 February 1891.
24. F.O. 881/6133. Dufferin to Salisbury, 24 March 1891.
25. F.O. 881/6133. Salisbury to Dufferin, 26 March 1890.
26. F.O. 881/613. Dufferin to Salisbury, 28 March 1891.
27. *Ibid.*
    F.O. 881/6133. Dufferin to Salisbury, 30 March 1891.
28. F.O. 403/124. King Menelek to Queen Victoria, received at the F.O. on 18 November 1889.
29. France D.D.F. Series 1, Tome VII, No. 514. L'Ambassade D'Italia to the French Foreign Ministry, 10 January 1884.
30. F.O. 403/124. Queen Victoria to Menelek, 19 November 1899.
31. Refer to Foot Note 34. Menelek to Queen Victoria.
32. F.O. 403/125. Queen Victoria to King of Ethiopia, 20 February 1890.
33. F.O. 403/124. Menelek to Queen Victoria, 18 November 1899.
34. F.O. 45/645. Salisbury to Dufferin, 12 December 1890.
35. F.O. 403/154. Salisbury to Dufferin, 20 January 1891.

36. *Ibid.*
37. F.O. 881/6133. India Office to the Foreign Office, 23 March 1891.
38. *Ibid*
39. F.O. 45/645. Salisbury to Dufferin, 12 December 1890.
40. F.O. 403/1890. Letter of Menelek to Queen Victoria, 27 February 1893; in the India Office to Foreign Office, 18 April 1893.
41. F.O. 881/6133. Viscount Cross to Lord Salisbury 23 March 1891.
42. Rosebury to Vivian, 4 May 1893.
43. F.O. 403/190. Queen Victoria to Menelek, 5 May 1893.
44. *Ibid.*
45. *Ibid.*
46. F.O. 881/6133. The Earl of Kimberley to Mangacia, 31 December 1894.
47. F.O. 369/658. Cromer to Kimberley, 4 January 1895.
48. *German Diplomatic Documents.* Vol. 2, p. 161 Baron Von Marschall to Bulow, 8 January 1895.
49. F.O. 369/658. Kimberley to Clairford, 6 February 1895
    F.O. 369/658. Clairford to Kimberley, 21 January 1895.
50. *Ibid, German Diplomatic Documents.* Vol. 2, p. 306 Count Metternich to Caprivi, 8 October 1894.
51. France D.D.F. Series 1, Tome XII. No. 240. Courcel to Berthelot, 18 December 1895.
    France D.D.F. Series 1, Tome XII. No. 212. Courcel to Berthelot, 20 December 1895.
52. F.O. 369/658. Kimberley to Clairford, 6 February 1895.
53. F.O. 78/486, Salisbury to Cromer, 29 February 1896.
54. Rubenson, Sven, *The Survival of Ethiopian Independence* (London, 1975), p. 403.
55. *Ibid.*
56. Rubenson, Sven, *Protest and Power in Black Africa* (New York, 1970) (Adwa 1896), pp. 165-66.

6

Menelek's Ethiopia Reorientation of British Policy and Frontier Negotiations

The battle of Adwa not only shattered the Italian dream of protectotare over Ethiopia but also Britain's defences for the eastern Nile Valley based on the Anglo-Italian protototocols. Since the British occupation of Egypt in 1882, Anglo-French relations had steadily deteriorated and by 1896 the French challenge to the British position in the Nile had become fierce. The French Government had despatched a mission under the command of Major Marchand to strike at the west bank of the White Nile through Congo and Ubhangi Sahrai to establish its claims to the Nile Valley. While Marchand might achieve this he could not be expected to occupy the territory unaided. However the French position would vastly improve if Emperor Menelek could be induced to align himself with the French in achieving effective occupation.[1] To achieve this the French Government sent Lagarde to Ethiopia in 1896. The British were nervously watching the French proceedings in Ethiopia. Salisbury suspected that "these French comings and goings"... had in view the opening of some communication with the White Nile through Abyssinia.[2] At the same time the situation in Ethiopia favoured the French having assisted Emperor Menelek against Italy. In contrast to British influence in Ethiopia which had reached its nadir, that of the French was at its peak; while France was trusted and respected[3] the British were distrusted and resented in Ethiopia. Just at a time when the French challenge to the British hold on the Nile Valley was becoming serious British strategy to protect eastern approach to the Nile had broken down. Uniquely among the European imperialist's aggressors of Africa Italy, Britain's surrogate had failed to follow her spheres of influence and treaties into effective occupation. The British had poor results from their surrogates. First Egypt and now Italy had failed them. They could no longer thwart the French through client states. In Ethiopia they had a backlog of ill will to overcome. Truly British policy over the past thirty years had been appallingly unsuccessful. Like most great powers Britain could employ force to make up for the failure of diplomacy, but that was not the right option in the new situation. Ethiopia had emerged as a strong power with a potential to obstruct British territorial claims, rights and interests in the Northeast and East Africa. These developments necessitated a reorientation of British policy towards Ethiopia.

First of all the British Government decided to preempt the French moves to acquire titles to the Nile Valley by reconquering and effectively occupying the Mahdist held Sudan. Military operations against the Mahdist Khalifa was ordered twelve days after the Italian defeat at Adwa. As British military operation on the Sudan bordering Ethiopia might make Menelek suspicious about British designs on his Empire Britain was keen to let him know that the military operations was solely against the Mahdist Khalifa and assure him of its friendship. At the same time Britain was anxious to get, if possible, Menelek's co-operation in the war against the Mahdists, if not at least his neutrality. Given the common frontiers of the Anglo-Egyptian Sudan, the British Somaliland and the British East Africa with Ethiopia Britain wanted to conclude agreement with Menelek concerning the frontiers. It had become necessary to win Menelek's friendship and achieve credibility at Addis Ababa. So the British Government decided to send a diplomatic mission to Menelek to achieve these objectives and "to personally assure him of goodwill and friendship of Her Majesty's Government."[4]

Rennell Rodd, the first Secretary at the British Legation in Cairo, was chosen to conduct the mission. However Rodd

Mission was at a disadvantage from the first. He could offer very little either to win Menelek's support or secure an acceptable frontiers for the Sudan. The British had very little knowledge of Menelek's diplomatic abilities or of Ethiopia's military strength. Menelek was in an *entente* with the Khalifa, having already, received two diplomatic missions from him. He had warned the Khalifa against the danger from the "Red English" and had told him to look upon the French favourably.[5] The French had just signed a treaty with Menelek regularizing the French Somaliland Protectorate's frontier with Ethiopia and had made large territorial concessions to Menelek. Though it was not known then, the French had also entered into a secret understanding with Menelek for Franco-Ethiopian collaboration in occupying the Nile Valley. In return for Menelek's support they had recognized Ethiopia's territorial rights to the Nile as far north as Khartoum.[6] In contrast what Rodd had been authorized to give Menelek was trifle.

Salisbury's instructions stated that the British Government offered to recognize Abyssinian frontier between the 10 and 15 parallel north latitude which would not exceed the sphere of influence assigned to Italy by the protocols of 15 April, 1891. The Government was ready to a further extension of the frontier between Famaka and Karakoja "if it should be necessary for the purpose of securing King Menelek's alliance and co-operation against the Dervishes."[7] Moreover notwithstanding, the Italian defeat at Adwa and the doubtful future of Italy's colonial empire in north-east Africa, the British had affirmed to the Italian Government the validity of the Anglo-Italian protocols—perhaps an insurance for the future—in case Italy should reassert her position in Ethiopia.[8] Rodd was explicitly told that any arrangement which recognized Ethiopia's territorial claims "should contain an explicit statement that such a recognition is made only so far as British and Egyptian rights are concerned and that any language which might be constructed as a claim to dispose of the rights or reject the claim of other countries should be carefully avoided."[9]

Rodd's assignment was formidable and frustrating. Even in the first meeting with Menelek, Rodd realized the difficulty in the way of reaching a territorial settlement. Menelek disclaimed any knowledge of the Anglo-German Agreements on which the British based their claims to the Nile Valley.[10] He advanced Ethiopia's claims to the whole territory from Lake Victoria Nyanza to Khartoum and from the Indian Ocean to the White Nile on the basis of his circular of 10 April, 1891 to the rulers of Europe. Though Rodd protested "that no such document was known to Her Majesty's Government"[11] the truth of the matter was different. Though Rodd himself was unaware of Menelek's territorial claims until he arrived in Addis Ababa and does not appear to have been briefed by the British Government, he was wrong in assuming that the British Foreign Office had been ignorant of them. Furthermore Menelek was right in insisting that he had notified the British Government of his territorial claims through his circular of 1891. Menelek's notification and the letter addressed to Queen Victoria did reach the British Foreign Office through the Indian Office[12] and were acknowledged. The Queen had written to Menelek: "We have received the letter which Your Majesty addressed to us April last relative to the limits of the Empire of Ethiopia. We thank you for the communication and send you in return copies of two protocols which have been signed by the representatives of ourselves and of our good brother, the King of Italy, for the demarcation of our respective spheres of influence in East Africa. So far as we are concerned it is our intention to abide strictly to our engagement to our brother, the King of Italy".[13]

The letter was handed over to the Italian Government to be forwarded to Menelek. Since Menelek and his deputy Makonnen disclaimed any knowledge of the protocols or of the British Government's response to his circular of 10 April, 1891, it may be assumed that the Italian Government choose not to pass on the Queen's latter to Menelek. Pretending friendship to Menelek and disowning any territorial designs on Ethiopia the Italian would have had great difficulty in explaining the existence of the Anglo-Italian protocols which recognized Ethiopia as an Italian sphere of influence. It seems apparent that the Italians had reason to suppress the Queen's communication to Menelek and they would appear to have done so. What is unclear is why the British Foreign Office did not brief Rodd about Menelek's territorial claims. Perhaps it was thought politic to pretend ignorance.

Rodd's insistence on Anglo-Ethiopian rights to the Nile Valley made no visible impression on Menelek who stood firm on his territorial rights as set forth in his circular of 10 April, 1891. More important he succeeded in impressing Rodd that unlike Britain. Ethiopian claim, was not mere paper claim but effective occupation. Rodd warned Salisbury that Menelek's claims were not mere declarations on paper, that the King had for years been actively engaged in rendering his occupation effective." Rodd felt that very little could be gained by a discussion of Anglo-Egyptian claims to the Nile Valley "under the limitations laid down by the official instructions." He confessed to Salisbury: that the utmost concessions proposed by the British Government to Menelek, even if he contemplated common action with Britain against the Mahdists, fell far short of the country which he claimed as a portion of his empire without reference to the larger area to which he has asserted his theoretical claims.[14]

He considered it pointless to discuss the question of the western frontier of Ethiopia until Britain had reconquered the Sudan. In the circumstances Rodd requested Menelek that pending a settlement of the disputed territory the emperor should not cede or promise any portion of it to others. Menelek replied that "he would give to none... whoever it might be." While the western frontier question was laid to rest, Rodd managed to reach an agreement with Menelek on the British Somaliland-Ethiopia frontier. It was a "most weary exercise."[15]

During the partition of Africa in the 1880's Britain acquired large tracts of territories in the east and north-east Africa. These were British Somaliland, the British East African Protectorates of Kenya and Uganda and the Anglo Egyptian Sudan. Britain's rights to these territories had been endorsed by Germany and Italy in the Anglo-German and the Anglo-Italian protocols of 1891 and 1894 respectively. Though all these territories shared frontiers with Ethiopia Britain had not seen fit to notify her about the extent of British colonial possessions in the region.[16] Such a course was inconceivable at the time when no African State had any legitimacy in European eyes and Ethiopia itself had been recognized as an Italian protectorate. But the magnificent victory of Ethiopia over Italy in 1896 forced Britain to reorient her policy, if not her attitudes, towards Ethiopia. Menelek's Ethiopia had emerged after Adwa not only as a strong power in the Nile Valley but also as a challenger to Britain's territorial claims in the region. Menelek had substantial territorial ambitions which clashed with those of Britain.

Menelek kept himself well informed of the happenings in Europe through his European contacts and French newspapers.[17] He knew of the arrangements among the practitioners of Africa and had an understanding of European imperialism and of the dangers which the European thrust into north-east Africa posed to Ethiopian independence. As early as 1891, as a reaction to the proceedings of the Berlin Congress, he had challenged the paper partition of east and north-east Africa by Britain, Germany and Italy in the Anglo-German and the Anglo-Italian protocols and notified those powers of Ethiopia's claims to "ancient frontiers." He had stated:

While tracing today the actual boundaries of my empire I shall endeavour, if god gives me life and strength, to reestablish the ancient frontiers of Ethiopia up to Khartoum and as far as Lake Nyanza with the Gallas.

Ethiopia has been for fourteen centuries a Christian island in the Sea of Pagans. If powers at a distance come forward to partition Africa between them, I do not intend to be an indifferent spectator.

"As Almighty has protected Ethiopia up to this day, I have confidence, He will continue to protect her and increase her territories in the future. I am certain that He will not suffer her to be divided among other powers.[18] Menelek believed that as an African he had better right to the adjacent African territories than the scramblers from distant Europe.[19]

As a determined expansionist Menelek set out to achieve his territorial goals systematically. Having learned how

Khedive Ismail had profited through the services of General Gordon, Samuel Baker, Hicks Pasha and other knowledgeable foreigners, Menelek surrounded himself with a number of Europeans who could assist him.[20] While Count Antonelli had advised Menelek to notify European powers about the extent of his territorial claims and to reinforce it by planting Ethiopian flags at its farthest limits, Alfred Ilg, his Swiss Counsellor, had impressed upon him the need to back up the claims with force.[21]

Menelek understood that effective occupation was the yardstick by which the scrambler's assessed the validity of each other's claims. He had been occupying territories which Britain claimed as her own and none of the British protectorates in the region had men or material power to resist his expansion. The absence of defined frontiers between British colonial possessions and Ethiopia and Menelek's disavowal of the Anglo-German and the Anglo-Italian treaties on which British titles to those territories rested raised serious problems for Britain. Menelek's Ethiopia could not be bamboozled like less powerful African States.

Notwithstanding her outdated war machinery, Ethiopia's ability to field at a short notice a huge army gave her an edge over her enemies as the recent experience of Egypt and Italy had shown. Britain was impressed sufficiently by the strength of Menelek's Ethiopia to realize that it could endanger the security of the adjoining territories claimed by Britain. Reversing the policy of ignoring Menelek's territorial claims Britain decided to seek a peaceful settlement of colonial frontiers with Ethiopia. This was achieved in three separate frontier treaties signed with Menelek between 1897 and 1907: these were the British Somaliland and Ethiopia frontier treaty of 1897, the Sudan-Ethiopia Border Agreement of 1902 and the British-East Africa and Ethiopia Border Agreement of 1902 and the British-East Africa and Ethiopia Border Agreement of 1907.

British Somaliland Ethiopia Border

The first warnings about Menelek's forward policy reached the British Government from its Somali protectorate which was very vulnerable given its structure, ethnic composition and poor finances. The protectorate was primarily made of the Somali coast including the ports of Zeila, Bulhar and Berbera and the hinterland comprising the Somali political groupings of Habr Awal, Mijjertan, the Gadabursi, Habr Tol Jaal, Esa, Habr Gechajin and Warrangali. The protectorate had interfered very little with those groupings confining itself to maintaining law and order and keeping trade routes open and safe. The Somali groupings had been split up between the British and the French protectorates and Ethiopia. They moved with their cattle to graze and water without regard to the frontiers which they hardly comprehended and clearly did not recognize. The British protectorate's meager revenue which came from port duties did not leave enough funds to maintain either a frontier force to protect its borders or an adequate administrative staff to supervise it. The British Government had become complacent about the security of Somali protectorate after securing its frontiers from its colonial rivals in the Anglo-French treaty of 1887 and the Anglo-Italian protocols of 1891. A threat to British interests in the Somali protectorate had hardly been anticipated. Consequently British Somaliland territories contiguous to Ethiopia became the object of Menelek's expansion because they were not administered and therefore could not be said to be "effectively occupied."

After conquering Harar in 1887, Ethiopian forces under the command of Ras Makonnen started coercing the Esa, Gadabursi, Habr Awal and the Somalis of Haud and Ogaden. The Ethiopians opened a post in 1891 at Bio-Kaboba among the Gadabursi Somalis who on paper lived under British protection.[22] The frequency and intensity of Ethiopian raids had increased so much that the India Office complained to the Foreign Office in early 1893 about "the oppressive proceedings of the Abyssinians" in regard to the levy of a daily tribute of sheep on the Yunas Jibril section of the Jibril Abokr Somalis and also of the repeated devastation of the Ogaden country.[23] Moreover towards the south the Ethiopians had penetrated the Jubah River and Lugh and in the north they claimed authority over the Esa.

Clearly the situation had become critical and the Indian Government proposed to send a mission to Ras Makonnen at Harar to resolve the issue amicably by dissuading him "from a course of action which was calculated to affect injuriously the British interests at Aden and the Somali coast." But having recognized the Italian protectorate the British Government could not deal with Ethiopia directly as Italy insisted that all negotiations should proceed through her.[24] The British Government could do nothing to stop the Ethiopian forays. The idea of arming the Somalis was dismissed as soon as it was raised since the armed men could use the arms as much against their official protectors as their present tormentors. Soliciting Italian intervention to check Ethiopian forays was counter productive since Menelek rejected their protectorate. There was a further objection for seeking Italian intervention even if it might help. The India office told the Forcign Office bluntly that if Britain used the Italian mediation to secure the cessation of the Ethiopian encroachment on Somali or Ogaden territory the object might be defeated by leading the Ethiopians to suppose that Britain followed a common policy with Italy on the coast. The effect of Italian mediation on the Somalis might also be disastrous and result in the loss of British influence over them.[25]

In the circumstances the British authorities decided to make direct but unofficial representation to the Ethiopian authorities to stop raiding British "subjects" in Somaliland.[26] Such approaches were unproductive. The Ethiopians continued to extend their authority by raiding people in British Somaliland, by establishing forts and collecting tributes in several places. In July-August 1896 the Ethiopians occupied Alalo in Gadabursi country, set up a number of huts and raised their flag.[27] The British, who had been in treaty relations with the Somalis of Gadabursi since 1884 and placed them under protection, requested the Ethiopian Governor of Harar to withdraw from there, but to no avail.[28] Regarding the Ethiopian act as "fatal to Britain's prestige and influence" the British officials asked London to act promptly to stop them. The Secretary of State for India ordered the Government of India to send a Marine ship and imperial gun boat to "afford effective support to British authority" in the Somali protectorate, obviously to scare the Ethiopians.[29]. Attaching great importance to peaceful commercial relations with Ethiopia the Government of India, however, "strongly objected to sending reinforcements to Zeila."[30] Lord Salisbury agreed and preferred a friendly representation to be made to Ras Makonnen, the Ethiopian Governor of Harar, not to aggravate the situation since a British mission would be sent to Emperor Menelek to arrange a frontier.[31] The Ethiopian Governor Maconnen replied that the occupied territory was Ethiopian, Menelek had informed all powers that Gadabursi was under his government, and that it cannot be abandoned.[32] Ferris, British Consul to the Somali coast advised the British Government that as Emperor Menelek had never accepted the delimitation of Somaliland between Britain and Italy. To avoid raids and further territorial acquisitions from Ethiopia, delimitation of the British East African frontier must be immediately arranged with Ethiopia through a "binding treaty" with Menelek.[33]

The India Office thought that without formally recognizing Ethiopia's *de facto* occupation in the Somali protectorate no agreement could be reached with Menelek.[34] From the very beginning the India Office and its consular officials had been correct in their assessment of the power relations in north-east Africa. London had studiously ignored them. As their advice demonstrates, even in 1893, when Italy seemed well on the way to absorbing Ethiopia, the India Office was advising caution. The imperial mind might well have paid greater heed. The battle of Adwa justified the policy of the India Office in a dramatic and outstanding fashion. The imperial mind had blundered against which it had been repeatedly warned. Following Adwa the British faced a host of frontier problems on three sides of Ethiopia without a drop of sympathy in that country. Menelek was wary. He was suspicious. He was hostile. Given the situation, the emperor could best seek revenge for the Italian invasion by striking at the British claimed territories all around his borders. The situation was grave. The British Government agreed with the suggestion of the Somali coast officials and sent the Rodd Mission to Ethiopia to negotiate a settlement with Menelek regarding British Somali-Ethiopia frontier.[35]

The British were ready to offer a number of inducements to Menelek for a definite understanding regarding the Protectorate's frontier. These included the facility for Ethiopia's trade and commerce through the protectorate to the sea coast, a "guarantee" that all goods coming to Abyssinia for the king's use would be duty free at Zeila, facilities for the importation of some arms and ammunition and permission to station an Abyssinian agent at Zeila. If necessary Britain would also transfer any tribe to Ethiopia. But Britain wanted an assurance from Menelek that "districts recognized as Abyssinian shall not be ceded to any other power."[36]

It is clear from these instructions that the British Government was ill-informed about the Ethiopian situation. Britain's proposed concessions were no concessions at all in Menelek's eye. The French had recently signed an agreement with him regarding the French Somali protectorate border with Ethiopia making substantial territorial concessions to Menelek. The French Somali ports had been made available to Ethiopia for importing arms and ammunition and the French had been endeavouring to attract Ethiopian trade to their port. As France had an honourable record from Ethiopian perspective Menelek settled with her quickly. France stood to reap commercial benefits as well. Britain's territorial concessions were too meagre, too pathetic and too late. A final demand that Ethiopia should not cede territory to another power was insulting the Emperor. The imperial mind had not yet understood the emperor with whom they had to deal.

Basing his demands on his circular of April 1891 to the European powers, Menelek claimed the Somali territories of Habr Awal the Gadabursi, the Esa and the Lake Asal as part of the Ethiopian empire. From Asal the Ethiopian frontier was traced to the northern limits of the Arafuile, skirting the coast line. Rodd countenanced theses claims with Britain's prior rights to the Somali territory on the basis of the Anglo-French and the Anglo-Italian protocols of 1887 and 1891 and the various treaties between the Somali political groupings and the British Government. Menelek disclaimed any knowledge of these treaties while Rodd disclaimed any knowledge of Menelek's circular of 1891.

Rodd was entirely wrong in this has been demonstrated earlier.[37] Consequently the British had sent their emissary to Menelek, ignorant of a document which he had circulated six years earlier. Notwithstanding Rodd's disclaimer, Menelek advanced his territorial claims to all of the British Somali protectorate east of Harar, as a part of Harar Dependency. Proposing the "extraordinary doctrine" that from times immemorial the Somali's had been Ethiopia's cattle keepers who paid regular tribute to their masters, Menelek claimed sovereignty on all Somalis and proposed that the British protectorate be limited to a hundred kilometers inland from the coast. The British rejected this claim.[38] They also opposed an artificial division of the protectorate ignoring the needs of the pastoral Somalis and their seasonal migrations. Instead they proposed a frontier based on Somali political divisions which did not find favour with Menelek. The British finally proposed the criterion of effective occupation. Menelek agreed but insisted on the maintenance of the *status quo*. The British agreed provided the *status quo* was defined and border was drawn on the basis of "the actual occupation." Once the principle was settled Menelek suggested that the British should work out the actual frontier with Ras Makonnen, the Governor of Harar.[39]

This was, however, not an easy task. Ras Makonnen reopened the entire issue proposing that the British Somali protectorate should be confined to a hundred kilometers from the sea shore and the rest was Ethiopian territory. He was apprehensive of any frontier which passed close to Harar which Menelek had incorporated only a decade ago. He also insisted on the British cession of the Somali town of Hergeisa. The British were in difficulty since they badly wanted a frontier agreement to check further Ethiopian expansion into their protectorate. They wanted this done without either alienating Menelek or ceding much territory. But the problem was that Britain had only paper claims against Menelek who had buttressed his territorial claims with effective occupation.

Explaining his difficulty Rodd wrote to Lord Salisbury that he was practically without a means of exercising any moral pressure, as while the French had just a few weeks ago accepted a conspicuous curtailment of their protectorate claims on the coast. It was obvious that without Britain being able to assert its rights in some more convincing manner than it had hitherto done... no understanding would be possible with Menelek without making much larger concessions than what had been proposed. The Abyssinians were to some extent in the position of *beati possidientes*.[40]

The Ethiopians had established a fort at Biyo Kaboba on the British side of the frontier as defined by the Anglo-French Treaty of 1888 and another at Jig Jiga just outside the British frontier as defined by the Anglo-Italian Protocols of May 1894. They had occupied Alalo in Gadabursi country. These territories had to be recognized as within the Ethiopian sphere.[41] Thus the British decided to do so without sacrificing their fundamental interests: these were to ensure a regular supply of meat and provisions to the Aden settlement and to keep the trade route from Harar to Zeila open since the customs derived from it would be the sole income to sustain the Somali protectorate. They refused to cede Hergeisa to Ethiopia since it was a "sacred city of the Somalis" who came to Berbera for trade. "To hand it over to the Abyssinians would have meant to loose all influence with many of the (Somali) tribes."[42] After securing these interests the British accepted a frontier which while giving away to Ethiopia some of the best food producing country retained in the Somali protectorate a number of groups who regularly traded to Berbera. While retaining Haabr Gerhaji group the British gave to Ethiopia a portion of the Esa and Gadabursi country.[43] Care was taken to draft the treaty in such a way as to specify the Ethiopian recognition of the British Somali protectorate without admitting Britain's cession of the Somali territory to Ethiopia. However it was evident that Britain ended up ceding much more territory to Ethiopia than she had intended notwithstanding the rationalization that much of the ceded country "was sparsely populated and barren region." Ethiopia extracted from Britain 67,000 square miles of what Britain had regarded as the Somali protectorate territory. Adept in the game of effective occupation Menèlek had turned it upside down against British adversaries to acquire some of the claimed Somali territory. As I.M. Lewis observed; "This represented a considerable concession to the Ethiopian Claims, which though not in 1897 supported by any firm Ethiopian occupation on the Somali soil beyond Jig Jiga, could not be challenged without the use of force, a course which Rodd rightly understood his Government could not countenance.[44]

It was ironic, yet typical of the age, that two imperialist powers argued about the welfare of a people over whom they intended to exercise hegemony. Probably neither knew anything about the pastoral Somali, far less their seasonal migrations. Probably the Somalis would have been highly incensed had they known of these negotiations. Probably all that the Somalis desired was to be left alone in the enjoyment of their independence. As pastoralists the Somali would ignore foreign frontiers as far as possible exploiting nature as they had always done.

Sudan-Ethiopia Frontier

Of the three colonial frontiers the Sudan-Ethiopia frontier was of greatest imperial significance since it was interwoven with the issue of Britain's sovereignty over the Nile Valley. Since occupying Egypt in 1882 Britain had been concerned with the fate of the Sudan through which the life giving Nile flows and on which Egypt's prosperity seemed to depend. Britain had for long been determined not to allow any rival power to lodge itself in the Nile Valley or to tamper with the Nile floods. The eastern frontier of the Sudan which flanked the White Nile and the western approach to the Blue Nile whose annual floods determined the quantity of water available to Egyptian irrigation in any year was of vital interest to Britain. Though the rise of the Mahdist State in the Sudan in 1884 had been a setback to British policy it had not diminished this vital British interest.

The Sudan-Ethiopia frontier had never been defined, and this shifting border had been the cause of a number of conflicts between Ethiopia and Egypt, the overlord of Sudan. Considering the 10 degree north latitude as the "recognized" southern frontier of Egypt, Britain claimed the territory to the west and south of the points between the intersection of 35 degree east longitude with 6 degree north latitude on the basis of the Anglo-Italian protocols of 1891.[45] Such claims clashed with those of Emperor Menelek based on his 1891 declaration which claimed for Ethiopia all the Sudan territory in the Nile Valley between Khartoum in the north and the Nile-Sobat junction in the south. More specifically the Ethiopian claims included the province of Gedaref up to Karakojah, Benishunqul and the adjacent territories as far as the junction of the Sobat with the White Nile.[46]

While the British ignored Ethiopia's claims until after the collapse of the Italian power at Adwa in 1896, during the Anglo-French competition for the Nile Valley, they hastened to conclude an agreement regarding the Sudan-Ethiopia border. However this settlement could not be achieved given the gap between the British and the Ethiopian positions.[47] The British Government learnt of Menelek's expansion into the claimed Anglo-Egyptian sphere in the Sudan from the Rodd Mission of 1897. To prevent further loss of territories to Ethiopia and to keep Menelek neutral in the expected Anglo-French confrontation on the Nile Valley there was clearly a need to make some generous concessions to Ethiopia. Realizing this Cromer advised the British Government to "allow a considerable extension of Abyssinian rule" in the Nile Valley.[48] This Lord Salisbury rejected as it would have implied "the possible admission of the claims of Menelek to occupy the west bank of the Nile within the British sphere."[49] However realizing that no agreement could be reached with Menelek without making territorial concessions, while no useful purpose would be served by starting negotiations before British control had been firmly established in the Sudan, the British Government put off the matter until the reconquest of the Sudan.

Kitchener's victory over the Khalifa at Omdurman on 2 September 1898 gave to Britain that "moral force," which Rodd had felt wanting while negotiating with Menelek in 1897. Nevertheless the British did not at once open formal negotiations with Menelek. In reply to an enquiry on this by its newly appointed agent in Ethiopia the British Government advised him "to receive and report any proposals which Menelek might make for the frontier", but it did not want to make any.[50] The unsubstantiated rumours communicated earlier by the British Agent that Menelek would take initiative to make formal proposals had encouraged his Government to think that Menelek would turn into a petitioner.[51]

This correspondence between the British Government and its agent in Addis Ababa has misled some writers into concluding that it was the British Government which was in a position to call the tune and it was Menelek's lot to play it.[51] This however was not so.[53] Barely seven weeks later the British Government alerted its agent, "that the time appears to have arrived to open the frontier negotiations and that they should be prepared to listen to any proposal which the Menelek might make regarding the modification of the old frontier."[54] Naturally one wonders why this *volta face* in British approach. As far as it can be deduced from documents it would appear that when Harrington asked for instructions on 28 September 1898 whether to open frontier negotiations the British reconquest of the Sudan had not been completed. Though the Khalifa's forces had been defeated at Omdurman the remnants of the Mahdist army was at large and remained to be subdued. At the same time certain territories in the Nile Valley adjacent to Ethiopia which Menelek had been claiming were yet to be reoccupied. Since it was known that Menelek had been endeavouring to achieve effective occupation of his claims, Britain too was determined to occupy those regions before opening formal negotiations.

The Anglo-Egyptian forces set about to accomplish their task speedily. In October they occupied Gedaref and by November had defeated the last remnant of the Mahdist forces in that region under Emir Ahmed Fadl. A British post was planted: At the same time general Hunter occupied Rosaries and Sennar and raised Anglo-Egyptian flags. In early November the British forces under Colonel Mason marched into Fazokl and Menelek was warned that any Ethiopian military operations against the Sheik of Fazokl would be considered unfriendly.[55]

Equally important the British had succeeded in forcing Menelek's ally, the French, to evacuate Fashoda and re-established the Anglo-Egyptian authority over most of the Sudan, except Benishunqul which was under Menelek's occupation. Thus having tightened their grip on the Sudan by late November 1898 the British felt ready to start discussions regarding the Sudan Ethiopia frontier and instructed Harrington to open formal negotiations with Menelek "when an opportunity occurs."[56]

Cromer's instructions to Harrington, approved by Lord Salisbury, required the British agent to show Menelek a strong fist in a velvet glove. While Menelek was to be assured of Britain's intentions not to encroach on any territory "which had always belonged to Abyssinia" he was to be firmly impressed of Britain's resolve to keep the whole territory between Ethiopia and the Nile "which formerly belonged to Egypt and which had nor been dealt in any existing treaties," Britain might make certain adjustments in the traditional frontier to accommodate Menelek but he was expected to take the initiative.[57] These instructions pleased Harrington who was an admirer of gun boat diplomacy and believed that a show of strength would force Menelek to acquiesce in Britain's wish. He had written cheerfully to Rennell Rodd that when the frontier negotiations commenced if they do not go smoothly a visit of the East India squadron to Berbera and the disembarking of a few blue jackets for gun practice might have a beneficial effect."[58]

Being new to Ethiopia and having very little knowledge of Menelek's abilities or diplomacy the British agent hoped for an easy resolution of the Sudan-Ethiopia frontier to Britain's satisfaction. In an effort to turn Menelek into a petitioner Harringlton at first pretended to be indifferent to the frontier question. So was Menelek. Exasperated of waiting the British agent turned into a petitioner and in March 1899 "emphasized on Menelek the necessity that he should discuss the frontier". When Menelek failed to oblige the infuriated British agent pondered whether an ultimatum should not be given telling him either to settle the frontier issue soon or face conflict with Britain.[59] A few weeks later Harrington correctly surmised that by refusing to open frontier negotiations Menelek was gaining time to occupy such posts as were not effectively occupied with a view to plead later that public opinion would not permit his withdrawal from them.[60]

Menelek was indeed attempting to occupy as much of Ethiopian claims in the Sudan as possible before starting negotiations. He was aware, as the Britain agent reported, that in territorial questions as far as Africa was concerned effective occupation constituted ownership.[61] During the Anglo-French competition for the possession of the Nile Valley Menelek took full advantage of the rivalry to extend his hold on the Nile regions bordering Ethiopia. In return for the promised Ethiopian aid to the French to establish their hold on the Western Nile Valley they had recognized his claims to all territory up to Khartoum.[62] He also despatched military expeditions under the command of his distinguished generals Wolde Giorgis and Dejaz Tesama Nadoo to Lado and Fashoda respectively and the Ethiopian flags were raised at the Nile Sobat confluence.[63] While Menelek could move rapidly into the sparsely populated neighbouring regions without visible state systems he could not do the same in the north-west. He was in a dilemma with regard to the much coveted Sudanese territories of Benishunqul and Gedaref which had been under the Mahdist State with which he wanted to be friendly.[64] He soon got his opportunity.

Taking advantage of the Mahdist military engagement with the British at Atbara, Menelek sent a military expedition under Ras Makonnen to occupy Benishunqul. After accomplishing this Makonnen also raised the Ethiopian flag at Rosaries.[65] Menelek also sent military expeditions under the command of Negus Takla Haaimanot of Gojjam to occupy Gedaref.[66] Before effective occupation of this could be achieved the Khalifa was defeated at Omdurman on 2 September 1898 and this brought Menelek face to face with the British. This, however, did not deter him. Though he had heard of Britain's forward movement to establish her authority over the Sudanese Chiefs of Fazokl, Agadi, Khumastra and the Mek of Zebel, Menelek despatched 5,000 soldiers under Deajaz Demissi's command to subjugate Benishunqul Chiefs who had reportedly solicited British protection. The commander was also instructed to occupy "the white Arab country" west and north of Benishunqul, obviously Gedaref.[67]

Menelek's entry into Benishunqul provoked a British protest for encroaching upon British territory. The Ethiopian flag was also raised at Gera though this had always been regarded as an Egyptian territory.[68] Demissi also re-hoisted the Ethiopian flag at Fazokl and was credited with the intention of occupying all territories in the neighbourhood which had not yet been reoccupied by the Anglo Egyptian troops.[69] Planting their flag at Gallabat the Ethiopian commander told the opposing British officer that he had Menelek's order to occupy all the country up to Doka.[70] Later the Ethiopian force struck southward with the declared intention of bringing the Nile Sobat region under Menelek's rule. Thus unperturbed by the British reconquest of the Sudan Menelek was occupying whatever territory he could until July 1899. He floated rumours that he would not stop until he had achieved the ancient frontiers of Ethiopia and warned the British that the Nile question was an international question and that he would have the French and Russian support in enforcing his rights.[71] Though the British were not unnecessarily worried by these threats they could not disregard them either given the Franco-Russian potential to stir up trouble. An amicable frontier agreement with Menelek seemed necessary to ward of any such complications.

The need for such an agreement was rendered urgent by the Sudan situation. Though the British had occupied Famaka, Fazokl, Gallabat and Rosaires and stationed a boat on the Sobat to "scare the Ethiopians should they return to occupy it", nevertheless they felt insecure.[72] The Sudan administration as,

Gromer observed, was a military executive and its effectiveness depended upon the loyalty of its soldiers. This however could not be taken for granted as many of the Sudanese soldiers were suspected to be sympathetic to the Mahdist cause, hence potentially anti-British. Moreover the enervating climate of the swampy Blue Nile district was having disastrous effects on the health of the British soldiers stationed there and the resultant unpopularity of the service in the Sudan was having demoralizing effect on the army.[73] For health reason it had become essential to diminish the size of the British garrisons on the upper Nile; this could not be done in view of the declared intention of the Ethiopians to reinforce their authority in the Nile-Sobat region. On the contrary a need had arisen to strengthen the Britishn garrison on the Sobat.

Cromer was greatly worried by his inability to move the British troops away from the Sobat into healthier regions because of the continued Ethiopian pressure.[74] He was no less concerned about the possibility of an Ethiopian offensive on the Sudan and warned Lord Salisbury not to disregard the threat. The British forces were so occupied in pursuing the remnant Mahdist forces and consolidating the reconquered Sudan that they could not be counted upon to repel by themselves any Ethiopian offensive. He also feared that an Ethiopian attack on the Sudan might incite hostile anti-British elements. This Cromer wanted to prevent at all costs.

A settled and defined border with Ethiopia would give the British in the Sudan the much needed security and to achieve this "Cromer was willing to allow Menelek "a considerable extension of authority in the Nile Valley." Should this be objectionable to the British Government then Menelek might be induced into a settlement with territorial concessions in British East Africa.[75] Although Cromer's fear of Ethiopia was exaggerated and Menelek would not have gone into a war with Britain to achieve his territorial goals, nevertheless his influential views prevailed with the British Government. Agreeing with the importance and urgency of a quick agreement with Menelek, Lord Salisbury advised the British Minister in Addis Ababa to press for one.. After achieving effective occupation of

Benishunqul and realizing the dangers of open confrontation with Britain which the continued Ethiopian incursions into the Sudan must cause, Menelek indicated to the British his readiness to discuss the frontier question.[76]

There is also reason to believe that the situation on his eastern border might have prompted Menelek to start the negotiations with Britain. The threat by Abdullahi of Somali to head a religious expedition against Ethiopia and the possibility large number of Ogaden Muslims joining hands with Abdullahi, who was from Ogaden, might have alerted Menelek. In March 1899, 15,000 Somalis under Abdullahi seized Jarso, twenty five miles east of Harar, posing a serious threat to Ethiopia. Menelek sent four thousand soldiers to expel them. Since Abdullahi's movement was as much a threat to Ethiopia as it was to the British in the Somaliland, Menelek perhaps decided to profit himself by making common cause with Britain against Abdullahi. So it was time to mend relations with Britain by calling off pressure on the Sudan-Ethiopia border.[77] So Menelek moved.

The Sudan-Ethiopia border negotiations started on 15 April 1899. The first issue to be resolved was the criteria for the settlement of the frontier. Menelek proposed that both historical claims and effective occupation must be the determinants. On the basis of his 1891 notification to European powers he claimed for Ethiopia all the Sudanese territory up to 14 degree north latitude. Advancing "historical claims" Menelek staked his right to Gallabat and Gera districts in the Sudan. The British rebutted this arguing that ancient history did not count in modern negotiations and that the criteria for territorial acquisitions in Africa was "conquest or effective occupation". Agreeing Menelek asked the British to state precisely Anglo-Egyptian claims in the Sudan. His strategy was to turn the British into petitioners and to retain powers of dispensation in his hands.[78] The British insisted that the whole of Sudan was theirs by the right of conquest including Benishunqul and the Sobat region. By claiming Benishunqul which was under Menelek's military occupation the British tried to check his territorial pretensions to those Sudanese territories which he had not occupied.[79] This did not surprise Menelek whose strategy was identical to that of the British negotiator. By claiming for Ethiopia all the territory up to Khartoum (14 degree north latitude) Menelek was attempting to force Britain to concede more than what he had effectively occupied. Rejecting the British claims ouright Menelek made fresh proposals. While dropping Ethiopian claims to 14 degree north latitude, Menelek demanded Benishunqul Sobat, Famaka, Fazokl and Gallabat arguing that they had been integral parts of the Ethiopian Empire. These claims however could not be substantiated as his effective occupation was limited to Benishunqul. In fact Famaka and Fazokl had been re-occupied by the British though Ethiopian flags had not been removed.

As neither seemed willing to withdraw from the occupied territory without a trial of strength it was agreed that Benishunqul should remain with Ethiopia and Famaka and Fazokl with the Sudan. The British were determined to keep Ethiopia as far as possible from the eastern approaches to the White Nile and refused to concede any territory in the region which had only been raided and not effectively occupied. Given the situation Menelek accepted a frontier far eastward of the Sobat dropping his earlier claim to all the territory in the neighbourhood of the Sobat, as far as White Nile.[80] This was indeed no great loss to him for he had never effectively occupied the Sobat region "whose climate is even more distasteful and unhealthy to Ethiopian Highlanders than it was to Europeans"[81]

Menelek however strongly opposed and foiled Britain's efforts to impose on Ethiopia a frontier farther east of the Sobat-Pibor junction as the Ethiopian influence had spread west of the proposed line into the neighbourhood of Wellega. He also refused to accept a frontier east of the River Juba as the territory west of it had already been under Ethiopian influence. In the north-west though Menelek could not sustain his claims to Gallabat province he wished to acquire its most important trade and commercial town Matemma. In an effort to secure by diplomacy what he could not by effective occupation Menelek staked Ethiopia's claim to the town on sentimental and patriotic grounds. He appealed to Harrington, to tell his Government that he did not claim Matemma as a right. Even if he did he did not have force to make it good against the British. He claimed it on sentimental grounds as King John and many Ethiopians had shed their blood, fighting the Mahdists there the place was sacred to Ethiopians who wished to have it. He asked the British to let him have the place for friendship's sake'.[82]

Finding it difficult to reject the appeal the British negotiator submitted the matter to his government's favourable consideration. With this all major issues had been settled amicably and Harrington agreed upon a tentative frontier.[83]

Britain was satisfied with the settlement as very little of former Egyptian territory, except Benishunqul had been lost and what had been ceded to Ethiopia had at any rate been a bone of contention. It was also agreed that as far as possible the frontier must follow ethnic and geographic lines. This was the best deal that the British Government could get from Menelek and had they sealed the treaty immediately with a formal ratification leaving necessary modifications to a delimitation commission they could have spared themselves several difficulties. This, however, could not be done because of Britain's excessive concern for the feelings of Italy with whom she had signed the protocols of 1894 relating to mutual spheres of influence in Ethiopia, even though the Italian protectorate of Ethiopia had died on the battle field of Adwa in 1896.

Since the proposed Ethiopia-Sudan frontier ran further east of the Italian sphere of influence as defined in the Anglo-Italian protocol of 1891, Italy insisted that such could not be done without her prior consent.[84] Though irritated, Britain agreed given the need for continued Italian support in Ethiopia against France, where Anglo-French rivalry was raging. Anglo-Italian discussions to resolve the difficulty were held in Rome in November 1899 and an agreement was concluded soon.[85]

Before signing the agreement with Ethiopia, deciding to acquire a better knowledge of the Lake Rudolph region to ensure that no vital British interests had been sacrificed, the British Government appointed Majors Gwyn and Austin to conduct surveys in the region. The surveys revealed that

Sudan-Ethiopia frontier was very difficult for the Sudan to administer as all possible communications to frontier posts would be on the Ethiopian side. If Sudan was to be given the facility of easy communications between possible frontier posts territorial changes would be required in the tentatively acquired frontier. Though the concessions required from Ethiopia would be trifle and that country might be compensated with the territory between Gemi and Mekir, Menelek might object and back out from the agreement. The British agent was advised by Salisbury to win Menelek's approval for the changes promising to sign the agreement without further modifications.[86] At the same time Lord Salisbury wanted to secure two imperial interests in the region: Ethiopia was to bind herself not to interfere with the free and natural flow of the Blue Nile and Lake Tana waters and recognize Britain's rights to free navigation on the Nile and construction of a Cape to Cairo railway through Ethiopia.[87]

Notwithstanding British trepidations and doubts that these demands might be objected by the fiercely independence-conscious Menelek, it met with his approval. These concessions did not seem to conflict with Ethiopian interests. Menelek had no intention of interfering with the Nile waters, through as an intelligent bargainer he exploited Britain's anxiety to secure an annual subsidy of ten thousand sterling by undertaking to keep away from the Nile.[88] The proposed Cape to Cairo railway through Ethiopia did not appear to compromise Ethiopia's territorial sovereignty. On the contrary Menelek saw it as a counter-weight to the French Jibuti-Harar railway which was feared as threat to Ethiopia's independence. Moreover the proposed British railway through western Ethiopia connecting Uganda and the Sudan might promote Ethiopia's economic development. So Menelek agreed to recognize Britain's right to build the railway. Britain succeeded in reaching an agreement with Menelek on all matters by March 1901 and it only remained to be formalized when the Italians interrupted unexpectedly.

Though the British and the Italian Governments had resolved their differences on the proposed Ethiopia-Sudan border through the Anglo-Italian notes of 1899, Italians official in Eritrea objected to serious divergences between the frontier line agreed in Rome and the actual frontier which Britain had arranged with Menelek. Though the Sudan-Ethiopia frontier, according to the map agreed in Rome was only two miles east of the town of Omberga in the Sudan, now it had been placed twenty miles east of that town near the junction of Setit-Maiteb thus including in the Sudan the trade route from Ethiopia which should otherwise have fallen to Eritrea. The Italians wanted the frontier line moved back by twenty kilometer. They advised Menelek not to sign the proposed treaty with Britain until this had been rectified.

The British were annoyed and angry with Italy for interfering with formalization of the treaty which they badly needed. Cromer was extremely panicky about the unsettled border given the rumours about the reported hostility of the Ethiopian frontier chiefs towards the British and the possibility of a hostile action against the Sudan. Cromer's anxiety and the sense of urgency for achieving a settled frontier with Ethiopia is revealed in the following instruction to the British Minister in Addis Ababa: Cromer instructed that main point of Britain's Abyssinian policy must be to avoid all risks of serious quarrels in the future with Abyssinia. This was far more important than any small territorial gains or concessions on the frontier.

"I want to see the army reduced (in the Sudan). I shall have to move cautiously as the soldiers will, of course find abundant arguments against any reduction.

This again tells in the direction of the absolute necessity of maintaining peace with Abyssinia. In point of fact, even without any Egyptian reductions, I do not think that any serious Abyssinian attack (on the Sudan) could be repelled without calling in the aid of British troops".[89]

The only way out for Britain was to come to terms with the Italians who appeared to be discontented "with their present territorial limit and keep steadily in their view the possibility of expansion."[90] During the negotiations with Italy Britain offered to leave the disputed Ethiopian trade routes outside the Sudan border if Italy bound herself not to interfere with the flow of the

Gash River, a tributary of the Nile.[91] While welcoming the reversion of the trade route which Eritrea might eventually exploit, Italy refused to compromise its sovereignty over the Gash River though she promised to deal with the waters by the principle of good neighbourliness. To avoid further delays the British accepted the Italian position and an Anglo-Italian accord at Rome sealed this understanding in November 1901.[92]

Now with all the obstacles cleared Britain and Ethiopia signed the Sudan-Ethiopia Border Agreement on 15 May 1902. The first article of the treaty defined the Sudan-Ethiopia border which ran from Khor-Um-Hagar to Melile and to the intersection of the 6 degree north parallel with the 35 east longitude. The second article provided for a delimitation of the frontier by a joint boundary commission; by article three Menelek bound himself not to construct or allow to be constructed any work across the Blue Nile or Lake Tana, or the Sobat except in agreement with the British and the Sudan Governments. By article four Menelek agreed to lease four hundred hectares of land on the Baro to the British to be used only for commercial and not for military or political purposes. The fifth article granted to the British Government the right to construct a railway through Ethiopia to connect the Sudan with Uganda.[93]

Britain was much pleased with the treaty. She had protected her interests in the Nile waters, secured the right to construct the Cape to Cairo railway through Ethiopia and retained more Sudanese territory than thought possible. This looked rather paradoxical given Britain's exaggerated fears of Menelek's strength and her anxiety to reach a quick agreement with him to strengthen the security of the Sudan. Britain's anxiety was such that in 1898 she had even considered handing him over the province of Gallabat were it necessary to reach an agreement. Yet she managed to keep most of the disputed Sudanese territory.

British East Africa-Ethiopia Frontier

British East Africa's frontier with Ethiopia was more thorny issue than that of the eastern Sudan border because Menelek's claims were better than those of Britain's. By his 1891 circular he claimed for Ethiopia all the territory down to the southern ridge of the Lake Rudolph and from the Indian Ocean to the White Nile.[94] This clashed with Britain's claims to the territory up to 6 degree north parallel as set forth in the Anglo-German and the Anglo-Italian protocols of 1891 and 1893 respectively.[95] Moreover while Menelek had been effectively occupying his claims Britain had done nothing to occupy or administer northern regions of her East African protectorates adjacent to Ethiopia. The Imperial British East African Company had established itself along the coast, to the north and south of Mombasa and inland at points along the road to Uganda only in the early 1890's.[96] Neither the British East African Protectorate nor the successor administrations of Uganda and British East Africa created in 1894 and 1895 respectively had neither the inclination nor means to bring northern territories under its control. Two years after its creation the Commissioner of the British East African Protectorate admitted to the Foreign Secretary that the whole vast regions from north of Mt. Kenya to Lake Rudolph and then eastward to Boran had yet to be brought within the area of direct British administration.[97] The undefined and unprotected British East African territories were vulnerable to Ethiopian expansion. Unlike the eastern Sudan which was more or less under effective administration of Egypt and the Mahdists and later of the Anglo-Egyptian military authority, the stateless and unprotected peoples of British East Africa could not resist the occupation of their territories by the well armed Ethiopians. Moreover the unprotected vast East African plain, especially the Lake Rudolph region, reportedly rich in ivory was of great interest to Menelek. To achieve expansion and power he needed arms and ammunition and to pay for this he needed ivory. Menelek aspired to bring this region under his authority; in fact Ethiopian expansion in this region had begun long before the European powers effected paper partition of East Africa in 1890-91.[98] Though Menelek had notified his claims Britain had disregarded them relying on the Anglo-German and the Anglo-Italian protocols.

This was the time when no African State managed to acquire full legitimacy in western eyes and the claims of a supposed Italian protected Ethiopia did not attract serious British attention. This was to misjudge Menelek a determined expansionist. Disregarding Britain's paper claims Menelek went on occupying territories south of Ethiopia. The British Government first realized this in 1897 when Rennell Rodd during his visit to Addis Ababa warned London that actual Abyssinian frontiers were then approximately within 80 miles of the Nile Valley at Gejeret Habeshi, within 200 miles of Lado and within 250 miles of the British protectorate of Uganda. Indeed Menelek's effective occupation extended into the British sphere of influence as defined by the Anglo-German agreement of 1 July 1890.[99]

Britain was shocked by the seriousness of Menelek's challenge to her claimed territorial sovereignty. But neither could she stop Menelek nor establish effective administration in East Africa given her preoccupation with other serious issues like the Mahdist problem in the Sudan and the French threat to the Nile Valley. It was only in 1898, prior to the Fashoda crisis, that the British Government attempted to establish its authority over the northern region of British East Africa. It despatched an expedition under Major Mcdonald to secure by treaty a continuous belt of territory between the Ugandan protectorate and the 10 degree north latitude, the recognized southern frontier of Egyptian dominion.[100] During his expeditions Mcdonald placed many northern frontier chiefs under British protection through treaties and proposed a military patrol to protect the treaty area. While confirming the treaties the British Government failed to provide a military patrol because of increased financial demands it would make on the already discredited grant-in-aid to Uganada which was under heavy fire in the Commons.

While the British were debating on the course of action to be pursued, Menelek was expanding into the protectorate territories unchecked. Exploiting European rivalries he used both the French and the Russians to achieve southward expansion. In March 1898 Menelek's general Ras Wolde

Georgis, accompanied by French explorer Daarogan and the Russian General Boulatovich, marched into paper protectorate of British East Africa and raised Ethiopian flags as far as third parallel north latitude.[101] Later Menelek appointed Leontiev, "the Russian bucaneer in grand style", as the Governor of as yet non-existent Equatorial province of Ethiopia, with the very considerable task of establishing Ethiopian sovereignty over the vast territories extending from the Indian Ocean to the fifth parallel of the north latitude on to the White Nile south-west.[102]

The Russian went about his job cheerfully sending reconnaissance parties in different directions, opening up new territories with the aid of local chiefs and establishing administrative posts where Ethiopian flags were hoisted to the sound of bugles and ceremonial war drums.[103] Leontiev crossed Rudolph, to the south of the frontier which Menelek had proposed. By September 1898 Leontiev was reported to have occupied Murle, in the British East African protectorate, after pulling down British flags.[104] He brought the Omo country and territories north-east of Lake Rudolph under Menelek's authority.

Emperor Menelek also ordered his southern chiefs to occupy maximum possible territory in the south and despatched four military expeditions for the purpose.[105] An Ethiopian expedition under the command of Fituarari Imani raided east and west side of Lake Rudolf in late 1898 and in March 1899.[106] Six months later the Ethiopians had penetrated the Boran country.[107] Another expedition under the command of Ras Wolde Giorgis proceeded to occupy Lado while Dejaz Tassamma was settling northern districts of the Boran Galla country.[108] A deputation of the Boran Gallas near lake Rudolph had come to Addis Ababa to render their submission to Emperor Menelek. The Ethiopians had also established a permanent post in Amare country between Lake Rudolf and Lake Stephanie. Worried about the undeterred Ethiopian expansion the British Minister warned London that he was convinced that Menelek was endeavouring to bring under his way all the territories claimed in his proclamation of 1891 and might not take any notice of the occupation of the territory claimed by Britain.[109]

Though Menelek was a determined expansionist he never liked to get into armed confrontation to achieve his goal. He was aware of the power and might of Britain. For instance, during their south-westward expansion when the Ethiopians sighted Mcdonald's expedition moving from Uganda towards the Sudan, and some of the Ethiopian troops had been forced back to the east bank of the Omo by British troops, to prevent an armed clash with the British Menelek ordered his generals not to go beyond the Boran land or south of Lake Rudolph.[110] He attempted to secure British recognition for his claims through a negotiated settlement.[111]

On 26 May 1899 Menelek proposed to the British a frontier line starting from the Juba river to the south of the Lake Rudolph passing Lake Achangi, Arabore Galla and Turkanna countries. The Lake Rudolph was to be in the Ethiopian sphere. From there the frontier line was to run due east bisecting Asehake to the Juba River.[112] Since this proposal heavily encroached upon British claims the British rejected it. However after further discussions with the British Minister Menelek made new proposals: The frontier to start from the termination of the Sudan frontier making a small curve to the Lake Rudolph on the north and the west of the Omo river; the Turkana would remain in the British sphere. On the southern side starting from the Junction of the Dawa River the frontier was placed in the tribal limits; the Maratha were to be in the British sphere. Whereas the Gere, Gabara, Sakaya, Saba and Turkana tribes were to in the Ethiopian sphere. After passing the Tartala tribes the frontier was to reach Lake Rudolf; Brunkendechi being in the British sphere.[113]

Since this frontier was based on effective occupation and its acceptance would stop Ethiopian expansion into the British sphere the British Minister in Addis Ababa recommended it to his Government.

The Foreign Office was however faced with divided counsels. British East African officials opposed Menelek's proposals. Having had only a limited experience with petty chiefs in the region, the protectorate officials regarded Menelek as another "petty chief" who could be manoeevered and bamboozled. They resented Menelek's "audacity" in claiming the British territory of Raheita, Stephanis and Boran land which was considered as rich in ivory and essential to the prosperity of the East African protectorate. Opposed to yielding to Menelek's effective occupation they proposed a frontier "that would limit Ethiopia to the north of Lake Stepahnie approximately at 5 north latitude."[114] The British Government was more sympathetic to the views of the protectorate official's than that of its their agent in Ethiopia.

Notwithstanding the intelligence brought by the Rodd Mission from Addis Ababa, the British Government had neither a full appreciation of Menelek's strength nor a true understanding of the effectiveness of his forward movement.[115] Regarding Menelek's occupation as nothing more than predatory raids and planting of flags, they hoped to flout it soon after they were ready to occupy the claims.[116] Virtually believing in the efficacy of Britain's paper rights against the Ethiopian expansion, British officials hoped that with the passage of time Menelek would only get weaker and be unable to contest Britain's rights. Pessimistic about the chance of Ethiopia remaining independent they feared that any region "which may eventually be admitted as Ethiopians would be open to the danger being some day claimed as the sphere of influence of some hostile European powers which may acquire or pretend to acquire rights in Ethiopia".[117] Cranborne went to the extent of not recognizing the principle of effective occupation with regard to African states noting that, "so long as it is only Abyssinian authority that is concerned we should not respect any plea of effective occupation."[118] No power had been more insistent than Britain upon the partition doctrine of "effective occupation". Now that Menelek had learned the lesson so well and had been playing the game so effectively to the disadvantage of Britain that power sought to elevate paper rights and dismiss Ethiopian occupation as mere raiding. Salisbury was in sympathy with British East African official view and felt that Menelek's proposals were unsatisfactory; but Menelek could not be coerced to accept the British East African Protectorate's proposals. Hence Salisbury decided to leave the matter hanging until better times.[119]

Menelek's effective occupation was not mere raiding as the British East African officials alleged. His method of expansion was as sophisticated as those of the neighbouring European powers, at the time, and more effective than theirs given the larger local resources he commanded compared to them. Garrisoning troops in the occupied territories, creating an administrative framework, distributing ploughs to peasants where agriculture was practicable besides making chiefs acknowledge his authority by visiting and paying him tribute under the pain of punishment, Menelek was extending his authority in much the same way as Europeans powers did.[120] Though the initial stages of occupation often produced hardships upon the inhabitants, once they had been subjugated they were well treated.[121] Donaldson Smith testified in his survey report that the Boran country was not only under Menelek's occupation but also was thriving.[122] Further confirmation of this was received by Baird and Maud who surveyed the Boran land in 1902.[123]

Menelek's methods of expansion were so effective that in February 1900 the British Agent in Addis Ababa frantically informed his Government that the Ethiopians were not only familiar with the territory to 4 degree north latitude but they had also been pushing further.[124] As the British Government neither protected them nor armed them for self defence the peoples in the British territory were giving themselves up under Ethiopian pressure.[125] The British East Africa and Uganda protectorates were unable to repel any serious Ethiopian incursions and their military strength "had been fixed to police the country in peace-time only and trust to outside assistance being given to them from other sources on emergencies arising."[126] Nor were the two Protectorates financially strong enough to raise the required troops locally to protect their borders.[127] British involvement in the Boer War since 1899, Abdullahi's rising in the Somali Protectorate, the revolt of the Egyptian and the Sudanese garrisons in 1900 had sapped Britain's resources so much that it was doubtful if she could have given much help to the protectorates had they been attacked by Ethiopia. Such an attack could not be ruled out.

Though Menelek himself was for a peaceful settlement any compulsion on him to accept the restricted frontier suggested by the British East African officials would surely drive him under the influence of his war-like chiefs who were opposed to the proposals with all their might. The British Agent warned his Government against protectorate official's view of Menelek as a "petty sqeezable African chief." Instead it would be wise to reappraise the frontier policy and adopt effective measures to protect the claims until an agreement could be reached with Menelek.[128]

The British Government welcomed the idea, but the available options were unattractive. Armed steamers could be placed on the Lake Rudolph to watch Ethiopian movements; local peoples might be armed to defend frontier posts against Ethiopian incursions. Britain might also consider buying Menelek's claims in the south for a sum of money. But all these proposals cost money to be implemented and the Treasury was opposed to increase money grants.[129] Besides, some of the proposals were dangerous. Arming of the Protectorate peoples was a double edged sword as arms could be used not only against invaders but also against their "protectors." Surrendering territory to Ethiopia to achieve a frontier was detestable to Lord Salisbury as it might be seen as Britain's weakness; preoccupied with the Boer War he put off the negotiation.[130]

The delay cost Britain more. Menelek began to claim as Ethiopian even the "indisputably British" territories. Being more belligerent than Menelek his southern chiefs, Ras Tassamma, Fitaurari Hapte Giorgis and Dejazmach Balcha, were determined to keep much of the Boran land in their control and they were familiar with territories down to 4 north latitude.[131] As the British Minister had feared the British East African Protectorate's proposal to limit Ethiopia to 5 north latitude so much infuriated Menelek that he suspended frontier negotiations for a long time.[132]

To save the situation Harrington had to reduce British claims and persuade Menelek to make fresh proposals.[133] Menelek agreed. By this the British East Africa-Ethiopia frontier was to start from their bend of Ganale Doria and run south of the Dawa River and then westward to Lake Stephanie leaving the Karayu and Waditu people to Ethiopia. The line was then to follow the southern shore of Lake Stephanie, due west to Lake Rudolf. The River Saachi was to be the border. Menelek promised to give Britain a healthy locality on the Baro River for a commercial station.[134]

Salisbury instructed the British Minister in Addis Ababa to secure maximum concessions possible beyond what Menelek had offered and also to get his undertaking not to alienate any territory adjacent to British East Africa to any other power without the consent of the British Government.[135] While Salisbury's concern for Britain's security was understandable his awful ignorance of Menelek's national goals was not. Menelek had not been fighting against the territorial claims of one European power to prepare the ground for another to move in. His policy was directed against European imperialism in general. Ethiopian territorial expansion was as much a reaction to the European scramble for Africa as a means to achieve its national greatness.

The frontier negotiations did not progress fast mostly because of Britain's indecisiveness. The British Government was caught between the moderate counsels of its Minister in Addis Ababa and the aggressive counsels of the East African Protectorate officials who wanted to restrict Ethiopia to 5' north latitude. They had insatiable land hunger notwithstanding their disclaimers. For instance Sir. Charles Elliot's wrote to the British Foreign Secretary: "that" the country to the north-west of Baringo hitherto considered worthless was an admirable grazing land equal to the finest in East Africa. There seemed to be enough good streak of land to give it a definite value for trade and colonization. In view of this and possible mineral discoveries, Britian should not abandon her claims to any territory which could be retained without undue difficulty and expense.[136]

Whatever its appetite for territory, the financial and military weakness of the protectorates did not warrant immediate occupation and administration of the northern region. To

Britain an ideal colony was one which was financially self supporting. Most of her colonial decisions unless related to larger imperial and strategical aims were made with reference to colonial finance. Imperial grants-in-aid were to be kept to a minimum and territorial budgets balanced. Moreover the British Government preferred to limit the protectorate to the coastal region and was against expanding inward among peoples who had very little to offer commercially and as yet were unused to having white men amidst them. It was also opposed to larger deficits in the protectorate's budgets and pleas for increased grants-in-aid which would be the result of extending administrative responsibility into the interior. Were it not for Menelek's challenge the British Government would have preferred to keep its paper rights to the territory to 6' north latitude and rest the matter until the region became economically viable to administer. But Menelek's expansion did not allow that option.

Finally the British Government decided to proceed on the criterion of effective occupation. They could not do otherwise least Menelek fall back on his 1891 claims and complicate the matter. Rather belatedly Britain recognized that her paper claims would not stand against Menelek's effective occupation. Count Gleischen of the British Intelligence Department stated honestly that Menelek "had much more right to the country than we have... We cannot assert that we have ever or in any way occupied or taken over any part of this country. In fact our sphere of influence is merely a map transaction not in the least recognized by the Abyssinians."[137] Britain found herself in an impossible position of wanting to undermine Ethiopia's claims while desiring to maintain influence over Menelek. Like other imperialist powers Britain believed that Ethiopia herself must fall to one of them. Whatever the future might hold, in the circumstances, Britain was being forced by the realities of the situation to recognize the Ethiopian territorial acquisitions.

The Maud-Butter survey showed that Ethiopian influence spread far beyond the proposed frontier down to 3.30' north latitude, that they had raided extensive territory from Lake Rudolph to Ganale Doria in the east and as far as Buna, Furrore and Turba in the south. Although it could not be established whether the Ethiopians had ever been south of the Lake Rudolph the Boran country had been under Menelek's authority and was fully pacified. The survey established that by virtue of effective occupation Menelek had better claims to the territory than the British had cared to admit.[138]

Captain Maud recommended a frontier based on the principle of effective occupation. This meant that Britain should drop her claims to territory north of 4′ north latitude and Ethiopia should drop her pretensions to the territories mearly raided. This would leave to Ethiopia much of the Boran land, Laban, Derri, Tertale, Gubbra Mago, Gabbra Alagan, Afota, Boran of the north-west Golbe, Arbore of the Hamran hills and the south-eastern part of the Liban which was waterless and uninhabited. Britain would claim as compensation a strip of the territory between the Sudan and the East African Protectorates which was rich in cattle and elephants with, perennial wells and good climate. Maud recommended the inclusion of the Lake Rudolph and the territories of Garre, Marrehum, Somali, Baladda, Idur Sakayyu, Azuran Boran, Lokob Summonder and Korro people in British East Africa.[139] He warned the British Government that a mere settlement of the frontier would not solve the problem. "Whatever frontiers are agreed with Menelek unless it were held by British posts it would not be respected by his very independent chiefs who ruled the Boran country."[140] This would affect Britain's prestige in the region. Maud's fears were confirmed by the British Minister in Ethiopia that although Menelek had ordered his chiefs to cease southward expansion, they knew that the emperor would be more pleased by their disobedience than compliance with the orders.[141]

Though Britain was anxious to sign a treaty with Menelek accepting the Maud-Butter line she was obstructed by Italy who insisted on her prior consent to any changes in the frontiers as determined by the Anglo-Italian protocols. She also wanted to include Lugh, which was a part of Ethiopia, in her Benadir colony in view of her expanding commercial relations with the Boran land. Italy hoped that "circumstances might arise in which Abyssinia might have to constrict her borders, and Italy would wish to keep an open road for expansion westward, north of the Juba." She did not want to see any other European power between Benadir and Ethiopia. Italian territorial aims in Ethiopia were at the root of Britain's difficulties there.

At the time Italy had been negotiating with Menelek Benadir-Ethiopia frontier. Menelek was reluctant to concede Lugh to Italy, instead aiming to push Benadir frontier to Berbera by proposing a border from there to Webbi. If the British agreed to a southern frontier from the intersection of Wabbi to 6' north parallel and recognized Menelek's proposed Benadir-Ethiopia border, it would confine Italy to the coast and interpose a block of territory between Benadir and Ethiopia thus checking Italian hopes of penetrating southern Ethiopia through Benadir.[142] Fearing this Italy pressed Britain to support her demand for Lugh in return for recognition of the proposed Ethiopia-British East Africa frontier.[143] Inspite of strong objection of its Minister in Addis Ababa the British Government agreed to the Italian suggestion.[144] The British and Italian colonial and commercial objectives clashed during the discussions in Rome in December 1903. The Italians proposed a southern frontier line running from Boranl and to Benadir in the hope of incorporating those territories when opportunity arose. This the British rejected, admitting the River Dawa as frontier. Italy was to have freedom of trade on all routes from Benadir to Boran land. Italy consented.

There was indeed something sinister in the British assurance to Italy that no changes would be made in the frontiers established by the Anglo-Italian protocols, though the Italian protectorate in Ethiopia had died on the battle field of Adwa. While negotiating an actual physical frontier between Ethiopia and the British East Africa, Britain had also been keeping alive a paper frontier with Italy, an imperial power which had failed in Ethiopia but had not given up her imperial ambitions. It would appear that Britain, like other European imperial powers, was sceptical about the long-term independence of Ethiopia. It was Menelek's Ethiopia which had defeated Italy. After Menelek's death should Ethiopia revert to Italy, Britain would not have to keep the constricted border which she was about to agree with Menelek. In re-endorsing a practically defunct treaty with Italy, without Menelek's knowledge, Britain would be keeping in tact her territorial rights for the future besides winning Italian support for herself in Ethiopia.

While Britain was negotiating with Italy Menelek was pushing the line of his effective occupation. His chiefs had entered Turkana, in the Britain East African Protectorate and it was feared that they may not stop until all territory to 2' north latitude had been brought into the Ethiopian Empire.[145] To check this the British Government would need a large frontier force which could not be organized due to want of money. However it appointed a frontier inspector with an escort of 50 riflemen to watch and report Ethiopian incursions into the British East African territories.[146] The cautious Menelek sent a few Ethiopian officers supposedly to help the travelling inspector but in fact to watch him.[147]

Notwithstanding these developments the frontier negotiations dragged on interrupted by Menelek's ill-health. Nor was he in a hurry as the British were. However in face of the threat posed to Ethiopian security by the Tripartie Agreement of December 1906, Menelek accepted the Maud-Butter line as the frontier with British East Africa. The British Minister to Ethiopia admitted to his Government "that we are a great deal luckier than I ever thought we should be over the frontier."[148] Though the British Government was anxious to sign the treaty at once Menelek insisted on actual delimitation of the frontier before its formalizations.[149] The British suspected that as Menelek's excuse to back out of the agreement which did not find favour with his southern chiefs. They were reluctant to be excluded "from almost the last remaining districts of no man's land where raid could be conducted with ease and impunity."[150] After much persuasion Menelek signed the treaty in December 1907.[151] Because of his illness and incapacitation he did not ratify. Though Major Gwyn delimited the frontier Menelek's Ministers refused to accept it on their own responsibility while he was alive. When Menelek died in

1913 the frontier agreement had yet to be ratified. But the British held firmly to the 1907 line and it remains today the boundary between Kenya and Ethiopia.

As an intelligent strategist and statesman Menelek would appear to have operated on the concept of three frontiers. First there was the actual frontier of Ethiopia as it existed in 1891 which he was determined to push further. Then there was the frontier he had claimed in his circular of 1891 which was an "ideal" frontier unlikely to be realized fully. Then there was the third frontier which he strove hard to achieve stretching from the Indian Ocean to the White Nile including all the Galla country, Benishunqul and Gedaref. While Menelek would insist that the real frontier was the one he had claimed in 1891 circular, this was in fact a bargaining ploy. There can be no doubt that Menelek succeeded in achieving most of his territorial goals. In the west he succeeded in including in Ethiopia Beni-shunqul, Shangalla land and Metemma which had been a part of the Mahdist State until its dismemberment and in the south he succeeded in stretching the Ethiopian frontier down to 3.30′ north parallel. Britain a great imperial power had been forced to withdraw from 6′ north latitude which had been conceded to her by Germany and Italy in the respective frontier agreements. Likewise he had succeeded in acquiring about 67,000 Square Kilometers of territory into Ethiopia British East African agreement prevailing over British adversaries.

Menelek had a good knowledge of the techniques of territorial acquisition and expansion of European imperial powers. Like them he notified to European powers in his circular of 1891, the claimed territorial limits of Ethiopia, more important he put into practice the technique of "effective occupation" and brought under his control as much of the claimed territory as he could beating his imperial rivals in their game. Wanting in local resources to contain Menelek's expansion, unable to deprive him of what he had grabbed from the claimed colonial territories, anxious to avoid a possible military confrontation, Britain conceded to Menelek the principle of effective occupation, a principle she had rejected in frontier settlements with Germany in East Africa and to some extent with France in Nigeria. This was a magnificent achievement for an African ruler of his time.

Nevertheless, unquestionably, Menelek became an imperialist scrambling along with the Europeans for as much territory as his forces would occupy. It was clear that centuries ago Ethiopia was much larger than she was when Menelek came to the throne. However no one would know where the "historic boundaries" had been. Nevertheless his claims were solid compared to the British, the new comers. For decades after his death Menelek stood as a hero over all Africa because he had the sense to expand to meet the incoming European scramblers. Every move he made outward raised the cost of the conquest to potential European aggressors. However during the de-colonisation and European retreat of Africa after 1945 Menelek's image dimmed. He became the only African imperialist whose successors refused to relinquish their hold on the imperial conquests. Major roots of Ethiopia's modern civil wars may be traced to "the subjects" seeking to liberate themselves.

REFERENCES

1. G.N. Sanderson, *England, Europe and the Upper Nile* (Edinburgh, 1965) pp. 290-324.
2. F.O. 141/324. Cromer to the F.O., 5 November 1897.
3. D.D.F. Series 1, Tome XI, No. 5, Menelek to Cornet, 5 January 1894, D.D.F. Series, Tome X1, No. 462, Menelek to Felix Foure 24 September, 1895.
4. F.O. 403/239, Salisbury to Cromer, 29 December, 1896; Cromer to Salisbury 29 December 1896.
5. G.N. Sanderson *England, Europe,* p. 190-314 Passium.
6. *Ibid.*
7. F.O. 1/32. F.O. Instruction to Rodd, 24 February 1897.
8. F.O. 403/255 Clairford to Salisbury 3 March 1897.
9. F.O. 1/32, Salisbury to Rodd, 14 May 1897.
10. F.O. 1/32, Emperor Menelek to Rodd 14 May, 1897. Enclosure in Rodd to Salisbury 16 May 1897.
11. *Ibid.*

12. F.O. 403/255. Menelek's Letter to Queen Victoria April, 1891. Enclosure in Rodd to Salisbury 16 May 1897.
13. F.O. 403/255. Queen Victoria to King of Ethiopia, 18 August 1891.
14. F.O. 1/32. Rodd to Salisbury 1 May 1897, 4 June 1897.
15. F.O. 1/32. Rodd to Salisbury 4 June 1897.
16. The Anglo-Italian Protocols were communicated to Menelek through the Italian Government; they suppressed it. See chapter 3 for details.
17. K.V. Ram "Diplomatic Practices of Ethiopia in the Nineteenth Century." *Trans-African Journal of History*. 1986.
18. F.O. 1/32. Menelek's Circular of 10 April, 1891 to European Powers, enclosed in Rodd to Salisbury, 4 May 1897.
19. F.O. 1/37, Rodd to Salisbury, 14 May, 1897.
20. Czeslaw Jesman, *The Russian in Ethiopia.* (London, 1958) pp. 119-21.
21. Richard Caulk, "Origins and Development of Menelek's Foreign Policy", Ph.D. Thesis. London University, 1966, p. 397.
22. F.O. 403/265. Ferris to India's Office, December 1896.
23. F.O. 430/190. The Indian Office to the Foreign Office, 6 January 1893.
24. *Ibid.*
25. *Ibid.*
26. F.O. 403/190. Foreign Office to the Indian Office, 13 January 1893.
27. F.O. 403/239. Asst. Resident at Zeila to Ferris, Consul Somali Coast, 31 August, 1891. The Resident at Aden to Hamilton, 7 September, 1896.
28. F.O. 403/239. Consul Ferris to Ras Makonnen, 31 August 1893.
29. F.O. 403/255. Hamilton to the Government of India, 5 January 1897.
30. F.O. 403/255. Salisbury to Cromer, 12 January 1897.
31. F.O. 403/255. *Ibid*; Ferris to Cunnigham, 22 December 1898.
32. F.O. 403/255. Ferris to Ras Makonnen, 1 August, 1896. Makonnen to Ferris, 22 December 1898.
33. I.O.L.R 20/F.I.A. The Indians Office to Foreign Office 22, February 1897.
34. F.O. 1/32. F.O.'s Draft Instructions to Rodd, 24 February 1897.
35. Refer to Chapter III, Foot Note No.
36. F.O. 1/32. Rodd to Salisbury, 13 May 1897.
37. F.O. 1/32. Rodd to Salisbury, 4 June 1897.
38. *Ibid.*
39. F.O. 1/38. Rodd to Salisbury, 9 May 1897.
40. F.O. 1/32. Rodd to Salisbury, 5 June 1897. The frontier was to stretch from Sonmudu at the intersection of the 44 meridian with the 9' parallel to the point of intersection of the 48 meridian with the 8 parallel.
41. *Ibid.*
42. *Ibid.*
43. F.O. 403/282. Macdonald to Salisbury, 31 July 1898.

44. I.M. Lewis. *The Modern History of Somaliland.* (London, 1965), p. 59.
45. F.O. 403/282. Macdonald to Salisbury, 31 July 1898.
46. F.O. 403/255. Menelek's Circular of April, 1891 in Rodd to Salisbury, 13 May 1897.
47. G.N. Sanderson, *England, Europe.* pp. 258-260.
48. F.O. 1/35. Cromer to Salisbury, 5 March 1898.
49. F.O. 1/35. Cromer to Salisbury. 5 March 1898; F.O. 1/35. Foreign Office to Harrington, 5 October 1898.
50. *Ibid.*
51. F.O. 1/35 Harrington to F.O. 28 September 1898.
52. H.G. Marcus, "Ethio-British Negotiations." *The Journal of African History,* Vol. 1. 1963; pp. 89-91.
53. K.V. Ram, "The Sudan-Ethiopia Border Negotiations and its Antecedents." *Trans-African Journal of History,* Vol. X, 1983.
54. F.O. 1/35. Cromer to Harrington, 24 November 1898.
55. F.O. 1/34. Foreign Office to Harrington, 14 October 1848; F.O. 1/35. Cromer to Foreign Office 15 November 1898.
    F.O 1/34. Harrington to Menelek, 17 December 1898.
    F.O. 1/35. Cromer to Foreign Office, 15 November, 1898.
56. F.O. 1/35. Cromer to Foreign Office, 15 November 1898.
57. F.O. 1/35. Cromer to Harrington, 14 November 1898.
58. *Ibid,* Harrington to Rodd.
59. F.O. 1/34. Harrington to Salisbury, 5 November 1898.
60. F.O. 1/36. Harrington to Salisbury, 3 March 1898.
61. Rome. Archivio Strico deell'ex Ministero dell' Africa Italian. Hereafter referred as ASMAI. Pos. 38, Fasicolo Ciccodicola to Foreign Minister, 18 February 1898.
62. F.O. 1/35. Harrington to Cromer, 21 March 1899.
63. F.O. 1/34. Harrington to Salisbury, 15 May 1898.
64. Sanderson, *England, Europe and the Upper Nile.* p. 294.
65. F.O. 1/34. Harrington to Salisbury, 15 May 1898.
66. Sanderson, G.N. "The Foreign Policy of Negus Menelek 1896-1898", *Journal of African History,* Vol. 1, 1962.
67. F.O. 1/34. Harrington to F.O. 30 April 1898.
    Harrington to Walker, 11 May 1898.
    Harrington to Salisbury, 15 May 1898.
68. F.O. 1/34. Harrington to Walker, 11 May 1898.
69. F.O. 1/34. Harrington to Salisbury, 16 November 1898.
    F.O. 1/36. Harrington to Menelek, 18 March 1899.
    F.O. 1/143/347. Cromer to Harrington, 30 January 1899.
70. F.O. 1/35. Harrington to Cromer, 1 March 1899.
    F.O. 1/34. Harrington to Cromer, 24 June 1898.
71. F.O. 78/. Cromer to Harrington, 17 July 1899.
72. F.O. 1/35. *Ibid;* Harrington to Rodd, 23 November 1898.

73. A/112, Salisbury Papers; Maxwell to Cromer, 9 June 1899.
74. F.O. 78/. Cromer to Salisbury, 7 March 1899.
75. F.O. 78/5025. Salisbury to Cromer, 6 June 1899.
76. F.O. 2/234. Cromer to Salisbury, 13 March 1899.
77. F.O. 78/5031. Hayes Sadler to Salisbury, 18 April 1899. In fact Ethiopia and Britain carried on joint military operations against the Abdullahi in 1903.
78. F.O. 1/36. Harrington to Rodd, 22 April 1899.
79. F.O. 1/36. Harrington to Cromer, 15 and 22 April 1899
80. F.O. 1/44. Harrington to Salisbury, 26 May 1899
81. Sanderson, G.N. "The Foreign Policy of Negus" Menelek. *Op cit.*
82. F.O. 1/44. Harrington to Salisbury, 26 May 1899.
83. *Ibid.*
84. F.O. 1/44. Sanderson's Note, 8 August 1899.
85. F.O. 1/44. Currie to Salisbury, 6 December 1899.
86. F.O. 1/44. Major Gwyn's Report on the Sudan-Ethiopia Border in Wingate to Foreign Office 1/44.
87. F.O. 1/44. Salisbury to Harrington, 29 September 1900.
88. F.O. 1/45. Sirdar to Cromer, 4 March 1901.
    F.O. 1/45. Lansdowne to Butcher, 29 August 1901.
89. F.O. 801/123. Lansdowne Papers, Cromer to Lansdowne, 5 June 1901.
90. F.O. 1/45. Wingate's Memorandum in Cromer to Lansdowne, 19 May 1901.
91. F.O. 1/45. Lansdowne to Buchanan, 29 August 1901.
92. F.O. 1/45. Buchanan to Lansdowne, 4 September 1901.
    F.O. 1/46. Lansdowne to Currie, 8 October 1901.
93. F.O. 1/46. Currie to Lansdowne, 27th November 1901, Vol. 13, p. 1901.
94. F.O. 1/32. Rodd to Salisbury, 15 May 1897.
95. Hertslet, *The Map of Africa by Treaty*, 3 Volumes (London; 1965) Vol. 3.
96. Gordon Mungeam, *British Rule in Kenya* (Oxford; 1964) p. 21.
97. Harrington to the F.O.C. 8683(1897) Quoted by Mungeam, *British Rule.*
98. F.O. 1/32. Rodd to Salisbury, 9 May 1897.
99. *Ibid.*
100. F.O. 403/282. Macdonald to Salisbury, 3 July 1899.
101. Barber, "The Moving Fronriers of Britain the Northern Uganda" *The Uganda Journal*, Vol. 29, 1965.
102. Ernest Work, *Ethiopia A Pawn in European Diplomacy.* (New York; 1936), p. 264.
103. F.O. 1/38. Sanderson's talk with Leontiev at the Foreign Office, October 1890.
104. C. Jesman, *The Russians in Ethiopia*, (London; 1958), p. 120.
105. F.O. 1/34. Harrington to Salisbury, 28 December 1899.
    F.O. 403/263. Harrington to Salisbury, 30 September 1898.

106. F.O. 1/36. Harrington to Cromer, 28 March 1899.
107. *Ibid*, Harrington to Salisbury,
108. F.O. 1/34. Harrington to Salisbury, 15 May 1898.
109. F.O. 1/34. Harrington to Salisbury, 15 May 1898, 7 November 1898.
110. F.O. 1/3. Harrington to Cromer, 28 March 1899.
111. *Ibid.*
112. F.O. 1/36. Harrington to Salisbury, 26 May 1899.
113. F.O. 1/44. Harrington to Salisbury, 3 June 1899.
114. F.O. 1/44. Jenner's Memorandum on Northern Frontier of British East Africa, 1 November 1899. Hardinge's Memo, 20 October 1899. F.O. 403/284 Thomas Sanderson's Memo is the same, 7 November 1899.
115. F.O. 78/5025. Salisbury to Cromer, 2 December 1899.
116. *Ibid.* Though this had reference to the Sudan Border this shows Salisbury's attitude towards the Ethiopian expansion in general.
117. F.O. 2/571. Cranborne's Minute, 1902.
118. *Ibid.*
119. F.O. 78/5025. Salisbury to Cromer, 2 December 1899.
120. F.O. 1/44. Harrington to Salisbury, 16 June 1900.
121. F.O. 1/44. Harrington to Sanderson, 17 February 1900.
122. *Ibid.*
123. F.O. 403/334. Maud and Baird Report on British East African Ethiopia Border.
124. F.O. 1/44. Harrington to Salisbury, 17 February 1900.
125. *Ibid.*
126. F.O. 2/515. Memorandum on the Organization of Military forces in B.E.A. and Uganda Protectorates.
127. Mungeam, *British Rule in Kenya*, p. 2.
128. F.O. 1/44. Harrington to Salisbury, 17 February 1900.
129. F.O. 1/44. Sanderson's Minute, 30 March 1900.
130. *Ibid.*
131. F.O. 1/4. Harrington to Salisbury, 5 May 1900.
132. F.O. 1/44. Harrington to Salisbury, 17 May 1900.
133. F.O. 1/44. Harrington to Salisbury, 16 June 1900.
134. F.O. 1/44. Salisbury to Harrington, 8 October 1900.
135. *Ibid.*
136. F.O. 1/41-1. Harrington to Butter, 2 August 1901.
137. F.O. 403/334. Memo by Count Gleischen, 30 May 1903.
138. F.O. 403/334C. Maud's Report. Encl. Harrington to Lansdowne, 28 September 1901.
139. *Op cit.*
140. *Op cit.*
141. F.O. 1/47. Harrington to Sanderson, 19 March 1903.
142. *Ibid*, Baird's note on Lugh.

143. F.O. 403/334. Rodd to Lansdowne, 1 January 1903.
144. F.O. 1/47-2. Lansdowne to Rodd, 23 January 1903.
145. F.O. 1/47-2. Harrington to Sanderson, 17 January 1903.
F.O. 1/54. Sadler to Lansdowne, 15 Febuary 1904.
Lansdowne's note n.d. on the Intelligence Division's letter to Foreign Office 18 February 1904. Foreign Office to Sadler, 22 Febuary 1905, F.O. 1/54.
146. F.O. to C.O. Harrington to Lansdowne, 30 November 1905. C.O. 879/88.
147. F.O. 371/190. Harrington's Minute, 19 January 1907.
148. F.O. 371/190. Harrington's Memo, 19 January 1907.
149. F.O. 371/190. Clerk to Gray, 17 April 1907.
150. F.O. 371/190. Clerk to Gray, 15 May 1907.
151. F.O. 371/395. Hohler to Gray, 1 January 1908.

7

Predominance Without Costs

Britain and the French Jibuti-Harar Railway

Since 1898 Britain had been watching with much concern the growing French hold on Ethiopia through the Jibuti-Harar railway which was under construction. This was Ethiopia's only means of modern transport, which on completion, would link the entire country from the Nile in the west to Shoa in the east to the Red Sea coast. To end the geographical isolation of Ethiopia and modernize the country Emperor Menelek had in 1894 granted a concession to Alfred Ilg, a Swiss national in his employment, to build and operate a railway from the port of Jibuti in French Somaliland to the White Nile through Addis Ababa, his capital. The concession was for ninety nine years at the end of which the railway with all its fixed assets was to become property of the Ethiopian State. The Ethiopian Government was responsible for the security of the railway and its permission was mandatory to transport troops and war materials.[1] Given the difficulty of attracting private capital for the venture Menelek tried to make the concession financially attractive by giving the concessionaires the right to levy a duty of 10 per cent on the railborne merchandise, besides binding himself not to allow any competing railways to be built in Ethiopia. In return for the concession Menelek was to get 100,000 thalers worth shares of the prospective railway company and half the profits whenever they exceeded three million francs a year.[2] Menelek was particular that the railway should remain a private venture.

With the help of Leon Chefneux, a Frenchman who had Menelek's confidence, Ilg founded a railway company in Paris, named Compagnie Imperial des Chemine de Fers Ethiopian. However at the time the railway concession was granted Ethiopia was regarded as a *quantite negligeable.* Its economic potential was unknown and the political future was uncertain. Italy was claiming a protectorate over Ethiopia and Emperor Menelek was strongly denouncing the Italian pretensions. War clouds were hovering over Ethiopia and prospects for an early construction of the railway did not look bright. Inspite of the virulent Anglo-French rivalry for predominance in Ethiopia, while France did not take immediate advantage of Menelek's railway concession waiting for the resolution of the Italo-Ethiopian conflict, Britain almost ignored it believing that the railway would not materialize and that her strategic interests had been secured through the Anglo-Italian Protocols of 1891.[3] However with the defeat of Italy at Adwa in 1896 and re-opening of the Nile question, Anglo-French rivalry for pre-dominance in Ethiopia intensified and the railway assumed a political character at once becoming a bone of contention between the two powers.

Realizing the economic and political benefits of a French controlled railway, the French Government approved the long ignored request of the French Railway Company for permission to build the first ninety kilometers through the French Somaliland Protectorate, appointed an engineer to superintend the construction and agreed to aid the collection of 10 per cent duties on the railborne traffic.[4] The British also entered the race hoping to wrest the railway from the French. Queen Victoria sent a graceful phonographic message to Menelek advising him to move the railway-head from the French Jibuti to Britain Somali port of Zeila.[5] It was becoming apparent that the Anglo-French rivalry would not allow the railway to develop as a private commercial enterprise.

Though the French Railway Company was a private concern France's official interest in the railway, which started from the French port of Jibuti, caused much trepidation to Britain. The Jibuti railway appeared to threaten Britain's imperial as well as local interests.

Located in the centre of British colonial possession in North-east and East Africa Ethiopia was strategically important. A French controlled railway would not only make France dominant in Ethiopia but also threaten British hold on the Nile and the neighbouring territories from the rear. Immediately the Jibuti railway seemed to undermine the economic survival of the British Somali Protectorate which survived on the duties collected on Ethiopian trade passing through the British Somali ports of Zeila, Bulhar and Berbera.

The approximate value of this trade was £ 500,000 sterling and it yielded an annual revenue of £ 29,000 sterling to the British Somaliland administration. Much of the merchandise was carried by camel caravans.[6] It took about six weeks to travel from the coast to Harar, the commercial capital of Ethiopia, and the journey was both hazardous and uncomfortable. If the railway from Jibuti to Ethiopia became a reality, trade would take that faster and easier route "depriving the very means of existence" to the British Somali protectorate. Shuddering the prospects British officials in the Protectorate, Cairo and Ethiopia urged the British Government to "neutralize the railway" immediately.[7]

Neutralizing meant building a branch railway from the British port of Zeila or Berbera to join the French Jibuti-Harar railway at some point on the Somaliland-Ethiopia frontier. As the French railway company now held a virtual monopoly over railway construction in Ethiopia, Britain could not build a railway beyond the British Somali Protectorate into Ethiopia. A railway which stopped at the frontier without reaching the commercial interior of Ethiopia would be worthless. British officials favoured a two pronged railway, one branch going to French Jibuti and another to British Zeila or Berbera, since it would give a fair share of Ethiopian commerce and parity of influence to both Britain and France. This solution however anticipated the willingness of the French railway company to accept a connecting railway from the British Somali Protectorate. If the proposal was rejected by the French railway company then Britain might persuade Menelek to grant Britain a concession to build an independent railway from Berbera to some place in Ethiopia.[8]

The British Government shared the concerns of its officials in North-east Africa. In September 1898, at the peak of Anglo-French rivalry for the Nile Valley, the British Government considered the possibility of building a neutralizing railway from Berbera to Ethiopia.[9] Prospects seemed encouraging as certain British investors, who had already acquired considerable holdings in the French railway company, were reported to be interested in promoting British interests in the railway "for patriotic reasons."[10]

The financiers of London interested in the French Jibuti railway and the economic exploitation of Ethiopia were grouped in three companies: The New African, the New Egyptian and the Oceana Consolidated. They were closely linked through mutual investments and interlocking directorships.[11] The companies had acquired wide financial interests in Africa through investments in the Mozambique, Pretoria-Petersburg railways, in the Beira Land Company, in the Katanga Copper Mines and rubber business, in the Van Ryan Gold Mines of Pretoria and Aboussa and Tarquah Gold mines in the Gold Coast. They were also involved in the Egyptian Land Reclamation Schemes and the Sudan Ferry Services. Equally impressive were their profits, the New African Company's dividends being 45 per cent in 1898 and 60 per cent in 1899.[12]

These companies had close links with British colonial administrators. For instance Charles Evan Smith, who was appointed the Director of the New African Company in 1898 and played a leading role in its affairs for over a decade, had considerable experience in economic imperialism in East Africa. In 1888, as British representative in Zanaibar, he had assisted the British East Africa Company's expansion into Uganda. Likewise Lieutenant Colonel Sir John Rogers and Gerald Fitzerald who had held high administrative positions in India and Egypt respectively were connected with the New Egyptian Company. The British aristocracy was also represented in these companies by the Marquess of Lothian and the Earl of Chesterfield.[13] These companies were connected with sections of British society which could bring influence to bear upon

British policy. They were profit oriented concerns, generally insensitive to nationalism or patriotism though they would readily embrace both to achieve profits.

African railways in general did not attract much private capital and the French Jibuti-Harar railway was no exception. The French Railway Company needed at least 34 million Francs to build 340 kilometers of the first section of the three stage railway and tried to raise 40 million Frances by issuing 28,000 shares and 50,000 bonds of 500 Frances each.[14] The French public invested much less than expected and the railway construction was begun with only half the required capital. Given the difficulty of raising funds internally, the French Railway Company began to look for external resources. The London financiers at once seized the opportunity to invest in the Jibuti railway. In fact during the first issue of the shares by the French Railway Company itself the English group had taken part; out of 8.5 million obligation 56,7000 were subscribed by a syndicate composed by Ochs and his French partners Rene Boudouy, Rousseau and Dessoudeix.[15]

The New African Company had acquired, as early as 1898, 17,000 debentures in the French Railway Company with option to buy further issues. In June 1900, along with the New Egyptian and the Oceana Consolidated Companies, the New African undertook to supply all the funds required to build the railway up to 215 kilometers and acquired construction rights in the railway. Holding 12,000 of the company's 36,000 shares with an option to acquire more seating four directors on a board of eight and acquiring voice in determining future issues the British group was close to controlling the management of the French Railway Company which was already under their "full power".[16] So considerable were their investments in the Jibuti railway by 1901, that the British group floated the International Railway and Construction Company to take over and develop their interests in the French railway. The British Government was watching these developments with satisfaction.

With its apparently influential position in the French Jibuti Harar railway, the New African Company was pre-eminently placed to play the role of an unofficial promoter of British policy and it did not waste the opportunity.

Familiar with railway politics of imperialism, involved as he was in the Mozambique railway, Albert Ochs, Manager of the New African Company, saw an opportunity to "milch the imperial cow." At the height of Anglo-French rivalry for the Nile Valley in July 1898, he approached the British Foreign Office with a proposal to neutralize the French Jibuti-Harar railway with a British line from Berbera to Harar. Both Lord Salisbury and his Under Secretary, Sir Thomas Sanderson liked the idea and authorized, Harrington, the British Agent in Ethiopia, to explore the possibility with Och's New African Company.[17]

During the discussions however Ochs dropped the original proposal for an independent British railway in favour of a fifty kilometer link line from Zeila, in the British Somali Protectorate, to meet the French Jibuti-Harar railway at some point along the Ethiopian frontier. Presumably it would ensure a fair share of Ethiopian trade to the British Somaliland while avoiding bitter Anglo-French rivalry which an all British railway from Berbera must cause by violating the monopoly of the French railway concessionaries.

Proposing to build the railway by winning the consent of the French concessinaries, the New African Company asked a British Government guarantee on the estimated construction capital of £ 300,000 sterling.[18] While winning the support of the British Foreign Office the proposal met with the Treasury's opposition. The very idea of a link railway, which could neither survive independently of the French railway nor really prevent the expected loss of revenue to the British Somali protectorate, was repugnant to the Treasury.[19] Notwithstanding the New African Company's assurance to secure a controlling Position in the French Railway Company, the unimpressed Chancellor of the Exchequer refused to "assume any financial responsibility in the matter..."[20]

The New African Company did not give up the hope. Trying to overcome the difficulty the Company suggested a British Somali Protectorate guarantee in place of an imperial one. This was not a novel idea. European colonies and protectorates in Africa had often been made to bear the cost of imperial railways even when such did not serve local interests. Supporting the idea the Foreign Office recommended it to the British Somali Protectorate.[21] Faced with declining revenues and lacking attractive revenue producing sources like the coastal trade of Lagos or the mineral wealth of the Gold Coast, the Somali Protectorate rejected the proposal.[22] Notwithstanding these setbacks the British investors and the British Officials in North-east Africa remained optimistic about the railway given Salisbury's admitted interest in it.[23] They coalesced their forces to manoeuvere the British Government into supporting the railway.

From Addis Ababa the British Minister kept up constant pressure on the Foreign Office to build the railway. His over agitated mind perceived disaster from the French railway not only to the British Somali Protectorate, which was apparent, but also to the Sudan, Aden and British and Indian Treasuries, which was farfetched. Arguing that the annual cost of servicing the construction cost of Berbera railway would be less than the expected grant-in-aid of £ 12,000, which would have to be made to the Somali Protectorate to off set its revenue loss caused by the French railway, he thought it would be a small amount to pay for the political and economic advantages to be gained. Moreover the issue was not just the economic health of British Somali Protectorate only, but of Britain's preponderance in Ethiopia also. Neutralisation of the French railway was essential to achieve this.[24] Besides soliciting Cromer's support the British Minister personally appealed to Salisbury to push the railway project.[25] Certainly Salisbury favoured a neutralizing railway but the time was inopportune to take it up. The Shire and Uganda railways, then under construction, and the Boer War were causing much expenditure and he did not wish to pressure the Chancellor of Exchequer for more money.[26]

While the British were becoming panicky about the French Jibuti railway, the French Railway Company was having difficulty in raising funds to complete even the first section of the railway to Harar. It had begun to lean heavily on British investors and barrowed a further sum of two million Francs from the New African Company.[27] Exploiting the opportunity the British Minister to Ethiopia endeavoured to induce the original concessionaries to sell Menelek's railway concession to the British investors for a profit. If they agreed, then the railway head could be moved from Jibuti to Berbera in the British Somaliland ending the French threat. Harrington's personal diplomacy had some success as the original concessionaries were reportedly ready to sell the concession.

Encouraged by the news the British Minister advised the British Government to buy the concession immediately or at least to influence British financiers like the Cassells or the Humbros to invest in the Jibuti railway. He reiterated that the opportunity should not be lost to seize the French-Ethiopian railway and financial parsimony should not deter imperial policy.[28] Supporting Harrington, while the Consul-General of the Somali Coast urged the Foreign Secretary to take immediate action, influential Cromer warned him that inaction would be a mistake and cost London more in the end if it the trade of Zeila were allowed to disappear.[29] Salisburry and Sir Thomas Sanderson were sympathetic to the proposal and referred the matter to the Treasury. Hoping to overcome latter's opposition, after favouring the Chancellor of the Exchequer with economic argument, that the French should not occupy predominant position in Abyssinia which the construction of the railway would probably give them, he warned that they would surely endanger British interests in the region and the matter was really worth considering.[30]

Joining hands with the official imperialists, the British investors had been lobbying for support in London for Berbera-Harar railway. Obviously these efforts had some success. Even the Treasury conceded that the matter needed an in depth consideration.

A high powered committee representing the Treasury, the Foreign Office and the Board of Trade discussed terms with the New African Company for building Berbera railway to connect the French Jibuti line.[31] For the first time in the last two years the British Government had taken serious interest in the railway and the matter needed to be handled adroitly. But the profit hungry New African Company failed to raise to the occasion. It asked the Government not only to guarantee construction capital of a million sterling to build the railway and improve Berbera port but also to invest half a million sterling in the shares of the French Railway Company. This was deemed necessary to control the management of the Jibuti railway to facilitate the connection of the Berbera line to the Jibuti-Harar railway and to ensure it favourable treatment. Regarding mere Government guarantee of capital an inadequate inducement, the New African Company proposed floating a syndicate, with monopoly, to build the railway and exploit mineral resources of the British Somali Protectorate.[32]

These demands were wide-ranging and extensive. The purposed investment of one and half a million sterling on Berbera railway would cost British Government £ 45,000 sterling annually at 3 per cent interest.[33] Spending so huge an amount to offset the revenue loss of the British Somali Protectorate seemed preposterous. Even if this was done there was no certainty the French Railway Company could raise enough funds to extend the railway to the Ethiopian capital.[34] Without such an extension the railway could not pay its way. Moreover opposed to guaranteeing any portion of the railway outside the British protectorate the Treasury refused to support the project, though agreeing to reconsider it if Salisbury wanted it.[35] Faced with an expenditure of £112,927,000 sterling for 1899-1900 against an estimated revenue of £110,287,000 sterling, and with the cabinet and Parliament opposed to increase taxes, the Chancellor of Exchequer was really in no mood to take up new railways.[36] Describing the latter's disposition Salisbury gravely minuted that the thought of African railways would make his Chancellor to have fits. This and the obvious financial constraints deterred Salisbury from pushing the project. Hence he decided not to press his Chancellor on the issue.

While refusing financial guarantees to build the railway, the British Government favoured setting up of a syndicate to exploit the Somali Protectorate economically. The other alternative to build Berbera railway was to influence the Hunbros or the Cassels to invest in it. Salisbury declined to consider the option lest the financiers conclude that they deserved a baronetcy.[37]

The New African Company, however, did not despair. Determined to pursue its financial interests the Company made new proposal to the British Government which would need a smaller financial guarantee to build a neutralizing railway. This involved buying Menelek's railway concession from the original concessionaries for £380,000 sterling and building a link railway from Zeila within £250,000 sterling. It would cost the Government £16,500 sterling annually to service the capital costs.[38] In its determination to win the support the Company left no stone unturned arguing that the railway was not merely an economic transaction, but a national interest. Since the French Government had been attempting to end the dominance of British capital in the French Jibuti railway, the company felt that it was the duty of the British Government to strengthen British hold on the railway. Though some officials like Ardagh, the Director of Military Intelligence, were won over by the plea, the British Government was unconvinced that national interests were so endangered as to pay for a neutralizing railway.[39] In any event the proposal was rejected by the Treasury.

While the British Government welcomed an arrangement with private investors to neutralize the French railway, as direct official intervention would have been opposed both by the French and Emperor Menelek, it looked for respectable partnership. The British investors failed to qualify for this. Claiming to be motivated by patriotism they were anything but patriotic. By asking too much from the Government too soon they fell in the government's estimation. While Salisbury regarded them as "pure and simple profiteers," his Parliamentary Under Secretary, Lord Cranborne, doubted if British interests could be advanced by "the so-called capitalists."[40] Their financial demands looked "extravagant" to Lansdowne, the new Foreign Secretary. The British investors were primarily interested in profiting from the railway, which the Government regarded as neither easily supportable nor absolutely essential to secure British interests; there was very little scope for co-operation between the two. The British Government welcomed imperialism on the cheap; the financiers shunned it.

The New African, the New Egyptian and the Ocean Consolidated Companies were pure commercial ventures organized for profiting. They were not imperially as inspired as the British South African and the British East African Companies. As financiers with investments in different parts of Africa, they had to accommodate policies of different European colonial regimes which were often opposed to those of Britain. So long as opportunities existed to invest and profit these companies wished to have less to do with their Government. It was only when their interest were threatened by rivals or foreign Governments they adopted strong national tones and sought the home Government's intervention.

Until 1901, when no great opposition was offered to British investments in the French railway, the New African Company and its associates kept low national profiles, though for commercial reasons they delved into imperial politics and offered to build neutralizing British railways. However when the French colonialists launched an aggressive campaign to oust them from the Jibuti railway, the British investors at once assumed belligerent national tone to win public support and force the British Government into aiding them. The directors of the New African Company "felt persuaded" that a policy which would give equal opportunity to both Britian and France in Ethiopia would be the best. Felt compelled to neutralize the French railway they promised "to do all in their power to...further this aim."[41] The Oceana Consolidated Company insisted that a British railway from Zeila was indispensable to protect British interests. The French were advised that the union of British and French capital and activity in Ethiopia would not only promote the interest of the railway company but also preserve good relations between the two countries.[42] The Earl of Chesterfield, Chairman of the newly founded International Ethiopian Railway Trust and Construction Company, warned that "the political importance of the railway with respect to

English and French interests in Abyssinia became daily more and more important... and its effects on the future of British and French commerce and policy in Abyssinia is carefully being watched.[43] Advising the construction of a British railway from Zeila, Chesterfield assured his audience, "I repeat we will do all we can to further this aim." Exuding self confidence, he concluded: "We have been able to increase our holding and we shall continue to do so." Trying to identify their commercial interests with Britain's national interests the British investors endeavoured to win the support of British imperial forces in the expected confrontation with France. While the strategy failed to win them support of the British Government, it ensured them bitter French opposition.

Though the French Railway Company had so far been forced to survive on British capital, because of the lack of French public support, once it was realized that the railway was about to pass into British hands through a simple commercial process, the French Colonialists mounted a campaign to free the railway from the tentacles of the British Inventors. A violent campaign was launched that French interests had been betrayed and once more rapacious England was seeking to supplant France. It was feared that the story of the Suez Canal would be repeated with the railway.[44] Moreover as the Jibuti railway was seen as a means to convert Ethiopia into a kind of French colony the colonialists wanted to preserve it as an exclusive French enterprises. The campaign seeking French Government intervention to save the railway reached its crescendo towards the end of 1901. Under public pressure, faced with the approaching elections, the Waldeck-Rosseau Government granted the railway an annual Government subvention of a half million Francs for fifty years clamping tight Government control over its management.[45]

By the terms of the Convention, the Railway Company was bound to remain a French enterprise with head office in Paris and its directors were to be French. The French Minister for the colonies was given power to regulate the Railway Company which was prohibited from contracting loans, accepting outside capital or issuing shares without his approval, thus in effect substituting the French State for a private company. Worse still, at the end of ninety-nine years, the French Somali Protectorate was to succeed to all rights of the company within Ethiopian territory. More important, by establishing control over the French Railway Company, which had a monopoly of railway construction in Ethiopia, the French Government had in fact succeeded to the monopoly rights.[46] Thus in their excessive zeal to prevent a possible British take over of the Jibuti railway, the French had disregarded Ethiopia's sovereignty and brought on themselves some unfortunate consequences.

The impact of the French Railway Convention on the British investors was shattering. Under official pressure the French Railway Company tried to free itself from the British investors. After clearing all debts owed to them, the railway company also annulled all contracts they held for railway construction in Ethiopia. Disappointed though the British investors were, they did not despair. They still had investments in the French Eailway Company. Trying to strengthen their position they mounted a campaign against exclusive French control and ownership of the Jibuti-Harar railway. Advocating a joint Anglo-French control of the railway they attacked the French Railway Convention as a grave threat to British imperial interests. The Earl of Chesterfield warned "that it was not in the interest of Abyssinia to allow her foreign trade to be placed virtually under French control or it was the interest of England to be excluded from all participation in the pegging out of such new and fertile field".[47]

The New African Company joined the chorus by urging the British Government to help build a neutralizing railway, while the Oceana consolidated insisted that such a railway was necessary to protect British interests.[48] Supporting them *The Times* lamented British ignorance regarding the magnitude of interests involved in the railway and the disastrous effects of French control.[49] Ignoring these pressures the British Government rejected the railway proposals.

Denouncing the French Government intervention, official imperialists in the Horn and Cairo supported the British investor's plea for a neutralizing railway. They were much concerned to check the ill effects of the Jibuti railway on the Somali protectorate's economy. Attempts to attract trade to Zeila by reducing custom duties from 5 per cent to 2 per cent had failed. Preferring the French railway to the old caravan route many business firms had moved away from British Zeila to French Jibuti. Facing an annual loss of £ 20,000 sterling, the British Somali Protectorate would sink into starved existence besides its flourishing neighbour Jibuti which was enjoying a boom.[50] A quick solution was needed to save the British protectorate.

British officials in North-east Africa were convinced that the only effective solution was to build a railway from the British Somaliland to Ethiopia, and they hoped that British investors like the Cassels could be persuaded to do this if an annual interests of 3 per cent on their capital was guaranteed by the British Government.[51] Even the sceptical Lansdowne agreed that a survey be ordered to determine the cost of the proposed railway, but the Treasury refused funds unless grave political interests were shown to be involved.[52] Even Cromer's influential opinion that Berbera railway could be justified on military considerations failed to convince the Treasury. The Chancellor of the Exchequer thought it preposterous to spend nearly two million sterling on a railway to prevent an annual revenue loss of £ 12,000 sterling to the Somali Protectorate.[53] When Salisbury had refused to exert pressure on the Treasury, Lansdowne preferred not to do otherwise. Disregarding these pressure the British Government refused to yield to the nationalist outcries of the private investors. Indeed there was no need to do so as the Government saw clearly.

Suddenly the political situation in Ethiopia had changed favouring British ascendancy and threating the French position. By stepping upon Ethiopia's sovereignty the French Government had provoked Menelek's indignation. By imposing official control on the French Jibuti railway the French had exposed themselves to the charge of secret territorial designs in Ethiopia. The French controlled railway seemed as harmful to British imperial interests in the region as to Ethiopia's independence and sovereignty. At once the two interests appeared identical. By strengthening Menelek's opposition to France the British could checkmate French Jibuti railway and ruin French influence. Now that the French blunder had provided an inexpensive alternative to safeguard British interests in the region there was no need to promote costly neutralizing railways.

The British had all along been opposing monopoly clauses of Menelek's railway concession to Ilg since it excluded all others, including the British, from building railways in Ethiopia. Now they prevailed on Menelek to cancel the concession without qualms since the French official intervention had destroyed private character of the railway.[54] Menelek did not rush to annual the concession fearing that is would embroil him in a dispute with the French Government, the railway company being no longer private. Exerting pressure the British warned him that they might treat with French to protect their interest unless he forced the French Government to relinquish its hold on the railway.[55]

Threatened though by the dark prospects, Menelek did not fall into the British trap. A farsighted ruler, he hoped to secure his interests by exploiting Anglo-French rivalry. Expressing reservations about opposing the French single handed he offered to cancel the railway concession if the British diplomatically and materially supported him against possible French attack on Ethiopia. He also requested British financial support to build his own railway from Harar to the frontier, which Britian might extend to the Somali coast.[56] The British Minister to Addis Ababa advised London to comply with Menelek's requests. These proposals were unpalatable to the British Government. While it was determined to end France's official control over the Ethiopian railway, she did not want an armed confrontation with France. Nor was the Government ready to commit funds for Menelek's railway. It advised its Agent in Addis Ababa not to emphasize British assistance to Menelek.[57] The shocked British Agent warned his Government that having encouraged Menelek to oppose the French, if he was denied aid, British influence in Ethiopia would suffer beyond repair. He advised that Menelek be supported strongly and vigorous opposition to the French railway be maintained. "France might fluster a great deal, but he doubted her doing much."[58]

The British Government did not like its Minister's uncompromising anti-French position. While attempt was being made to harmonies Anglo-French interests in many parts of the world it would be out of character to escalate Anglo French rivalry in Ethiopia. While the Jibuti Harar Railway was of material interest to Britian it was not important enough to "cross swords with France."[59] Even if France monopolized the Jibuti-Harar railway and dominated the eastern approach to Ethiopia Britian still could command the western approach through the Sudan and the Nile. Moreover the British Government had concluded that British policy needs in Ethiopia scarcely warranted an expenditure of millions on a neutralizing railway unless it could be justified on commercial and financial grounds. It might be better to protect British interests in Ethiopia through a negotiated settlement with France. Making a virtue out of necessity Lansdowne advised, Harrington, the British Minister to Ethiopia, that it would be unwise of Menelek to agree to French Government acquiring possession of railway within his territory, for same reasons it is not in his interest that Britain should undertake railway from Berbera into Abyssinia.[60]

Harrington deprecated this policy. Having led Menelek to count on British support in opposing the French, he thought it immoral to let him down. Menelek was in serious difficulty with the French Government having annulled the railway monopoly and withdrawn the right to collect a 10 per cent duty on the rail-borne goods. This had ruined the company's ability to raise the much needed construction capital. Urged by the Company the French Government was pressing Menelek to withdraw his opposition to the railway. Menelek was threatening to reach an agreement with the French if the British let him down. If Menelek did so Britain would loose a powerful tool to wring concessions from France. Certainly London did not want Menelek to jump out of British net. With characteristic vagueness the British Government assured Menelek that it would help him to resist France from imposing "a disagreeable solution on the railway."[61]

Meanwhile Menelek's continuing opposition had placed the French Railway Company in great difficulty. Having spent all money raised by pledging the French Government subvention it was unable to finance further construction. The Jibuti-Harar railway which had been plying up to Dire-Dawa since December 1902 was not even paying operational expenses. While its monthly receipts were 15,000 Francs the expenses were 115,000. The Company's efforts to raise capital on Paris market had failed since public was afraid of investing in a railway which was the centre of political rivalry and faced bleak commercial prospects. Faced by acute financial pressures the railway company was wooing British capital ignoring legal restrictions imposed on external borrowing by the convention of 1902. It was pressing the French Government to end Anglo-Ethiopian opposition to the railway through an agreement with those powers and fund the extension of the line to Addis Ababa.

Obviously the French Government was in difficulty. The French Chamber could not be persuaded to pay for the railway until it could be shown that the company had been permitted to extend the railway into the Ethiopian interior. Menelek was unlikely to permit it to do so, so long as he had British support. Apparently the solution to the French difficulty lay with the British. If the British were made to withdraw their support to Menelek alone and unsupported, he might not continue his opposition to the French railway.

The French business and commercial groups interested in the Jibuti railway had felt so harassed by 1904 that they were pressing for a peaceful resolution of the difficulty with Britian. The French Colonists, including Etienne and Deloncle, who had fought far so long to keep the railway exclusively French had realized the need for harmonization of Anglo-French interests.[62] Agreeing that the time was opportune to do so the French Government opened negotiations with Britian.[63]

Inspite of the success which Britian had in ruining French influence in Ethiopia, she was unsure of the situation. Her major weapon in fighting the French had been Menelek. But he was now annoyed with Britian for not supporting him adequately in overcoming the French threat and not assisting him to build a railway. He could not be appeased with mere assurances. Financially expensive, commercially indefensible, Menelek's railway could only be supported on political expediency. But the warming Anglo-French relations would make a mockery of it. A diplomatic settlement with France to protect British interests would be preferable to senseless competition and ruinous investments on a non-paying railway. Lansdowne confided to Balfour:

> We dislike the French railway scheme and the concession containing some objectionable clauses. But I doubt we should encourage Menelek to place himself entirely in our hands... But as the French are apparently on good terms with us... We might approach the French Government informally and endeavour to bring out a friendly solution.[64]

The British Government advised its Minister in Addis Ababa that it was not prepared to promise aid to Menelek in opposing the French.[65] This *volte face* in British policy could not be explained to Menelek. It placed the British Minister in impossible position in Addis Ababa.

Whatever Harrington's disappointment, British investors in the French Railway Company welcomed the policy of harmonizing Anglo-French interests in Ethiopia. Anglo-French rivalry was hurting their interests. Because of the French Railway Company's financial and political difficulties the value of British investments in the railway was depleting. It could only prosper and produce handsome profits if the Jibuti railway was extended to Addis Ababa and flourished commercially. This was unlikely to happen sc long as Anglo-Ethiopian opposition to the railway continued. Having failed to muster British Government's support for themselves and faced with the hostility of the French Government, the British investors planned to protects their investments in the railway by promoting Anglo-French understanding. They spearheaded the move to bring about a joint Anglo-French control and management of the Jibuti railway. "This policy was made known to the shareholders of the New African Company: "While loyally supporting the French railway and the French Government in their endeavour to push forward the railway the Board has never lost sight of the desirability of harmonizing English and French commercial interests concerned therein. Although these views have not hitherto met with general favour, the Board hopes, the friendly accord now existing between England and France will tend to a conclusion of friendly understanding in respect of the railway and in that case our position as shareholders would be materially increased".[66]

Proposing the construction of a British line from Berbera to join the Jibuti-Harar railway at Dire-Dawa and its prolongation to Addis Ababa as a joint Anglo-French venture, the British investors, led by Ochs, established contact with the French colonial group in Paris to achieve the objective.[67] Some of the French colonists, including Waldec Rosseau, and the French Railway Company responded favourably.[68] He arrived at an understanding with the French colonialists on a scheme for an Anglo-French accord on the railway;[69] supported by Lord Cromer and the British and French Ministers to Ethiopia, Ochs advised London to take the matter up with the French Government officially.[70] Despite Lansdowne's scepticism about the role and intentions of the British investors, his Under Secretary, the Earl of Cranborne, thought it unwise to repulse them in view of "international policy" on the railway which the British Government might adopt.[71]

On Albert Ochs' initiative the British and French Ministers to Ethiopia met in Paris in December 1903 and reached a tentative agreement harmonizing British and French interests in Ethiopia and recommended it to the acceptance of their Governments. By this the French Jibuti railway was to be allowed to reach Harar. From there the railway was to be extended to the Ethiopian capital as a joint Anglo-French venture. In return for free hand in the Hawash Valley, France was to make Jibuti a free port ensuring free and equal treatment to British goods and subjects at that port and on the railway. All railway construction to the west of Addis Ababa, a British sphere of influences, was to be carried under British auspices. Both powers were to guarantee Ethiopian independence.[72] Strongly recommending the agreement to British Government Ochs considered it as "practical and generous".[73] The British Government rejected the proposals as too "generous" and "extreme" concessions to France, though it would settle for less favourable terms in the Tripartite Agreement of 1906.

Notwithstanding this set-back the British investors continued their pursuit in Paris for an Anglo-French understanding. Thus they paved the way for official British and French negotiations. But, during the negotiations, the British Government ignored them completely without consulting even on matters which affected them most.

Anglo-French negotiations on Ethiopia began in May 1904, in the friendly environment of the *entente cordiale*. The French objective in opening the negotiations was to give "a precise direction" and to pursue a "firm policy" to keep the railway "absolutely French".[74] Anglo-French *entente* was pressed into service to achieve this goal. Both Lansdowne and Cambon thought it possible to reach a quick agreement despite the apparent divergences in the British and French positions on the railway question. The British wanted to end France's exclusive control on the railway, to secure equal treatment on it to British subjects and merchandise and if possible to internationalize the entire line. Certainly they preferred Menelek building the railway from Harar to Addis Ababa instead of the prolongation of the French railway to the Ethiopian capital.[75] Determined to maintain her hold on the first two section of the Jibuti-Harar railway France rejected internationalization as "inadmissible to public opinion."

France tried to win over Britain with some important concessions. Assuring free participation to British capital in the railway and its management, France offered to relenquish her right to build the third section of the railway from Addis Ababa to the Nile, in return for a British recognition of the Jibuti railway as a French interest. While agreeing with the essentials Britian disagreed on details. Satisfied with the French offer to keep out of the Nile region of western Ethiopia's British sphere, Britain opposed France's claim to absolute control on the first two section of the Jibuti railway since that would leave "the neck of the bottle" (railway head at Jibuti) in her hands. Britian wanted a share in the control and management of Jibuti railway which was strategically and militarily important besides being the commercial life-line of Ethiopia. She offered to end her opposition and recognize the railway as a French interest if the terms were accepted.[76]

While the negotiations were going on in London Menelek was worried about its implications for Ethiopia. Unimpressed with British and French assurances to safeguard Ethiopian independence, Menelek strove to promote his interests by exploiting local Anglo-French hostilities. He gave Britain a concession to build a railway from Berbera to the Nile through Ethiopia.[77] Strongly supporting Menelek the British Minister to Ethiopia advised his Government not to regard Menelek's railway concession just as a bargaining ploy to extract concessions from France but as an opportunity to neutralize France and strengthen British influence in Ethiopia. However if British did not like to work out the concession, Harrington recommended that Menelek be allowed to hypotheticate the Egyptian annual subsidy of £ 10,000 sterling to raise the required construction capital to build his own railway. Supporting the hypothetication of the subsidy Cromer proposed that Egypt be made to assume direct obligation to the lender and Britain obtain a "lien" on the Menelek's proposed railway.[78] This was an ingenious plan. Britian would acquire control of Menelek's railway if he should build one. British would supplant France.

Clearly these suggestions were unacceptable to London. Given the Treasury's opposition to African railways, Lansdowne considered it "idle to proceed on that assumption."[79] Even were Menelek allowed to hypotheticate Egyptian subsidy adequate funds could not be raised for the proposed railway: moreover, he preferred the payment of subsidy tied down to "good behaviour" of Menelek. Above all Déclassé, the French Foreign Minister, was implacably opposed to an independent Ethiopian railway. The success of Anglo-French negotiations required that Britain ignore Menelek's requests.[80]

The French were opposed to any proposal which disallowed the extension of the French Jibuti railway to Addis Ababa. It was a French company which held the railway concession, it was French money that had gone into the railway construction and it was French Government subvention that has helped it to survive independently.[81] The French considered it most unreasonable that other powers should wish to control the French railway. While regarding the French objection "perfectly natural" the British Foreign Office considered that the best arrangement would be to lay down a general principle that all railways in Ethiopia should be constructed by Menelek himself and financial assistance be provided on an international basis.[82] Lansdowne urged the French to accept it. It would please Menelek, save Ethiopia from railway politics and give the concerned European powers equal opportunity for investment in that country. Rejecting the suggestion, the French insisted that no agreement could be reached unless the first two sections of the railway were recognized as exclusive French interests. Allowing the French to have their way Lansdowne let Menelek down.

Fearing that this volte face in Britian policy would discredit Britain with Menelek, Harrington warned London that the Ethiopian Emperor would give a serious rebuff both to Britain and France if a disagreeable solution was imposed on him. He urged the British Government not to give into French pressure and support Menelek.[83]

Harrington was considering the issue in the local context and not from the wider angle of Britain's European diplomacy. His views "looked much belated" to Lansdowne, the architect of the *entente*. Loath to offend the French he confessed to the British Ambassador in Rome: "the railway is what the French care much about... I don't see how we can—considering our present relation—put up that potentate (Menelek) to oppose the construction of the Dire-Dawa section."[84] There was a big gap in the positions of the British Foreign Secretary and his Minister in Ethiopia. To Harrington the maintenance of Ethiopian independence was as much an important end of British policy, at least until 1906, as the protection of vital British interests in the region. To Lansdowne the strengthening of Anglo-French friendship based on the *entente* and an inexpensive arrangement to protect British interests in the region were more important objective than the preservation of Ethiopian independence. He might help maintain Ethiopia's independence as long as it did not clash with other primary British objectives; but he would not commit Britain to that end.

Given Britain's refusal to aid his projected railways, Menelek tried to solve his problem ingeniously. Since heavy capital was his need and this could not be raised without European support, he planned to establish a bank in Ethiopia. Hopefully the Bank would not only finance his railway but also promote Ethiopia's economic development. Since Italy appeared to be the weakest and most compliant of the European powers interested in Ethiopia, Menelek asked her to float a Bank in Addis Ababa.[85] While the Italian Foreign Ministry liked the idea that Italian Treasury opposed Government intervention.[86] Rome's efforts to induce private financiers to exploit Menelek's offer however failed, as the latter demanded a Government subsidy to cover their initial operation which was refused.[87] The matter was left hanging and the delay cost them the opportunity.

Menelek needed an urgent solution for the railway problem. Impatient of waiting he proposed the offer to the British. Perceiving an excellent opportunity to augment British influence Harrington requested his Government to induce some British capitalists or a British Bank to take up Menelek's concession. The British Government influenced National Bank of Egypt, a British institution, to take up the concession.[88] The British succeeded where the Italians had failed. Though Menelek welcomed Italian participation as well in the proposed bank, as he instinctively disliked its exclusive ownership by any one powerful European nation. The Italians too believed that it would be a joint Anglo-Italian venture. But the British considered that, from a political point of view, it should be exclusively British—under British control and auspices."[89] But other European powers were unhappy. The Italians, the French and the Germans, who had lately been evincing interest in Ethiopia, opposed the establishment of a predominantly British Bank as it would tip the scales in Britain's favour.[90] Failing to be co-concessionaires with Britain, the Italians warned Menelek against the danger of placing such an important monopoly in British hands.[91] However, Mc Gillivrey, the adroit negotiator of the Bank, gained Menelek's confidence by displaying sympathy for his cause.[92] The National Bank of Egypt secured Menelek's concession to establish Bank of Abyssinia with a monopoly for fifty years.[93] The French feared that the British would use the Bank to impose their control over the administration and finance of Ethiopia and endanger Ethiopian independence.[94]

The establishment of the Bank of Abyssinia had a decisive impact on Menelek's railway policy. Though it is doubtful if he ever wanted to build a railway of his own, certainly he did not want one under exclusive French control. Strengthened by Mc Gillivrey's friendly assurance of financial support and Rosen's[95] indication that German help might be forthcoming for his railway, Menelek exerted pressure on the Italian, the French and the British Governments to produce an acceptable railway solution.[96] In a special meeting with European Ministers in Addis Ababa, in April 1905, Menelek warned them unless they neutralized and internationalized the Jibuti railway and extended it to the agreed destination within the stipulated time he would build his own railway.[97]

Menelek was, however, wrong in thinking that he could alter the policy of the concerned European powers. Britain, France and Italy were closing their ranks in Ethiopia. The first two powers were very sensitive to Germany's professed interest in Ethiopia. Suspecting Germany's hand behind Menelek's ultimatum they hastened to conclude an agreement on Ethiopia. Convinced that Menelek's opposition without Britain's support would be ineffective, the French disregarded Menelek's warning. Though the Italians were opposed to exclusive French control of the railway and preferred its internationalization which Menelek was also demanding, they were neither strong nor influential to push it. The British alone were in a position to force international control on the French railway, but they did not.

It is unfortunate that the British Government did not exert enough pressure to internationalize the French Jibuti railway, a solution favoured by the British investors, the French railway company and even the French colonialists. In fact there was a growing movement within France for such a solution. Menelek's opposition to the French railway had made investments in it almost worthless and French dreams of making the railway an instrument for economic exploitation of Ethiopia could not materialize unless Menelek allowed the railway to reach Ethiopia's interior. This was unlikely unless the Jibuti railway was internationalized or French Government's control was ended. Moreover, as Lansdowne pointed to Cambon, the internationalization would relive the railway company from its financial problems by freely attracting international capital. Exasperated by waiting, determined to end the stalemate and interested in profiting by promoting trade with Ethiopia many members of the French Chamber of Commerce were urging internationalization of the railway.[98] Had the British capitalized on this they could have provided a railway solution acceptable to most. But they did not succumbling to French official pressure.

Déclassé and the extreme right wing of French colonial party, were committed to the doctrine of French paramountcy in eastern Ethiopia, and the Jibuti railway was its essential component. Comite de 1, Africa Francaise fully opposed any dilution of French control on the railway while influential colonialists including D, Aunay were insisting that it should remain French. They opposed any proposal for internationalization seeing it as "la ingerenza dell inghilterra." (meddling by the British). Rejecting Lansdowne's allusion to growing support for internationalization in French business circles and media, Déclassé argued that such were a minority, "obedient" to financiers involved in the railway, and their opinions did not count for much. He insisted that both French Parliament and French Colonialists were committed to keeping the Jibuti railway as a French preserve and opposed its internationalization.[99]

Déclassé and his supporters warned the British that their support on the railway question was seen as touch stone to the *entente cordiale*. Count D'Aunay, a Déclassé supporter, declared that the *entente cordiale* would be an object of derision did it serve to diminish French influence in Ethiopia.[100] The French Government emphasized that future Anglo-French relations would much depend on Britain's stand on the railway.

The British had little choice given the importance they attached to the new found friendship with France. Lord Lansdowne, the Foreign Secretary admitted this to the British Minister to Addis Ababa: "The French continue to press for the extension of the line to Addis Ababa by the existing company and are entirely opposed to internationalization. In the present circumstances no other solution seems possible, and we shall not be able to conclude an agreement with France on the subject except upon this condition".[101]

Britain did want to conclude an agreement with France and she had no reason to displease her to merely please Menelek. She acquiesced in the French demand. The British Government decided to end its opposition to the French railway. Lansdowne told Cambon that the British cabinet had agreed to the French proposal that the railway from Jibuti to Addis Ababa must remain French while any construction from Addis Ababa to the Nile must be British.[102]

Since the British Government had been forced to let down Menelek on the railway question she tried to make the issue look insignificant by comparing it to the larger issue of Ethiopian independence. Menelek was told that Britain had been trying to safeguard Ethiopian independence through a tripartite agreement and it could not be achieved were the French disallowed to keep the railway. Such a failure would be a greater menace to Ethiopia than the French controlled railway itself.[103] The message was clear: Britian would not oppose the French railway; better Menelek did likewise.

This change in British policy looked a betrayal to Menelek. A seasoned statesman that he was, he did not display his anger or distrust towards Britian. Instead we urged the British Government to build a neutralizing railway, warning her that if she failed to use his railway concession he would allow some other European power to work it out. The Italians too joined the chorus. Disappointed by the British acquiescence in the French wish, and prompted by Menelek they pressed the British Government to reverse its position and to promote a "commercial railway". But Britain was in no mood to consider these views having committed to France. Menelek however did not give up his preference for internationalization of the Jibuti-Harar railway. There is adequate circumstantial and inferential evidence to suggest that he used Germany, Italy and the Bank of Abyssinia to change their railway policy to meet his views.

Menelek's threat that he might use some other European powers aid to promote his contemplated railway did create much anxiety and many ripples in the British and French diplomatic circles. Both suspected German hand behind Menelek's moves. In the light of the Moroccan incidents it seemed likely that Germany might stir up trouble in Ethiopia and oppose Anglo-French policy on the railway. Flying rumours in Addis Ababa and Cairo that the Germans were going to finance Menelek's railway from Harar to Addis Ababa and claim a share in the French-Jibuti only strengthened the suspicion.[104]

Indeed there was some basis for the French concerns. The timely, perhaps the intended shocking disclosure of Dr. Rossen, Head of the German Mission to Ethiopia, to Cromer and Rouvier, that Germany might claim a share in the Jibuti-Harar Railway of Ethiopia made the French nervous. Reporting this to Paris Paul Cambon fulminated that Germany had no *raison d'etre* for such pretensions, but her moves only showed the true "colour" of her politics.[105] However Dr. Rosen, had hinted at the same time that Germany could not interfere if the railway remained exclusively French.[106] Answering the agitated French Chambers Rouvier concluded that "so long as the railway remained French no trouble would be encountered"; hence no suggestion for the internationalization would be entertained.[107]

The French urged the British to conclude an agreement on the railway immediately to prevent possible German intervention.[108]

It is difficult to comprehend the German designs in Ethiopia. However it is presumable that by strengthening the French opposition to internationalization of the railway, and by encouraging Menelek to build his own railway from Harar to Addis Ababa, the Germans were hoping to intensify Franco-Ethiopian rivalry and strengthen German influence in Ethiopia. But the German moves only spurred Britain, France and Italy to reach an accord on the railway soon.

Even more interesting than the German feelers was Menelek's manòeuver to win over Mc Gillivrey of the Bank of Abyssinia to finance his railway in opposition to the wish of the British Government. Bank of Abyssinia was a British sponsored Bank. Though the British Government had described the Bank as "non-political", certainly it was far from being so. As the Italians rightly saw that in the African context it was difficult to say where the purely economic role of such institutions ended and where their political role started. Usually the sponsoring European Governments found them useful in promoting their political goals. Though the British Government had no direct hold over the Bank, it had been understood from the beginning that its actions would conform to British policy in the region.[109] The statutes of the Bank had been framed on the advice of Lord Cromer. An Italian, a German and a French member had also been added to the Board of Directors on the British suggestion to smoothen the ongoing tripartite negotiations.[110]

While the British Government did not interfere in the day to day administration of the Bank, its policies were certainly watched. The British Government wanted the Bank of Abyssinia to keep away from the railway question. However sympathizing Menelek's aspirations, Mc Gillivery, the Bank's first governor, promised financial aid to Menelek's proposed railway and this stiffened Menelek's opposition to Anglo-French policy on the question.[111] Clearly the British Government was unhappy about Mc Gillivrey's role. Cromer expressed the British position: Manifestly, Menelek relies on the Bank to provide him funds to make his own railway... Until I got the correspondence (Mc Gillivery's letter to the Governor of National Bank, Cairo) I did not appreciate the important part which the Bank negotiator had played... It is so far awkward that it will strengthen French suspicions that we have been acting against them.[112]

Anxious to avoid any misunderstanding with France, the British Government instructed the British Minister in Addis Ababa to prevent Mc Gillivery from doing anything that might encourage Menelek to reject the railway proposals which the tripartite powers were about to make.[113] Refusing to bow down to the officials policy the strong-willed Mc Gillivrey insisted on supporting Menelek. His actions, of course, had as much been motivated by prospects of making profits for his Bank through investment in Menelek's railway as his sympathies for the latter. At the same time the British investors in the Jibuti railway favoured German participation in the railway while the German Director of the Bank of Abyssinia favoured the Bank taking up the construction of the Harar-Addis Ababa railway in place of France. Germany seemed to be keen in staking her claim for a share both in the Jibuti railway and the Bank.[114] The policy of Mc Gillavrey which the Germans and the British capitalists seemed to be supporting and its impact on Menelek were obviously irksome to the British.

Meanwhile enraged by the indifference of the European powers to his earlier warning Menelek gave them an ultimatum stating that he would build his own railway "with the support of the Bank" if they failed to provide him with an acceptable railway agreement within the stipulated time.[115]

Unfortunately both Mc Gillivrey and Menelek were mistaken in assuming that they could have their way. Menelek was as knaive in equating Mc Gillivery with the Bank as Mc-Gillivrey was in assuming that the Bank, though a private institution, would be permitted to operate in opposition to British policy. The tentacles of British power reached the Bank's Governor and through Board of Directors in Cairo. They knew that it was their interest to have British Government behind them. Mc Gillivrey's intervention in the railway infuriated the British Government which feared that the French might suspect its complicity. So great was the concern for the *entente* that though the French themselves had not bothered to protest against Mc Gillivrey's action, the British thought that it would be "breach of faith with the French" if Mc Gillivrey was not chastised.[116]

Since the British Government lacked legal rights to interfere in the Bank's affairs, it considered exerting "moral pressure" to have McGillivrey recalled.[117] However the British Government abstained from so doing to avoid giving impression to Menelek that the Bank was a political institution intended to serve British policy.[118] Moreover the recall of Mc-Gillivrey who enjoyed Menelek's confidence would only have added to Britain's difficulties in Ethiopia. Thus Britain was most anxious to avoid.

While the British Government's displeasure at Mc Gillivrey is understandable its cynicism towards the Bank's financial future is not. That the Bank's participation in Menelek's railway might have contributed to its financial stability and generally strengthened British economic interests in the region did not impress the British Government. In its strategically inspired and politically oriented Ethiopian policy economic considerations played a very insignificant role. British institutions would be allowed to pursue economic interests only so long as such did not conflict with official policy; even then they could be sacrificed for higher imperial considerations.

This becomes more evident in British policy towards British investors in the French Jibuti railway.[119] Refusing to withdraw from the French railway company inspite of ruinous effects of the French Government's hostility on their financial prospects, the British investors hoped to improve their position. Their hopes were well founded. Ignoring the French Government's limitations on its powers of external burrowing, the French railway company, in its financial difficulties, had sought British investments. Lending large amounts to the French railway company the British investors had improved their holdings[120]. Though the French Government had allowed this to enable the railway company survive financially, it was nevertheless hostile to the British group.

By 1906 the French Government had taken steps to eject the British investors from the Jibuti railway. Neither the *entente cordiale* nor subsequent improvement in Anglo-French relations had removed French hostility towards the British investors. There were rumours that once Britain had recognized the Jibuti-Addis Ababa railway as a French interest, the French Government would liquidate the railway company to "ecraser le groupe Anglais" and find a new one amenable to its official policy. Frightened British investors repeatedly requested the British Government to protect them adequately in any agreement which might be reached with France. Ignoring their appeals the British Government made no attempt to secure their interests. They were not even consulted in the on-going negotiations with France since their views on the railway question was opposed to that of the French. When it was realized that Britain might sacrifice their interests for an accord with France and demanded to know what was being done to protect them, the British Government tried to silence them saying that they should not complain "if they received no worst treatment than the French investors."[121]. The British Government's unconcern so demoralized the British investors that they threatened to withdraw co-operation from the Government in other African projects, such as the Mozambique railway.

Neither threats nor economic arguments dissuaded the British Government from its policy. [122] In the Tripartite Agreement of December 1906 the British Government recognized the French Jibuti-Harar railway as a French interest in return for her recognition of British interests in Ethiopia. The British Government made no provisions to protect British capital in what was to be a virtually French railway.[123] The Tripartite Agreement was a rude shock and a bitter disappointment to the British investors as well as Menelek. This did not bother the British Government. The "so called British capitalists" had neither sufficient political influence nor capable spokesman to embarrass the government. Their protests were easily ignored. Menelek's protests and disappointments too could be ignored. Ephemeral influence with an ageing African monarch could be sacrificed for an adequate guarantee of British interests by an European adversary who alone was in a position to challenge those interests in the region.

This was a clear case where the needs of finance capital made no impression on British policy which was solely pursued with an eye to British strategic interests. First, the British government's refusal to use British capitalists to build a railway from the Somaliland protectorate, and later to protect their investments in the French Jibuti railway can only be attributed to the non-economic nature of British policy in Ethiopia. The railway from the first to the last was a political question to Britain and so it was viewed and resolved.

REFERENCES

1. F.O. 1/41. Monson to Salisbury, 22 July 1897.
2. Richard Pankhurst, "The Franco-Ethiopian Railway and its History", *Ethiopia Observer*, Vol VI, No. 2, 1962. p. 344.
3. For details see chapter 2 of this study.
4. Same as foot note 1.
5. *Letter of Queen Victoria*. 3rd Series, (London; 1932.) 3 Volumes, Vol. 3, p. 263. Queen Victoria to Menelek 8 August 1898,
6. Gleischen, *With the Mission to Menelek*. (London; 1898). pp. 169-170.
7. F.O. 1/41. Harrington to Salisbury, 25 July 1898.
   F.O. 1/41. Sadler to Salisbury, 25 July 1898.
8. F.O. 1/41. Harrington to Salisbury, 25 July 1891.
9. F.O. 1/35. Salisbury to Cromer, 19 December 1898.
   F.O. 1/34. Sanderson to Rodd, 7 December 1898.
10. F.O. 1/34. Sanderson to Harrington, 15 July 1898.
11. Leonard Woolf, *Empire and Commerce in Africa*, (London; 1961) p. 206.
12. *The Times*, 24 and 29 June 1899; 22 June 1900; 14 December 1901.
    Woolf, *Empire and Commerce*. pp. 206-210.
13. K.V. Ram, "British Government Finance capitalists and the French Jibuti-Harar Railway". *The Journal of Imperial and Commonwealth History*. London. Vol. XI. 1981.
14. F.O. 1/36. Monson to Salisbury, 22 July 1897.
15. Mario Pigli, L, *Ethiopia Nella Politica Europa*, Ter za Edizione. 9 PADOVA; 1936), p. 43.
16. *The Times*, 6 July 1901.
17. F.O. 1. Sanderson to Harrington, 15 July 1891.

18. F.O. 1/42. Harrington's memorandum, 25 July and 15 August 1898. Harrington to Salisbury, 7 November 1898.
19. F.O. 1/36. Sanderson's Memo, 25 July 1898. F.O. 1/36. Harrington's Memo, 25 July 1898.
20. F.O. 1/36. Harrington's Memorandum, 25 July 1898. F.O. 1/34. The Treasury to the Foreign Office. 7 January 1899.
21. F.O 1/36. Sadler to Salisbury, 29 March 1899.
22. F.O. 1/36. Foreign Office to the Somali Protectorate's Consul General, 2 March 1899.
23. F.O. 1/36. Harrington to Salisbury, 31 August 1899. F.O. 1/35. Salisbury to Cromer, 19 December 1898.
24. F.O. 1/36. Sanderson's Memorandum, September 1899.
25. F.O. 1/46. Sanderson to Bertie, 9 September 1899. Sanderson to the Treasury, 9 September 1899. *Ibid.* F.O. 1/44. Lord Salisbury's Minute. 4 October 1899.
26. Mario Pigli, *Ethiopia Nella Politica Europea* (Padua; 1936), p. 43.
27. F.O. 1/39. Harrington to Salisbury, 14 April 1900.
28. F.O. 1/41. Sadler to Salisbury, 24 February 1900. F.O. 1/37. Cromer to Sanderson, 15 May 1900.
29. F.O. 1/36. The Somali Protectorate's Consul-General to Foreign Office. May 1900
30. F.O. 2/82. Foreign Office to the Treasury, October 1899.
31. F.O. 1/41. Sanderson's Memorandum on the Ethiopian Railway Scheme, 20 November 1900.
32. F.O. 1/41. Sanderson's Minute 15 and 25 October 1900.
33. F.O. 1/41. Sanderson to Cromer, 25 October 1900.
34. F.O. 1/4. Sanderson to Ochs, 1 December 1900.
35. Lady Victoria Hicks Beach, Life of Sir Michael Hicks Beach 2 Volums, (London; 1932) Vol. 2. p. 111.
36. F.O. 1/37. Cromer to Sanderson, 15 May 1900.
37. F.O. 1/41. Cranborne's Minute 26 January 1901.
38. F.O. 1/41. Ardagh's Memorandum 29 July 1901.
39. F.O. 1/44. Cranborne's Memorandum, 26 January 1901. Also see Lord Salisbury's note 4 October 1899.
40. *The Times*, 6 June 1901.
41. *The Times*, 27 December 1901.
42. F.O. 1/41. Excerpts from Chesterfield's Speech, 31 October 1901.
43. Pankhurst, "The Franco-Ethiopian Railway". pp. 152-153.
44. F.O. 1/41. Monson to Salisbury, 7 February 1901.
45. Skinner, *Abyssinia Today*. (London; 1960) pp. 104-107.
46. Chesterfield, "England and Abyssinia", *The National Review*, XXXVIII, (1902) p. 977.
47. *The Times*, 26 May 1902.
48. *The Times*, 11 May 1902.

49. F.O. 1/41. Harrington to Sanderson, 29 July 1902. Cromer to Lansdowne, 17 October 1902. Sanderson's Memo, 8 March 1902.
50. F.O. 1/41. Harrington to Foreign Office. 12 April 1902.
51. Same as foot note 55.
52. F.O. 1/43. The Treasury to Foreign Office. 1 December 1902.
53. F.O. 1/41. Sanderson to Cromer, 19 December 1902. Treasury to Foreign Office. 14 November 1902. T/12/26., 14.09.19
54. F.O. 1/41. Harrington to Salisbury, 30 May 1900.
55. F.O. 1/41. Harrington to Foreign Office, 12 April 1902.
56. *Ibid.*
57. F.O. 1/41. Harrington's Memo. 29 July 1902.
58 F.O. 1/43. Lansdowne to Harrington, 3 February 1903.
59 F.O. 2/802. Cromer to Harington, 18 March 1903.
F.O. 1/43, Lansdowne to Harrington, 3 February 1903; F.O. 2/802 Cromer to Harrington, 18 March 1903.
60. F.O. 1/43. Harrington to Sanderson, 8 February 1903.
61. F.O. 1/43. Instruction to Harrington, in Sanderson to Cromer, 17 March 1903.
62. F.O. 1/43. *Ibid*: Cromer to Harrington, 18 March 1903.
63. F.O. 1/43. Harrington to Lansdowne, 14 April 1903.
64. F.O. 1/43. Lansdowne's Minute to Balfour on Cromer to Harrington, 14 April 1903.
65. F.O. 1/50. Harrington to Cromer, 2 May 1904.
66. F.O. 1/50. Bunson's Memorandum, 8 March 1904.
67. France *Documents Diplomatique* Lagarde to Déclassé, 25 February 1904. *Francaises*, Second series, Tome IV.
68. F.O. 2/802. Hill to the Treasury, 2 March 1903.
69. F.O. 1/43. Lansdowne to Balfour, 14 April 1903.
70. F.O. 1/43. Cromer to Lansdowne, 26 December 1903.
71. F.O. 1/43. Excerpt from a copy of Address of the Directors of the New African Company, 31 December 1902.
72. The New African Company's Report to the Annual Meeting, 31 July 1903. *Ibid.*
73. F.O. 1/43. Harrington to Sanderson, 20 November 1903.
74. F.O. 1/43. Ochs to Sanderson, 18 August 1903.
75. F.O. 1/43. Sanderson's Minute, December 1903.
76. F.O. 1/43. Cranborne's Memorandum, 12 April 1903.
77. F.O. 1/42. Harrington to Sanderson, 10 December 1903.
78. F.O. 1/50. Bunson's Memorandum of 9 March 1904.
79. France D.D.F. Series 2, Tome IV, No. 348: NS Ethiopia 12. Lagarde to Déclassé, 25 February 1904,
80. France D.D.F. Series 2, Tome IV, No. 348: Lansdowne to Monson, 14 May 1904. F.O. 1/50. Cambon to Déclassé, 18 May, 1904,

81. France D.D.F. Series 2, Tome V, No. 40882. Cambon to Déclassé, 29 October 1904.
82. F.O. 403/346. Menelek to Harrington, 28 August 1904.
F.O. 1/50. Harrington to Lansdowne, 28 August 1904.
F.O. 1/50. Lansdowne to Harrington, 9 June 1904.
83. F.O. 1/50. Harrington to Lansdowne, 31 August, 1904.
F.O. 403/346. Cromer to Foreign Office. 12 November 1904. Cromer to Lansdowne 9 December 1904.
84. F.O. 1/50. Gorst to Cromer, 18 September 1904.
85. F.O. 1/50. Lansdowne to Harrington, 18 September 1904.
86. France D.D.F. Series 2, Tome V, No. 436. Cambon to Déclassé, 8 November 1904.
87. F.O. 1/56. Foreign Office Memorandum, 14 February 1905.
88. F.O. 1/53. Cromer to Lansdowne, 15 March 1905.
89. F.O. 800/160. Lansdowne to Bertie, 13 January 1905, *Lansdowne Papers*.
90. Italy, Rome. Archivio Storico dell 'ex Ministero dell' Africa Italian. ASMAI. Fascicolo 1, Martini to Tittoni, 27 September 1903.
91. ASMAI, Pos. 50. Fascicolo 1. Tittoni, 25 December 1903.
92. ASMAI. Pos. 50. Fascicolo 1. Tittoni to Ciccodicola, December 1903.
93. ASMAI. Pos. 50. Fascicolo 1. Tittoni to Ciccodicola, 24 November 1904.
94. F.O. 401/8. Peccori to Bon Giovani, 23 December 1903. *Ibid*. Cromer to Lansdowne, 28 December 1904.
95. F.O. 78/5430. Mc Gillivery's letter to the Governor of the National Bank of Egypt, 21 April 1905.
96. F.O. 401/8. Cromer to Lansdowne, 29 December 1904.
97. F.O. 401/8. Harrington to Cromer, 14 March 1905.
98. F.O. 401/8. *Ibid*. Terms of the Bank Monopoly. Harrington to Cromer, 14 March 1905.
99. 1. The National Bank was to establish in Ethiopia a banking company called the Bank of Abyssinia and its statutes were to be fixed by the National Bank of Egypt.
    2. The Company was to have a capital of £500,000 sterling and the shares were to be offered for public subscription in London, Paris and Rome, Berli, New York, Cairo and Addis Ababa.
    3. The Emperor bound himself not to allow any other bank to be established in his kingdom and the National Bank was to hold the monopoly for fifty years.
    4. The Bank was given eight exclusive previleges like the minting of the coinage and issue of Bank notes etc.
    5. After all expenses had been defrayed 10 per cent of the profit placed on reserve and a 7 per cent dividend paid to the shareholders, 20 per cent of the reminder was to go to Menelek.
100. He was the Head of the German Mission to Ethiopia. The British and the French feared that Germany would make troubles for them in Ethiopia.

101. F.O. 401/8. McGillivrey's letter to Palmer of the National Bank of Egypt. 21 April 1905.
102. F.O. 1 /53. Harrington's Telegram in Cromer to Lansdowne, 13 April 1905.
103. F.O. 1/53. Berie to Lansdowne 18, 15, 24 and 27 February and 3 March 1905.
104. France D.D.F. Series 2. Tome VI. No. 65. Déclassé to Cambon, 20 March 1905.
105. Gilmour, *Abyssinian Railway* (London; 1906) p. 49.
106. F.O. 401/8. Lansdowne to Harrington, 23 March 1905.
107. France D.D.F. Serie 2. Tome VI. No. 196. Cambon to Déclassé, 27 March 1905.
108. F.O. 401/8. Lansdowne to Harrington, 23 March 1905.
109. France D.D.F. Series 2. Tome VI, No. 324. Geofffrey to Déclassé, 19 April 1905.
110. France D.D.F. 2. Series 2, Tome VIII. No. 139. Cambon to Déclassé, 21 May 1905.
111. France D.D.F. Series 2. Tome IX. No. 398. F.O. 401/8. Lansdowne to Bertie, 22 November 1905. Cambon to Rouvier, March 1906.
112. D.D.F. Series 2. Tome VIII. No. 139. Rouvier to Geoffrey, 19 November 1905.
113. D.D.F. Series 2. Tome VIII. No. 164. Rouvier to Berrere, 28 November 1905. 13. N.S. Ethiopie Vol XI & XII. Jeffrey-Rouvier, 17 March 1905. No. 382.
114. F.O. 1/44, *Jenner's Memorandum on Northern Frontier of East Africa*, 1 November 1899, Hardinge's Memo of 20 October 1899.
115. F.O. 401/8. Cromer to Harrington, 1 December 1905.
116. F.O. 78/5430. Cromer to Gorst, 21 April 1905.
117. *Ibid.*
118. *Ibid.*
119. F.O. 371/1. Cromer to Gray, 19 March 1906.
120. F.O. 401/8. ASMAI. POZ. 41/1 Tittoni to Tornielli, 7 June 1905, Lansdowne to Bertie, 19 April, 1905. NS Ethiopie, XIV. Lagarde to the French Foreign Minister, 10 February 1906.
121. F.O. 371/1. Harrington to Grey, 15 March 1906.
122. F.O. 371/1. Gray's Minute, April 1906.
123. F.O. 371/1. Gorst's Minute, April 1906.
   F.O. 371. Harrington to Cromer, 23 March 1906.
   Gray to Harrington, 6 April 1906. F.O. 371115. The French Railway Company obtained permission from the French Government to raise these loans from the British group. The Ethiopian Railway Trust and Construction Company to the F.O. 1907. F.O. 371/1.
   K.V. Ram. "British Government, Finance Capitalists and the Jibuti Harar Railway". *The Journal of Imperial and Commonwealth History*. V. XI. 1981.

8

Sharing the Ethiopian Cake

The Earl of Cromer, influential British Consul-General in Cairo, pontificated, in July 1904, to the British Foreign Secretary: "We have to consider what is our main political interest in Abyssinia. In my own opinion that interest consists in maintaining native rule in that country. We do not want to annex any part of Abyssinia ourselves and we do not want part of it annexed by France or Italy."[1] British policy in Ethiopia since the 1840's surely bears out Britain's want of enthusiasm for territorial acquisitions in that country. This did not mean however that Britain was committed to the maintenance of Ethiopia's independence; far from it. In the 1890's, to secure her interests in the Nile Valley, Britain bartered away Ethiopian independence in the Anglo-Italian Protocols by reconfirming Italian protectorate over Ethiopia; moreover to protect British interests in the Sudan Cromer prevailed upon the Italians to confine their colonial aspirations to Ethiopia and not to extend into the Sudan.[2]

It was Menelek's brilliant victory over Italy at Adwa in 1896 which produced a healthy respect in Cromer for Ethiopia converting him into a protagonist for "native rule in Ethiopia." After the demise of the Italian Protectorate in Ethiopia British attitude towards Ethiopia changed drastically.

Given Ethiopia's strategic position in relation to the Nile and the British Protectorates in East and North-east Africa, Britain preferred the existence of a technologically backward "native rule in Ethiopia than a European one, so long as it accepted British predominance. However Britain did not have a free hand as she had to reckon with French and Italian aspirations in that country.

France had been interested in Ethiopia since the mid-nineteenth century and had built considerable influence with Emperor Menelek by backing him in his struggle against the Italian aggression. Further, to strengthen their local position the French Government headed by Hannotou had gifted 10,000 rifles and 2.5 million cartridges to Menelek.[3] Moreover having acquired control over the Jibuti-Harar railway through which she aimed to promote economic prosperity of the French Somali Protectorate, which depended on Ethiopian trade, France looked on eastern Ethiopia as her sphere of influence. She was determined not to allow either Britain or Italy to undermine her position in Ethiopia.[4]

Then there was Italy, the defeated colonial power, which was anxious to re-establish her position in Ethiopia. At the time she had two colonial possessions in North-east Africa, Eritrea to the north and Benadir to the South-east of Ethiopia. Eight hundred miles of Ethiopian territory stretched between the two colonial possessions. It was Italy's ambition to create an Italian empire in East Africa extending from Eritrea in the north to Benadir in the south including all the intervening Ethiopian territory. Italy wanted to keep the Eritrean and Benadir hinterlands free from British and French influences so that she might acquire those regions if Ethiopia was partitioned. Continuing to regard Ethiopia as her sphere of influence Italy was opposed to British or French predominance there.[5]

Given the raging Anglo-French rivalry which lasted until the conclusion of the *entente cordiale* in 1904, opposition to the French was a basic tenet of British policy in Ethiopia and its corollary was co-operation with Italy which was equally hostile to France. Notwithstanding their common enmity towards France, she could not count on Italian support automatically. There was a price to be paid for her co-operation which consisted in supporting Italy's colonial aspirations in the region at Ethiopia's cost. Britain was not averse to this though her methods and approaches to achieve varied according to the changing perceptions of Ethiopian Power and altering patterns of European alliances.

After the battle of Adwa in 1896, though Ethiopia had emerged as a strong power in the Nile Valley and many European States had rushed diplomatic mission to Ethiopia to cultivate Menelek's friendship, most European powers, including Britain, doubted Ethiopia surviving independently for long. To most Europeans Emperor Menelek personified Ethiopian independence. Moderate in victory, conciliatory in disposition, and a farsighted ruler, Menelek knew how to profit from European contacts without compromising Ethiopian independence. In 1903 Menelek was sixty years old and was not expected to live long. It was generally believed that the subdued warring groups which were quiescent before Menelek's power would erupt and clash after his death and an enfeebled Ethiopia would be partitioned by the interested European powers. That Ethiopia had survived independently throughout her existence, had only lately frustrated Italian efforts to impose a protectorate on her and that she might continue to be an independent state did not impress the interested European powers.

Moreover prospects for an independent Ethiopia did not seem encouraging given the dismal political pattern of Africa of the time. By 1903, the whole of Africa except Morocco, Tripoli and Liberia had been partitioned by European imperial powers: even these countries were by no means free from the tentacles of European imperialism. While Morocco was about to fall to France and Tripoli to Italy, Liberia was almost a colony of the United States. It was inconceivable that Ethiopia could remain independent for long, especially after Menelek's death. Britain, France and Italy, the three European powers interested in that country knew that none of them could establish exclusive dominance over Ethiopia. Each sought to secure its interests against its colonial rivals through a diplomatic settlement. The negotiations among these powers to share Ethiopia spanned three years culminating in the paper partition of that country in the Tripartite Agreement of 1906.

Italy was most anxious about Ethiopia's future. She wanted to develop Eritrea and Benadir economically by expanding their trade into the Ethiopian hinterlands; build railway connecting the two colonies swiftly and provide them adequate defence. Ambitious as her colonial programmes were inadequate were her resources, both economically and diplomatically. Italy was unhappy with the attitude of European powers, including her allies in the Triplice, towards her colonial ambitions: while Austria was totally indifferent, Germany was only mildly supportive. While Britain was lukewarm France was decidedly hostile. She needed British support to realize her colonial aspirations, but her usefulness to Britain had declined with the forced annulment of the Italian protectorate over Ethiopia. Though Britain had continued to recognize the Anglo-Italian protocols of 1891 and 1894 to prevent a political vacuum, she did not regard seriously the underlying Italian political pretention to Ethiopia.[6] Since 1897 Britain had been cultivating close friendship with Emperor Menelek to safeguard British interests in the Nile Valley, and each of her triumphs there strengthened Italy's fears regarding Britains territorial designs in Ethiopia.[7]

Italy was painfully aware that her recognition of Ethiopian independence had depleted the value of the Anglo-Italian protocols, and without their re-endorsement by Britain she lacked the basis for her colonial enterprise in Ethiopia. Concerned about the inadequacy of her resources to defend her Eritrean and Somali possessions from a possible French attack, and convinced that her interests in the Red Sea and the Mediterranean seas could only be effectively safeguarded with British support, Italy was anxious to reach an accord with Britain. This she wished to achieve before the value of her support to British policy in Ethiopia was reduced further by the successful conclusion of the on-going Anglo-French negotiations[8]

Italy had achieved considerable influence with Menelek. Distrusting Britain which had sided Italy in the Ethiopia-Italian war and suspecting France which had virtually seized the Ethiopian railway, Menelek was displaying friendship for Italy, the defeated weak European power. The Italian Consul Ciccodicola had much clout with Menelek and it could be of help to Britain in the ongoing Anglo-French confrontation in Ethiopia. In May 1903 when the British Government sought Italy's support to end French control on the Jibuti-Harar railway, the Italian Government proposed to Britain an Anglo-Italian understanding to promote mutual interests in Ethiopia.[9]

Italy suggested "open door" policy to end all economic monopolies in Ethiopia, which clearly meant opposition to the French monopoly over the Jibuti-Harar railway, the major Ethiopian outlet to the sea; she offered support to promote the contemplated British Berbera-Sudan railway a British undertaking to connect it with Eritrea. More important, Italy proposed to Britain a mutual guarantee of Italian territories in Eritrea and Somaliland and the British possessions in East and North-east Africa.[10]

These proposals were obviously inconvenient to London. As in European questions so in colonial matters, the British Government shunned formal alliances which would commit British military support to the defence of allied territories. Despite the inherent limitations informal co-operation with Italy had worked well in the past and the British preferred only a "frank exchange of views" with the Italian Government to pursue "concurrent policy in Ethiopia".[11] Deciding to avoid "inconvenient entanglements" with an "undesirable" partner,", Britain informed Italy that mutual guarantee of territories could not be considered until British Somaliland had been effectively occupied[12]; nor could Italian support be sought for the Berbera-Harar railway before deciding on its feasibility. The British offered co-operation to Italy in all other matters, especially in opposing French monopoly on the Jibuti-Harar railway.[13]

Britain's "dilatory reply" only enhanced Italy's suspicion regarding British aims in Ethiopia. Resolved to protect its interests Rome offered in September 1903, modified proposals to Britain.

Italy sought regulation of the British East Africa-Ethiopia frontiers in accordance with the Anglo-Italian Protocols of 1891, a definition of British and Italian interests in Ethiopia with reciprocal guarantee to secure them, and an understanding on Ethiopia's future *if the status quo was ever disturbed*, and support for Italian commercial enterprises in Ethiopia including the extension of the proposed British Khartoum to Kassala railway to Eritrea whenever it was taken up.[14] Italy sought a definite understanding with Britain to act together to safeguard their respective interests and to neutralize hostile influences.

It was clear that Italy wanted to check not only the French but also possible British expansion in Ethiopia. The Italian Foreign Minister, Admiral Morin, and the Head of the Colonial Department Signor Agnesa, believed that Britain had gained much in Ethiopia from Italian support and Italy must be compensated by her. Exploiting the British need for their support, the Italians threatened to act independently if a definite agreement was not reached soon.[15]

To Britain it was a undesirable alternative. Despite her antipathy to a formal agreement with Italy, she did not want to alienate her. The King of Italy with his Foreign Minister was scheduled to go on a state visit to Paris. Italy was aiming to improve her relations with France and reduce her dependence on the Triplice which was lukewarm to her colonial aspiration. After the fall of Crispi, Viscounti Venosta, the Italian Foreign Minister in the next government, had closed the dispute over Tunis by recognizing the French Protectorate there. The Franco-Italian trade war was ended in 1898. Trying to loosen Italy from Germany Déclassé had succeeded in making her Sign Notes of Exchange with France, in June 1902, which bound them to neutrality if either of the signatories was attacked by a third power. Italy's efforts to achieve a working entente with France, while in the Triple Alliance, had angered Von Bulow, the German Chancellor to reprimand Italy to make a choice between "matrimony and concubinage." Ignoring the German displeasure Italy was attempting to cultivate France. Obviously Italy's moves had the intended effect on the British. Sir Francis Bertie, the British Ambassador to Rome, urged London to do something quickly to prevent the Italians from coming into some arrangement with the French who "were a danger to Britain's Nile interests in Abyssinia."[16]

The Foreign Secretary agreed that such a diplomatic shift would hurt Britain given the raging Anglo-French rivalry in Ethiopia and some efforts must be made to keep Italy on Britain's side.[17] Britain also needed Italian co-operation to conclude successfully the ongoing military operations against the rebel Abdullahi in the Somaliland. Given the pressures, the British Government agreed to discuss with Rome an arrangement for the protection of Italian and British interests in Ethiopia.[18]

The British and Italian delegates confabulated in Rome in December 1903 to work out draft proposals for a treaty. Italy sought not only formal British endorsement of the Anglo-Italian Protocols of 1891 and 1894 but also safeguards for Italian and British territorial interests in Ethiopia, if that country disintegrated after Menelek's death.

This might mean not only joint Anglo-Italian intervention to place on the throne a candidate favourable to the two powers, but also measures to defend Anglo-Italian spheres. Clearly this was a suggestion for paper partition of Ethiopia in expectation of the hoped for disintegration of that State.

British delegates opposed provisions for an *ipso facto* political intervention in Ethiopia fearing possible military conflict with that country. They favoured only "consultation and joint action", as circumstances necessitated. They also rejected a mutual guarantee of respective territories as it virtually meant Britain guaranteeing Italian territories in North-east Africa against possible French attack. Hence Britain declined any commitment for armed intervention in Ethiopia.

Finally the Italian and the British delegates agreed that their Governments should guarantee the territorial and political *status quo* of Ethiopia, maintain her independence and abstain from intervention in her internal affairs. However if the Ethiopian State broke down, Britain and Italy were to partition her on the basis of the several agreement between them with special regard to British interests in the Nile Valley and Italian interests in Eritrea and Benadir, especially in providing communication between the two colonies. If partition proved impracticable the two powers were to oppose any other country from occupying and exercising power in the spheres reserved for the signatories. Clearly this provision was directed against France. They also undertook to further each other's commercial objectives in Ethiopia and maintain "full and frank exchange of views" on all matters of mutual interest. A special agreement was to be worked out later on the *modus operandi* for intervention.[19]

Though the British and the Italian delegates stated that the maintenance of the territorial and political integrity of Ethiopia was their common objective, the agreement itself was more concerned with the eventuality of its break down and partition than with measures for its prevention. Italy succeeded in enforcing her right to Ethiopia through the inclusion if the Anglo-Italian protocols in the draft proposals. The British delegates made sure to get a *quid pro quo*. As the existing agreements between Great Britain and Italy recognized Ethiopia as an Italian sphere of influence inspite of the remoteness for realization of the possibility, they did not want to reaffirm the protocols without remodelling of the frontier towards the Valley of Upper Nile, more favourable to British interests in the Sudan than had been able to obtain the negotiations with Menelek.[20]

The British delegates departed radically from their earlier position in recommending to their Government joint responsibility with Italy to oppose any power which might violate the Ethiopian *status quo*. As the British Ambassador in Rome observed this meant that Britain and Italy would "forcibly resist" French occupation[21] It was an onerous burden, yet it was recommended as a concession lest a disgruntled Italy drift into an alliance with France facilitating its drive to the headwaters of the Nile.[22] The British Ambassador to Italy advised his Government that to obtain contingent support and aid of Italy some sacrifice must be made to satisfy her dream for the future.[23]

The British delegates had still been operating within the old framework of Anglo-French rivalry. Perhaps they were ignorant of the 'secret' Anglo-French parleys in London for resolving their differences and improving relations. The British Government was close to concluding an *entente cordiale* with France and Lansdowne was reluctant to rush into a basically anti-French agreement with Italy. The British Government did not take up the Rome proposals for negotiating a treaty with Italy. Worried about the possibility of a secret Anglo-French understanding on Ethiopia behind Italy's back Tittoni, the Italian Foreign Minister, proposed immediate conclusion of an Anglo-Italian treaty on the basis of the Rome proposals, deprecating" Lansdowne's suggestion of taking the French into confidence.[24] Certainly the British Government was in no hurry to oblige Italy. Italian support for neutralizing France had been the British objective while approaching Rome in May 1903. Now the situation had changed because of drastic improvement in Anglo-French relations. Italian support was not a prime objective, while good relations with France was. Naturally it was only after the conclusion of the Anglo-French *entente* in April 1904 that the British acceded to the Italian request for negotiations to conclude a treaty—that too after ensuring that Italy voted on the Egyptian decrees as desired.[25]

When the much belated Anglo-Italian negotiations started in London to consider the Rome proposals of December 1903, the British Government was unenthusiastic about a bilateral agreement with Italy. The anti-French character of the Rome proposals made Lansdowne very uncomfortable. Having concluded a friendly alliance with France Britain could not, at the same time, enter into an agreement with Italy partly directed against France. Moreover the Rome proposals referred to a number of treaties which concerned not only Britain and Italy but also France. It was necessary to keep France informed of what was intended. He told Italy that it was not right to dispose of so large an African issue behind France's back and he did not propose to keep France ignorant of the Anglo-Italian negotiations. Obviously Lansdowne wished to bring France also into negotiations and to conclude a tripartite agreement on Ethiopia.[26]

From the British point of view the complicated Anglo-Italian negotiations which lasted until 1905 hinged on two questions: in the context of improving relations with France what was an alliance with Italy worth? What attitude should Britain maintain towards Ethiopia? While Italy's diplomatic co-operation in Ethiopia was desirable and her logistic support against Abdullahi in Somaliland would be helpful their value was not so great as to commit British military and diplomatic resources to defend and promote Italian territorial interests in North-east Africa. Even at the height of Anglo-French rivalry, when the British Government was better disposed to the Triplice, it did not rate highly the value of Italian support to British policy. Lord Salisbury confided to Baring: "A good deal of exaggerated language is used in diplomatic conversation and post-prandial oratory as to the value of Italian alliance to England. It is valuable to us because it is essential to Germany and the friendship of Germany is very important to us because she keeps Russia and France in order. In itself the Italian alliance is not very advantageous and has several drawbacks... I do not see the friendship of Italy so high as some other objects of political desire. It is desirable but it is not worth a great price even in African square miles".[27]

Now that Britain had signed *entente cordiale with* France and was less sensitive to German's feelings the value of an Italian alliance to British policy had depleted further. Yet in Britain's imperial strategy Italy could play a useful role. Italy's military weakness made her a harmless neighbour in the eastern Nile Valley. Despite the recently concluded Anglo-French *entente* it would be useful to keep Italy on Britain's side than to let her drift into an alliance with France.[28] To achieve this Britain would support her in North-east Africa so long as it did not call far heavy demand on Britain's military and diplomatic resources. Now that the Rome proposals for an Anglo-Italian accord were demanding both, the British Government was unenthusiastic. Moreover weighty British military opinion considered Italy a liability. Her resources were too inadequate to support her colonial aspirations, which in British view, were "wild" and "impractical".[29] The British War Office feared that any treaty with Italy for reciprocal guarantee of territories in East Africa would only saddle Britain with heavy responsibilities.[30]

Britain's attitude towards Ethiopia also differed from that of Italy. Italy sought a paper partition of Ethiopia, notwithstanding the language used to cover it up and remoteness of the possibility[31]. Was it necessary to acquiesce in the Italian wish and effect partition? In 1903 Britain enjoyed preponderant influence with Menelek, both France and Italy having been discredited in Ethiopia for different reasons. Britain had settled the frontiers of the Sudan and the British Somaliland with Ethiopia while negotiations were proceeding for an agreement on the British East African frontier. Given the coterminous frontiers of Ethiopia with the adjacent British possessions Britain preferred to see that country remain independent. She was only particular that Ethiopia should not fall under hostile European influences lest British position in the Nile Valley be threatened. Even from a practical point Britain preferred the existence of an indigenous Government in Ethiopia which would keep its agreements with her rather than acquiring Ethiopian territory. Nor did Britain want Ethiopia annexed by France or Italy. The British Minister to Ethiopia had argued that: surrounded by British or semi-British territories it is better in British interest that the present state of affairs should continue as long as it means independence to Ethiopia rather than another power should dominate that country.[32]

This view was shared by Lord Cromer, the British Consul-General in Cairo. Favouring a policy of maintaining Ethiopian independence not only did he criticize Italy for proposing the partition but also regretted the British Government was considering it. He complained that contrary to the declared interest in maintaining Ethiopian independence, the Rome proposal emphasized what was to happen in the event of disintegration, thus indicating that partition was not "merely possible but highly probable." Criticizing the basic assumption that Menelek's death would inevitably lead to the break up of the Ethiopian Empire he preferred to assume that, inspite of a probable civil war for succession, Ethiopia would survive independently. Cromer recommended that the common object of British and Italian diplomacy should be to prevent a division of Ethiopia and that Britain, France and Italy should sign a self-denying ordinance against acquiring Ethiopian territory, regarding the disintegration as evil and pledging to prevent it.[33]

While Lansdowne agreed that it was a British interest to keep Ethiopia independent, as a pragmatist he took a less idealistic view of Ethiopian independence than Cromer. Britain did not have a clean slate to start with. Having recognized the validity of the Anglo-Italian protocols, Britain could not deny the existence of an Italian sphere of influence in Ethiopia without zeopardising Anglo-Italian relations. Italy had been pressing for a redefinition of the spheres of interest. A rejection might induce Italy to enter into a secret agreement with France and deny Britain the needed support to end absolute French control over the Jibuti railway. Hence the British agreed to a definition of British and Italian sphere in Ethiopia, rationalizing that an agreement foreseeing the dissolution and partition of that country need not prevent Britain from "keeping Abyssinia on its legs."[34] However if Ethiopia fragmented and came up for partition she should fare as well as other partitioning powers, and Lansdowne proceeded to safeguard British interests through an agreement with Italy and France; one major obstacle to achieving this with Italy was the anti-French character of the Rome proposals. If this was divested agreement could be reached soon.[35] Rome was informed.

Ever since the commencement of the Anglo-French negotiations to harmonize their relations Italy had been concerned about its implications for herself. Prinetti, the Italian Ambassador to Paris, had been advising Rome that France and Britain might conclude a secret treaty injuring Italian interests there and the best way to check this was for Italy to take up the issue of "her rights and interests" for discussion with France soon. The Italian Foreign Minister Tittoni, however, felt sure that continuation of Anglo-Italian negotiations for a treaty would prevent France and Britain from modifying the *status-quo in Ethiopia without Italian consent*. As the Anglo-French *entente* had not covered Ethiopia, Italy hastened to reach an agreement with Britain before France set in. She offered revised proposals to Britain for a treaty.[36]

The British and the Italian Governments soon resumed negotiations for an accord on Ethiopia. Once a decision was made to define British and Italian spheres, whether Ethiopia would eventually be partitioned or not, Britain tried to tighten its control over the entire Nile system in western Ethiopia, while Italy endeavoured to retain all the territory conceded to her in the Anglo-Italian Protocols. Britain refused to re-endorse the Italian claim unless Italy recognized "absolute control over the Nile and all its affluents" as a paramount British interest. While conceding this, Italy vehemently opposed Britain's claims to regulate the waters of not only the Nile River but also all its affluents.[37] Italy feared that by that doctrine Britain might gradually extend her control over the hinterlands of the Blue Nile, the Taccaze, the Solit and the Atbara rivers which spanned the whole of western Ethiopia, and take away much of "the territory conceded to her. It would also frustrate the Italian hopes for developing close commercial relations between Eritrea and western Ethiopia. Opposing the British demand Italy claimed interest in the Nile tributaries which flowed through Eritrea. Infuriated Britain warned Italy not to insist on such "infelicitous" proposals, under the threat of denying her the much coveted corridor between Eritrea and Benadir through Ethiopia.[38] Italy had won British diplomatic support for this concession at the Rome Conference of 1903 against the opposition of several British officials, who feared that the Italian strategy was to separate Anglo-Egyptian Sudan from western Ethiopia with a block of Italian territory.[39] She did not want to zeopardise this important interest.

Frightened by the British threat, Italy backed down offering to recognize Britain's rights to the Nile waters and all its affluents, "without prejudice to local Eritrean interests."[40] The British accepted the Italian reservations. An Anglo-Italian agreement was reached on 18 January 1905. Britain and Italy undertook not to seek concessions in Ethiopia injurious to each other and to co-operate for mutual benefit. They agreed to maintain the political and territorial *status quo* of Ethiopia.

However in the event of disintegration they agreed to co-operate to achieve a territorial re-arrangement to safeguard the Anglo-Egyptian interests in the Nile Valley and western Ethiopia, and the Italian interests in Ethiopia relating to Eritrea and Benadir colonies, especially an uninterrupted territorial link between them.[41] The Italians had succeeded in making Britain to enter into an agreement with them. But it could not be signed immediately as Britain insisted to defer it until France's adherence had been secured.

Long before the commencement of the Anglo-Italian negotiations in London in April 1904, the British Government had concluded that any agreement on Ethiopia which did not include France would only be a partial solution to Britain's Ethiopian problem. A primary interest of Britain was to secure a political solution to the French Jibuti-Harar railway question and this anticipated direct negotiations with France. However the British preferred to include Italy also in any negotiations with the French as that country had been interested in the Ethiopian railway and had supported Britain in opposing French monopoly over it. From the British point of view a tripartite agreement was essential to harmonize conflicting French and Italian interests in Ethiopia.

France had started in Ethiopia hoping to convert her into a "sort of colony" and benefiting without seeking formal control. The French policy of supporting Ethiopia against Italy had paid her handsomely. France was the most favoured European power in Ethiopia by 1897 with predominant influence with Menelek. The vanquished Italy and her ally Britain had become a suspect. However the anti-climax followed soon. France's unconcealed efforts to turn the private French Jibuti-Harar railway into a political instrument to dominate Ethiopia had destroyed her credibility in Emperor Menelek's eye. Britain had seized the opportunity to ruin French influence in Ethiopia and augment her own by strengthening Menelek's fears regarding France's territorial ambitions in Ethiopia. French influence in Ethiopia had reached the nadir.

Determined to force the French Government to withdraw its official hold on the Jibuti Railway, Menelek had penalized the Railway Company by withdrawing the concession to leavy 10 per cent duty on the rail-borne goods and refusing the permission to extend the railway to Ethiopian capital Addis Ababa. France's efforts to pacify Menelek and end his opposition to the Jibuti railway had failed. The railway had come to suffer and France saw Britain's anti-French policy at the root of her difficulties in Ethiopia, ignoring the fact that it was her move to establish official control over the private French Jibuti railway that was the heart of the problem. She also feared that a successful conclusion of the Anglo-Italian negotiations might intensify Britain's anti-French policy and she might end up dominating Ethiopia.[42] The continuing financial difficulties of the Jibuti-Harar railway, the failure of the French Minister to Ethiopia to persuade Menelek to end his opposition to the railway and the need to secure French interests in Ethiopia through an accord with Britain induced Déclassé, the Foreign Minister, to approach the British Government for a settlement.[43]

Paul Cambon, the French Ambassador to Britain broached the matter with the British Government in May 1904. He assured Lansdowne that since the French Government had recognized British occupation of Egypt in the Anglo-French *entente* she could have no designs to harm Britain, and there should be no difficulty in reaching an Anglo-French accord on Ethiopia. While France would make concessions to British interests in western Ethiopia she would not relinquish her control on the Jibuti railway, a vital French interests. France's "absolute control" over the Jibuti railway was just the thing that Britain had been opposing and she would not acquiesce in the French demand. Moreover Britain wanted French assurance for an "unrestricted use of the line as far as the sea," before an agreement could be reached.[44]

While France lacked the means to exert exclusive influence on Ethiopia she was opposed to its domination by Britain or Italy. Aiming at a balanced solution, in June 1904, the French Government made a four point proposal to the British for an agreement on Ethiopia. These were: maintenance of the *status quo* in Ethiopia; provision for joint action to protect Anglo-

French interests there if law and order collapsed after Menelek's death; definition of spheres of influence, and economic questions, specially the Jibuti railway.[45] Sceptical of Ethiopian independence France, like Italy, was sure that Ethiopia would be partitioned after Menelek's death. Inspite of her professed concern to maintain Ethiopian independence France was keen on dividing that country into spheres of influence and securing the consent of her colonial rivals to her claims to the whole of eastern Ethiopia.

Refusing to provide Italy the claimed territorial corridor through eastern Ethiopia on the pretext that it would cut through French sphere, France sought British recognition to the Jibuti-Harar railway as an exclusive French interest.[46] To win British support France offered to relinquish her rights to build the third section of the railway from Addis Ababa to the Nile in western Ethiopia which Britain considered her sphere of influence. She proposed equal treatment to British goods and passengers on the Jibuti railway and to make Jibuti a free port.[47] Suggesting that respective spheres of influence in Ethiopia be named as "economic zones" to avoid provoking Menelek, France warned Britain that her reactions to the French proposals would reveal the usefulness of the recently concluded *entente cordiale*.[48]

Though these French proposals were significant concessions to British interests in Ethiopia, they were inadequate to meet Britain's formal commitments to Italy to provide a territorial link between Eritrea and Benadir through Ethiopia, and informal commitment to Emperor Menelek to prevent French domination of the railway. In the meantime Britain was under heavy pressure from Menelek to fulfill her promises. The circulating rumours that the Tripartite powers intended to partition Ethiopia had created an explosive situation in Addis Ababa.[49]

Given the determined efforts of France to turn the Jibuti railway into a political instrument, and the known colonial aspirations of Italy, Menelek was becoming highly suspicious of the proceedings of those powers. He was furious.

Notwithstanding Britain's assurances regarding Ethiopian

independence and her opposition to French domination Menelek was unsure of her real intentions. He was aware of the Anglo-Italian protocols and Britain's failure to explain how foreign spheres of influence could exist in an independent country made him only doubt Britain's *bonafides*.[50] Menelek was so nervous that the British Minister to Ethiopia had requested his Government to administer him a "strong sedative" in the form of an assurance that the proposed tripartite treaty would guarantee Ethiopian independence.[51] But the prescription had failed.[52] In the circumstances Britain's acceptance of the Jibuti railway as an exclusive French interest would not only make it look like a betrayal to Menelek but also destroy British influence in Ethiopia.

Determined to end French hold over the railway Menelek favoured a joint Anglo-French or international control over the Jibuti railway. Favouring Italian participation in the railway, Menelek asked the tripartite powers to guarantee Ethiopia's independence and territorial integrity. Supporting Menelek the British Minister in Addis Ababa warned his Government against an Anglo-French accord which left the railway in the French hands disregarding the Emperor's wishes.[53] Notwithstanding the obvious advantages of an Anglo-French accord it would still be desirable to maintain British preponderance in Ethiopia. Cromer too advised his Government to listen to Menelek for internal reasons and internationalize the railway. He reiterated his opposition to creation of spheres of influence as it would only hasten the partition of Ethiopia. If France could not be persuaded then "economic zones" might be recognized for purposes of railway construction only without political or territorial rights.[54]

While appreciating the moral soundness of Cromer's views and Harrington's insistence on British primacy in Ethiopia, Lansdowne was more concerned for the strengthening of the *entent cordiale* with France convinced that unless France was conceded "real control" over the Jibuti railway and right to the Hawash Valley in eastern Ethiopia no agreement on Ethiopia could be reached, Lansdowne did not mind displeasing Menelek.[55] While willing to concede Italian and

French interests in Ethiopia he was opposed either to a precise definition or a distinct recognition of territorial spheres in that country. Arguing that a contingency for partition would arise only if Ethiopia disintegrated and that might not happen he pressed France not to insist on a definition of respective spheres of interests.[56]

Disagreeing that a definition of spheres of influence would necessarily hasten the break up of Ethiopia, France considered it a folly to wait to define what was obvious until the country disintegrated. Having "irrevocably committed' himself in French Chambers to uphold French interests and honour in Ethiopia Déclassé claimed for France all territories which did not fall within the watershed of the Nile including Addis Ababa, Ethiopia's capital.[57]

While dismissing the French claim as "far-fetched and preposterous...", Britain realized the futility of opposing the French demand for a definition of spheres of interests.[58] Britain suggested instead that if it became impossible to maintain Ethiopian independence, then the signatories might concert measures to protect French interests in the hinterland of Jibuti, British interests in the Nile and its tributaries and the Italian interests in securing a territorial corridor through Ethiopia between her Eritrean and Benadir possessions.[59] Such a territorial link for Italy, could be provided outside the French sphere.[60]

Though Britain pressed for internationalization or Ethiopianizaion of the Jibuti railway in preference to a French controlled one, eventually she gave into the French demand offering to recognize the railway as French interest, were it given an "international appearance" and goods and subjects of all nations were given equal treatment on it.[61] While welcoming the relinquishment of the French right to build the railway from Addis Ababa to the Nile, Britain sought a recognition of her right to build a railway from the British Somaliland tó the Sudan through Ethiopia.[62] Obviously this was seen as an insurance against any future French threats to British interests. Convinced that Britain would not really build a railway from the Sudan connecting Ethiopia and there would in reality never be competition from that quarter to the Jibuti railway, France conceded to the British demand.[63]

Now that Britain was willing to admit a French sphere of interest in eastern Ethiopia and allow the substance of control over the railway, the French Government agreed to sign a treaty with Britain. Through the Anglo-French accord Britain had succeeded in warding off the French threat to the security of the eastern Nile Valley through Ethiopia and reinforcing her rights to the Nile basin. However Britain deferred signing the negotiated accord with France for the same reasons she had put off the formalization of the Anglo-Italian accord earlier. Lansdowne suggested that Italy should now be brought in as "it would be impossible to deal with the Abyssinian questions except with the full knowledge of the Italian Government."[64]

Given the nature of European interests in Ethiopia a tripartite agreement between Britain, France and Italy was indispensable to harmonize their interests. A dual agreement between any two would only be a partial solution to the difficulty. But Italy was not for bringing in France and insisted on signing a bilateral arrangement with Britain. However she gave in given Britain's refusal to sign an arrangement excluding France.[65]

By the time the tripartite negotiations began in London in April 1905 there were no new issues to be resolved relating to Ethiopia. In the recently concluded bilateral negotiations Anglo-French and Anglo-Italian interests needed to be adjusted and all these had to be included in an agreement. The tripartite discussions between 1905 and 1906 were thus primarily concerned with harmonizing French and Italian interests in Ethiopia. Since British interests were not in dispute, these having been secured in the Anglo-Italian and the Anglo-French negotiations, Britain was in an advantageous situation. Commanding the trust of both France and Italy, she found herself placed more in the position of a mediator than a negotiator.

London was the venue of tripartite negotiations and Lord Lansdowne, the British Foreign Secretary, was its moving spirit. With innate tact to gracefully wade through sticky diplomatic waters Lansdowne was uniquely fitted to handle the volatile

Italian and the prestige conscious French colleagues. The sauve and sensible Paul Cambon, the French Ambassador to London, brought into the tripartite negotiations not only wisdom and sincerity but also the stability and continuity which the frequently changing French Foreign Ministers could not provide after Délcasse's exit. The persistent and some what irritable Tommaso Tittoni, who alternated as Italy's Foreign Minister and Ambassador to London during the time the tripartite negotiations spanned, contributed both to its initial delay and ultimate success. Given the Franco-Italian hostility and the want of weighty and influential Italian representation in Paris, the French Embassy in Rome occupied a very important and sensitive position. Camille Barrere, the French Ambassador to Italy, with his vision, tact and foresight had been highly successful in bringing about Franco-Italian *detente.* A mentor and friend of Déclassé, his influence at Quai d'Arsay outlasted the latter's fall. Respected in Rome and trusted in Paris Barrere ensured that the *detente* was never derailed by passing and flying tempers of the two Latin adversaries trying friendship. Mellowing the raging outbursts of Rome and softening the hardened heart of Paris Barrere helped the tripartite negotiations succeed.

Though, at first, it appeared that a tripartite agreement could easily be arrived by blending the Anglo-Italian and the Anglo-French agreements with some amendments to meet French and Italian interests in Ethiopia it did not turn out to be that simple. Franco-Italian differences could not be easily reconciled. Consequently British diplomacy during 1905 and 1906 was directed to promoting a Franco-Italian rapprochement and achieving the Tripartite Treaty.

The issues which concerned the three powers in Ethiopia had been discussed and solutions arrived in the just concluded Anglo-Italian and Anglo-French discussions. These were, as discussed earlier, their economic and political interests in Ethiopia and what was to happen when the expected disintegration of that country occurred. Britain had tried in those negotiations to obtain a general agreement on Ethiopia avoiding a definition of territorial spheres of the powers. Such a territorial description would have looked to Menelek a crude partition of his empire and provoked his bitter opposition.

Though Britain held on to the same position in the tripartite negotiations, she was outnumbered by both Italy and France who were insisting on a definition of their spheres of influence. Britain preferred that she, France and Italy should declare the maintenance of Ethiopian independence as their common interests and abstain from interference in Ethiopian affairs. However if Ethiopia "broke up" in the future the three powers might concert measures to secure for Italy a territorial corridor through Ethiopia between her Benadir and Eritrean possessions, to France territory "in the rear of her actual possessions east of the Nile watershed" in the Hawash Valley and to Britain in the watershed of the Nile and its affluents. Only if it became inevitable were they to proceed "with the actual settlement of their frontier in Ethiopia."[66]

Making proposals for a treaty Britain suggested to France and Italy to freely exchange their views to arrive at an agreement soon.[67] The British also communicated draft of the recently concluded Anglo-Italian agreement for France's consideration.

Concluding that the Anglo-Italian Treaty draft violated the Anglo-French Treaty of 1884 on Harar and ignored French interests in eastern Ethiopia, the French Government made counter proposals in March 1905 for a tripartite treaty.[68] Ignoring the recently concluded bilateral arrangements with Britain, France revived her claims to the whole of eastern Ethiopia including the capital Addis Ababa. Opposing the territorial corridor for Italy between Benadir and Eritrea through eastern Ethiopia, France also rejected Italian claims to build railways in the adjoining Ethiopian territories. Determined to keep the Jibuti railway as an exclusive French interest, she warned Britain and Italy that no agreement could be reached unless this demand was conceded.[69]

These French demands were most infelicitous and unacceptable to Britain. Having conceded to Italy a territorial link between her Benadir and Eritrean possessions in the recently concluded Anglo-Italian agreements, Britain could not back out of her commitments under French pressure. Nor could shė recognize the Jibuti railway as an exclusive French interest given the Italian and Ethiopian opposition to such a course, without sacrificing her influence with both. At the same time she did not want to weaken the recently concluded Anglo-French *entente* by opposing France preferring a solution which kept her influence intact with all three powers Britain attempted to moderate the French demands by supporting the Italian objections.

Certainly the French claims clashed with Italy's aspirations in Ethiopia. Italy wished to limit French and British spheres of influence to small zones in eastern and western Ethiopia respectively, so that much of middle Ethiopia might fall to her in any future partition. An uninterrupted territorial link between Eritrea and Benadir colonies through Ethiopia, seemed indispensable to Italy to achieve her colonial objectives. However the French railway and territorial claims cut directly across the corridor which Italy so desperately wanted. Trying to overcome the French opposition, Italy suggested a *quid pro quo,* offering Italian support to French railway policy in Ethiopia in return for their support to the Italian territorial claims. France was unenthusiastic.

The French-Italian rivalry was so deep that inspite of their recent efforts to improve relations, their mutual suspicions and colonial rivalries persisted. Italy's membership in the Triplice which was directed against France was obviously a deterrent to close relations. Moreover France had no sympathy for Italy's colonial aims, and was embittered at Italy for her role in strengthening Menelek's opposition to the French railway. France despised Italy's duplicity of professing friendship in Rome and Paris and opposing French interests in Ethiopia whenever she could. She was in no mood to make concessions to Italy in Ethiopia. Equally embittered was Italy about France's continued opposition to Italian aspirations in Africa, especially French contribution to the demise of her protectorate in Ethiopia.

Geography also added to the Franco-Italian problem. Benadir protectorate was to the south-east of Ethiopia while

Eritrea was to its north and north-east. A direct territorial link between those possessions could only be provided through eastern Ethiopia which interposed. But France claimed eastern Ethiopia, which was contiguous to the French Somaliland and through which her Jibuti-Harar railway passed, as her exclusive sphere[70]. Déclassé held that an Italian territorial corridor through the region "would cut through French territory, French railway" and "undermine French rights". Such could never be permitted.[70a]

Enraged by the French opposition Italy retaliated. Opposing the extension of the French controlled railway to Addis Ababa, Italy supported Menelek's proposal to build the line himself.[71] She insisted on the deletion of the French Railway Convention of 1902 from the proposed tripartite agreement as it implied territorial sovereignty of France on the territory through which the railway passed. The railway convention was an understanding between the French railway company and the French Government. Without reference to the Government or the Emperor of Ethiopia, arrogating to itself the right of succession to the properties of the railway company including the railway track, (fifty years after the signing of the convention) France posed a threat to the sovereignty and independence of Ethiopia.[72] Italy suggested the suppression of all references to the French railway in the proposed treaty which might be considered separately as a purely economic issue.[73] Opposing the French pretensions to a sphere of influence up to Addis Ababa and cricizing it for failing to consider Italian interests adequately, Italy rejected the French proposals.

The Jibuti railway and the Hawash Valley in Ethiopia were France's important interests and the Italian opposition to them only hardened French attitude towards Italy. Instead of harmonizing relations with her, the French asked the British to sign at once the recently negotiated Anglo-French accord, leaving it open for Italy's later adhesion.[74] Obviously the French move provoked strong Italian protest. Rome warned that such a step would be seen as a deliberate attempt to exclude Italy, cause violent public reaction and jeopardies Franco-Italian relations.[75] Though the Frenchequipped that they had only been inspired by a spirit of "*perfaite loyalte et un espirit enetente reciproche*" they did not try to assuage Italy.[76]

Endeavouring to save the *detente* Barrere spoke highly of the commitment of Tittoni, the Italian Foreign Minister, to the successful conclusion of the tripartite negotiation on which he had placed "un-grand price." Furthermore describing to Déclassé the Italian Foreign Minister's "sentiment de penible surprise" at the unhappy turn of events Barrere asked him to reconsider the matter.[77] In the mean-time Italy requested Britain to assist her to overcome the French opposition and to moderate French demands.[78]

The Italian demand came handy to the British in checking the French pretensions supporting the Italian objection to the inclusion of the French railway convention in the proposed agreement, the British favoured Menelek's building and controlling the Harar-Addis Ababa railway. Certainly that would save the Ethiopian capital from the French stranglehold. In view of Ethiopia's determined opposition to an all French railway the British advised France to "meet King Menelek's objections" in some way. Meeting with strong French opposition they proposed that the Jibuti-Addis Ababa railway be given at least an international appearance with a Board of Management made up of British, Italian and French members.[79]

Giving up her long and bitter opposition to the proposal France concurred finally, warning Britain not to press for real internationalization as Germany would claim a share in it and create difficulties. To protect the Jibuti-Harar railway from any future unfair competition by the proposed British railway from the British Somali Protectorate, France sought and obtained British assurance not to build a competing railway, while relinquishing her right to build the railway from Addis Ababa to the Nile.[80] Britain withdrew her objection to the extension of the Jibuti railway to Addis Ababa[81]. Appeasing France Britain ignored the Ethiopian and Italian objections to an all French railway.

Though greatly disappointed by this reversal of British policy Italy knew that very little could be done against Anglo-French combination. Nevertheless she tried to prevent the

Jibuti-Harar railway from becoming a French Government enterprise by demanding France's written undertaking against such happening, besides claiming exclusive rights for herself to build railways between Benadir and Eritrea.[82]

The British were unenthusiastic about Italian objectives in Ethiopia and their officialdom was more in sympathy with France, their traditional enemy, than with Italy, their traditional friend. Considering the Italians a troublesome people who "can't run straight" and disregarding their objections, Cromer suggested leaving the entire Hawash Valley, in eastern Ethiopia to France. The Italians might object, but it was their business."[83] Persuaded that the French objections to the Italian territorial demands were reasonable, Sir George Clerk of the Committee of the Imperial Defence opined that Italy should withdraw her territorial pretensions of Ethiopia.[84]

Though Lansdowne did not disagree with these views and the improved Anglo-French relations made Italian support to British policy in Ethiopia more dispensable than ever, he considered the matter differently. Having committed to Italy too deeply Britain could not ignore Italian views and interests. If an agreement was not concluded with Italy she might claim the whole of Ethiopia by the Anglo-Italian protocols and "give more trouble than she would under the proposed agreement"[85] Supporting the Italian objections Lansdowne demanded from the French Government a commitment not to convert the private railway company into an official French enterprises and maintain its commercial character. As Italy had earlier been conceded the territorial corridor in the draft Anglo-Italian agreements, and now that could not be denied, the British requested the French to accommodate the Italians.[86]

France had no choice but to work with Italy if an agreement was desired. In the renewed negotiations at Rome though Barrere and Tittoni arrived at a formula to harmonize Franco-Italian interests, Déclassé rejected it under the pressure of the French Colonists who wanted exclusive French influence over the Jibuti railway and the Hawash Valley maintained.[87]

There followed an impasse, neither France nor Italy initiating further negotiations. Obviously the Moroccon heat had paralized them. They were scared of signing a large African agreement behind Germany's back lest German wrath be directed against them more scartchingly. In the light of the Moroccon crisis such fears could be understood though its magnitude was unrealistically out of proportions. Nevertheless as the German fear cast its shadow on the tripartite negotiations it helps to understand it.

Germany had very little interest in Ethiopia except for very infrequent diplomatic forays. Replying to Emperor Yohannes's request the German Emperor had offered mediation in 1882 to settle Ethiopia-Egypt frontier question though nothing materialized. Again in 1887 Bismarck had pressed Britain to undertake a diplomatic mission to help Italy out of her difficulties with Ethiopia. Having ignored Emperor Menelek's appeals against the Italian pretensions to a protectorate over Ethiopia and having had neither economic nor political interests in that country, when the German Emperor suddenly decided to send a commercial mission to Ethiopia in November 1904, the tripartite powers began to suspect trouble. A German commercial mission, headed by Dr. Rossen, head of the Eastern wing of the German Foreign Office, visited Ethiopia in 1905 and concluded a treaty of friendship and commerce with Emperor Menelek which required him to follow a policy of "Porta Aperta". Expressing his misgivings to the British Government the British Military Attachee from Berlin wrote: Whether it (the German Mission) is intended to introduce few more rifles and guns into the country I do not know. It may be flying at a higher game in the direction of establishing a colony or leasing some land or even trying a hand at weltpolitik with the Emperor Menelek. In any case from what I have the honour to know of that dusky monarch, I do not expect the results will be bounteous.[88]

As the British stand in the Moroccon crisis had upset the Germans, the British feared that they may capitalize on Britain's failure to meet Menelek's wishes on the railway to augment German influence in Ethiopia.[89] There were rumours that Germany might lend money to Emperor Menelek to build his own railway from Harar to Addis Ababa.[90]

Such a step would be prejudicial to both British and French interests. Though the British resented German intrigue and commercial competition in Ethiopia, they tried to keep her in good humour by offering her a Directorship on the newly created British controlled Bank of Abyssinia. Lascelles, the British Ambassador in Berlin, assured the German Emperor that "this was a proof of British willingness to meet the wishes of the German Government."[91] Nevertheless fearing complications from Germany's latest interest in Ethiopia, the British urged the French to expedite the negotiations.

More than any, the French were absolutely scared of Germany. The French diplomatic sources from Cairo and Addis Ababa had warned Paris that Germany was planning to claim a share in the Jibuti-Harar railway with a view to challenge France.[92] The Rosen Mission in Addis Ababa was reportedly encouraging Emperor Menelek to stiffen his opposition to France and was certainly behind his ultimatum to Britain, France and Italy.[93]

The French Foreign Ministry feared that Germany was watching for the first opportunity to start a conflict with France in Ethiopia and she would attempt to profit from the situation. They were perturbed by the news that the German Emperor had spoken of establishing a legation in Ethiopia for promoting "intimate contacts" with that country and that he might even visit Addis Ababa.[94] So anxious was France to prevent another Moroccon incident, that the Foreign Affairs Committee of the French Chamber of Deputies passed a resolution abstaining France from concluding an agreement with Britain and Italy to avoid giving a pretext for "German intervention in Ethiopian affairs."[95] Most concerned not to provoke German wrath Rouvier, the French Prime Minister and Foreign Minister, suspended the tripartite negotiations.[96]

No less anxious was Italy about German reactions, though she was a member of the Triplice. It was reported in diplomatic circles that the Italian Foreign Minister Tittoni would be frightened by a German frown while his successor San Guiliano kept postponing the tripartite talks for the same reason.[97] Already suffering German wrath for their neutral stand in the

Moroccon crisis, the Italians had become preoccupied "with German susceptibilities".[98] They did not want to sign an international agreement without German blessings.[99] Italy wished to put off the negotiations until the Moroccon heat had cooled of.[100] Passing this confidential information from the Italian Ambassador, Rouvier told the French Ambassadors in Rome and London that he agreed with the Italians, "de ne pas chercher au precipiter la conclusion de 1' arrangement projete"[101] Because of the German fear France and Italy suspended the negotiations from July to November 1905 notwithstanding Britain's ploddings.

When the tripartite talks resumed in November 1905 France and Italy were still in disagreement about their respective claims in eastern Ethiopia. Italy wanted an exclusive zone in Ethiopia over which she would some day exercise sovereignty and as Barrere reported she would "accept nothing less."[102] France refused to admit such pretensions.[103] Unhappy about the deadlock Britain tried to expedite the agreement by offering to provide the much disputed territorial corridor between Italy's Eritrean and Benadir possessions in western Ethiopia outside the zone which might fall to France. While this was acceptable to France, Italy wanted a clear description of the corridor to be specified in notes of exchange. Moreover the French refused to admit the Italian demands until Italy ended its opposition to the French policy in Ethiopia. This did not help matters. Having supported the French on the Moroccon issue at the cost of German wrath, Italy expected the end of French opposition to her colonial aims in Ethiopia.[104] Irritated by the French opposition Italy considered withdrawing from the tripartite talks altogether and urged Britain to sign at once the already concluded draft Anglo-Italian treaty on Ethiopia. The British disagreed fearing that such a step would not only be unfriendly to France but also might block a lasting solution to the Ethiopian problem.[105]

Whatever her opposition to Italy, France desperately wanted an agreement on Ethiopia. The French railway company was in grave financial difficulty and the French Chambers had refused to finance it unless it was shown that

French interest in the railway had been adequately protected. This could not be done unless Menelek permitted the extension of the railway to Addis Ababa and let the French railway company to collect the 10 per cent transit duty on the rail borne goods. Even the French Prime Minister's personal appeal to Menelek to do this by endeavouring to convince him that without any sacrifice on his part and without any threat to Ethiopian independence the French Jibuti railway would increase the economic importance of his country and that he had more to fear from the territorial imperialism of Britain and Italy than France had no success. Menelek refused to discuss the railway question with the French until the completion of tripartite negotiations with Britain and Italy.[106] In the circumstances the need to reach an agreement with the two powers compelled France to comply with the British position.[107]

But instead of expediting the tripartite negotiations by conceding the Italian demands, the French Government asked Britain to sign at once the draft Anglo-French treaty on Ethiopia. The British refused to sign for the same reasons they had declined a similar Italian request.[108] The French complained that the British Government was showing undue consideration to the susceptibilities of the Rome cabinet."[109]

Since the British would not sign separate treaties with either, France and Italy tried to resolve their differences. Italy demanded clear identification and precise description of her territorial corridor in Ethiopia offering to end her opposition to France in Ethiopia. In the negotiations at Rome France allowed Italy the territorial corridor between the Benadir and Eritrean colonies to the east of Lake Thana but west of Addis Ababa, clearly outside both the British and French spheres of interests.[110] The exact location and description of the line was to become the content of a note of exchange among the tripartite powers.[111]

While accepting the proposed Italian territorial corridor France objected to an exchange of notes fearing that it would be tantamount to a secret agreement, and if divulged, it would ruin French influence with Menelek further.[112] Fearing the ill effects of Paris's refusal, Barrere persuaded Rouvier to accept the arrangement, pointing that the requested note would only be an explanatory letter and not a secret protocol or an annex to the main treaty. While the note of exchange would not hurt France it would please Italy, which, at the cost of suffering German wrath, had maintained "equivocal" attitude at Algeciras.[113] In the same tone Barrere questioned whether it would be in the French interest to leave "the right hand man of Germany" disgruntled.[114] Paul Cambon too advised Paris not to bruise or offend Italy. These arguments won the day. The French Government agreed to give the suggested explanatory note.[115]

With the advent of 1906, inspite of changes in governments of all the three countries, tripartite negotiations progressed. The catalyst was Germany. The failure of the three powers to provide Menelek an acceptable railway solution and their protracted negotiations had strengthened his suspicion that they were scheming to partition his country. He had warned the tripartite powers that he would take his own steps to solve the railway question if they failed to provide him an acceptable solution by May 1906. The Germans seemed to be exploiting his fears for their own purposes. The information that Coates, Minister Plenipotentiary of Germany, had landed in Jibuti to meet Emperor Menelek and he had been followed soon by 38 German families worried the French Government.[116] Fearing that Menelek may transfer the concession to build the railway to Addis Ababa to a German company, the French were watching against surprise at Menelek's court.[117] London too was aware that the German Mission in Ethiopia had been hoping to "secure some successful fishing in the troubled waters" there had been interfering in every matter.[118] Both Britain and France agreed that Emperor Menelek was adept in exploiting the situation and that Germany would create troubles in Ethiopia soon the British Minister in Addis Ababa was urging them to expedite an agreement on Ethiopia.[119]

While the need for a quick conclusion of the tripartite negotiations was pressing it was rumoured that the pro-German Sonnino-San Guiliano Government, which had come to power in Italy in December 1905, was dissatisfied with the concessions made to Italy and was considering to renegotiate for a better deal.[120] To forestall this the British exerted pressure on Rome to conclude an agreement soon. Sir Edward Gray, the new Foreign Minister of Britain, warned Italy that it would be regrettable if Italy found herself separated from France and Britain, her neighbours in the Mediterranean, by not signing the treaty.[121] Britain wanted the ongoing tripartite negotiations to be considered in the wider context of European relations and not in the exclusive context of their interest in Ethiopia. Though the British attributed the Italian reluctance to expedite the negotiations to their fears to sign such an important African agreement behind Germany's back, they were mistaken. In fact the Italians had revealed the terms of the proposed agreement to Germany in April 1905.[122] The delay was due to the failure of both Britain and France to appreciate the Italian colonial aspirations. Italy was keen to achieve commercial penetration of Ethiopia both from Benadir and Eritrea. Expecting that the entire territory between Benadir and Eritrea would fall into her hands Italy wanted the region recognized as an Italian sphere. That would provide her the "legal" basis for territorial claims if Ethiopia was partitioned. Unless France and Britain conceded this demand Italy did not want to recognize Anglo-French interests in Ethiopia. In pursuit of this policy Italy proposed the omission of all references to the dissolution of Ethiopia and British and French interests there, instead expressing support to *Porta Aperta*-open door policy.[123]

Absence of all references to spheres of influences, and declaration of open door policy would also please Germany and win that power's approbation for Italy. This move did not help Italy. Not only the infuriated British threatened to sign the tripartite agreement with France alone, leaving the door open to Italy to join whenever she cared, but also rejected the Italian proposals as it went against British interest. Edward Grey wrote to the Italian government: The proposal that all those parts of the agreement which have references to the contingency of dissolution should be entirely suppressed, I fear, is not likely to commend itself to His Majesty's Government.

These articles, together with those which provide for future railway concession in Ethiopia, are in the opinion his Majesty's Government Vital Portion of the agreement, and represent guarantees which they consider indispensable for the future protection of British interests.[124] Grey's letter is also very significant as it clearly reflects the change in Britain's Ethiopian policy from one of maintaining its independence to that of the expected vivisection.

Realizing the futility of pressing Britain any more, and fearing the dangers of isolation the Italians endeavoured to win their claims by persuasion. Tittoni the Italian Foreign Minister argued that the Italian public would consider it as "marche le dupe" if Italian claims to the Tigrean hinterland was not recognized while admitting French claims to eastern Ethiopia. Complaining that France had deliberately contrived to destroy the concessions which Italy had procured in the Anglo-Italian negotiations to promote her own interests, Tittoni urged Britain to pressure Paris to moderate its claims and to ensure that Italian interests were not sacrificed. Italy expected this from Britain not merely because of traditional friendship but also out of "moral obligation."[125] Clearly unimpressed and out of sympathy with Italy, Britain refused to reopen the issue and threatened to sign the Ethiopian agreement with France immediately leaving it open for Italy to join later.[126]

With Britain hardening her position and France keen on signing the agreement with her the situation seemed grave to Italy—*"pericoloso i per nostri interessi"*. The conclusion of Tripartite treaty was very important to Italy as France would, for the first time, recognize Italian sphere of influence in Ethiopia reversing her policy; without this, Italian possessions of Benadir and Eritrea would be exposed to the danger of French expansion. If she did not sign the treaty Italy's influence in London, Rome and Ethiopia would not only decline but an opportunity would also be lost for "the reorientation of her international relations given her desire to lessen her dependence on the Triplice. Worse, Anglo-French agreement, excluding Italy, would have made a mockery of Italian diplomacy, possibly ruptured her relations with both France and Britain, besides creating bad public opinion in Italy. To avoid it Tittoni, the Italian Ambassador at London, urged Gray and Cambon not to sign the agreement promising Italian adherence as soon as he took over as Foreign Minister in the new Geoletti Ministry.[127] He wanted not only to protect Italian interests in Ethiopia but also demonstrate that Italy had excellent relations with both Britain and France.[128]

While the diplomatic wrangle was going on between Rome and Paris, the Ethiopian situation was worsening. In the last week of May 1906 Menelek had suffered apoplectic fits and his death was expected shortly. If Menelek died and a civil war for succession ensued, there should be an arrangement among the powers to act jointly to protect their interests and life and properties of their nationals in Ethiopia. The British Minister in Ethiopia advised his Government to sign immediately an agreement with France to achieve this.[129] The Italians could not delay longer. On 7 June they conveyed their readiness to sign the treaty.

Hoping to overcome the French opposition the Italians sought Anglo-French recognition of the Eritrean and Benadir hinterlands as Italian interests, renouncing their exclusive claim for the intervening Ethiopian territory.[130] Considering this as adequate concession to the French, though the British accepted the Italian proposals, the French rejected it and refused to sign the treaty.

This was unacceptable to the British who at the cost of being considered unfriendly had pressed the Italians into making concessions to the French views. Not only the deteriorating health of Menelek but also the danger of German intervention in Ethiopia required an urgent conclusion of the treaty. Britain was determined that the arrangement should not collapse because of French opposition, to the not unreasonable Italian claims. Moreover, with an eye on the European situation, Britain considered it unwise to displease Italy over the doubtful and uncertain future partition of Ethiopia. Inspite of being a member of the Triple Alliance Italy had indirectly supported France and Britain at the Moroccon conference and Britain thought it time that the French should consider the Italian requests from the wider European perspective. They warned France that it would be "most unfortunate if the whole thing collapsed because of the French opposition. Such a fiasco could not but prejudice the willingness of co-operation of Italy in other questions, such as the Mediterranean questions, in the future, and an excellent opportunity would have been lost for setting the Ethiopian question as well, besides producing very unfavourable impression on Italy".[131]

The Earl of Grey advised Bourgeois, his French counterpart, to reconsider the matter positively.

Although the British Foreign Secretary was now no more sympathetic to Italian colonial aims he certainly brought a measure of statesmanship to the negotiations. Though he did not set out to detach Italy from the Triple Alliance deliberately, his move must have influenced beneficially those processes which were to see Italy out of the Triple Alliance, on the side of the Allied Powers, in the First World War. While urging France to take a broader view the British threatened Paris that England and Italy might sign the agreement leaving it open to France to sign later. Paul Combon French Ambassador in London, reasoned with his Foreign Minister to consider the issues broadly. Aware that Bourgeois, the Foreign Minister was withholding consent not only because of his dislike to the Italian territorial pretensions but also because of the fear of Germany Cambon advised him: "It is only right we declared that we are ready to sign a general agreement on Abyssinia and join Britain and France in communicating it to Germany. I don't see any danger in doing it. If we don't sign our good faith will be suspected; it will be impossible to find a solution to the railway and we shall face strong opposition to the Menelek's court. Harrington will revive anti-French policy. He will not wait to eliminate French influence completely. Our withdrawal from the agreement would be a blow to the *entente cordiale* with Britain which constitutes an essential guarantee of French security".[132]

He also opined that it was futile to reject the Italian request. They were essential to Italy and would not hurt France. Italy was only craving for equality among the signatories. Even if the French succeeded in imposing their views on the Italians any agreement that did not recognize the Eritrean and Benadir hinterlands as Italian interests might be rejected by Italian Parliament.[133]

The French Government was convinced of the strength and fairness of Cambon's arguments. It would also appear to have realized that continued opposition to Italy in Ethiopia might upset the process of weakening the Italian connections with Germany and Austria which had begun to loosen with Prinetti-Barrere Agreement of June 1902. Moreover the French dared not sign the agreement without Italy because of the fear of Germany. The new French Foreign Minister, Bourgeiois feared that Germany might pick up a "quarrel" with France if she signed the agreement on Ethiopia with Britain alone. Britain's assurances to the contrary, and even her willingness to communicate the essential of the intended treaty to Germany before its formalization, did not relieve Bourgeois of this fear.[134] He enquired whether Britain would stand by France if a critical situation arose because of German opposition.[135]

However neither Cambon nor Grey feared such a contingency. They hoped to overcome possible German opposition to the treaty by making Italy to be the "carrier of the news" to Berlin in the first instance. London and Paris were to make simultaneous communications to the German embassies later.[136] The Italian participation in the treaty was thus seen as essential, in the French view, to ward off possible German wrath.[137] So the French withdrew their objections to the Italian proposals finally. They recognized Italian claims not only to the Benadir Eritrea territorial link but also to the hinterlands. Britain was asked to give a written undertaking that such link would be provided to the west of Addis Ababa, clearly outside the French zone.[138] There was no difficulty as the British had only to put on paper what they had already conceded verbally. It was soon done. Now that all major difficulties had been overcome the Tripartite Treaty was initialled on 6 July, 1906.[139]

The Tripartite Treaty which was formalized in December 1906, was a most ambiguous document, full of contradictions.

Though the signatories declared the maintenance of the territorial and political *status quo* of Ethiopia as their common interests, in reality, it was a paper partition of Ethiopia. The *status quo* itself was to be determined by the "affairs actuellement existent et les arrangements" cited in Article 1 of the treaty. They bound themselves not to interfere in the domestic affairs of Ethiopia and to remain neutral in the event of internal changes in that country. However, if the Ethiopian *status quo* was disturbed, they agreed to concert measures to maintain the "integrity" of the country and to take necessary steps to protect their legations and lives and properties of foreigners. Should it be found difficult to preserve Ethiopian integrity the powers would concert measures to protect British and Egyptian interests in the Nile Valley, particularly in controlling the floods of the Nile and its tributaries; Italian interests in the hinterlands of Eritrea and Benadir, particularly in establishing a territorial connection between those two colonies and French interests in the hinterlands of the French Somali Protectorate, particularly in the Ethiopian territory necessary for the construction of Jibuti Addis Ababa railway.

The powers agreed that the Jibuti Addis Ababa railway was to be owned and operated by the French company and that it should ensure equal treatment to subjects and commerce of all nations. On the railway board were to sit an Englishman, an Italian and an Ethiopian. Like privileges were to be conceded to France on the boards of any British and Italian railways which might be built in Ethiopia. All railway construction west of Addis Ababa was to be carried out under British auspices. Britain was confirmed the right, which she had secured from Menelek in 1904, to build a railway from the British Somaliland to Anglo-Egyptian Sudan through Ethiopia, while Italy was given the right to construct railways joining Eritrea and Benadir. The powers undertook not to compete with one another's railways in Ethiopia.[140]

The Tripartite Treaty was more concerned with common interests of the guaranteeing powers than the interests of the guaranteed power. It had been arrived with an eye to the future. Each of the signatories had fears that the other two powers might secretly partition Ethiopia. Both France and Italy had no doubt that Britain, with adjoining territories in Africa and her interests in the Nile hinterlands, would absorb Ethiopia the moment it became possible to do so. Likewise Britain feared that France with her railway and declared interests in the Hawash Valley would, sooner or later, dominate Ethiopia. The naive belief of the French colonial party that Ethiopia could become "a sort of French colony", only strengthened such suspicions. Neither France nor Britain really feared Italy whatever might be her designs in Ethiopia. However the Italians suspected both. Inspite of her defeat in 1896, Italy considered Ethiopia her sphere of influence and was much concerned for her future position there. As France had not recognized the Anglo-Italian protocols of 1891, Italy suspected utmost danger from her in Ethiopia. The Tripartite Treaty relieved Italy from this anxiety. The inclusion of the Anglo-Italian Protocols in the Tripartite Treaty not only meant their re-endorsement by Britain, whose attitudes towards them since 1896 had been doubtful, but also their acceptance by France which had never endorsed the Italian claims over Ethiopia. In addition the treaty reduced French menace to Italian interests in Benadir and Eritrea. As any future territorial divisions of Ethiopia had to take place with as much regard to the Anglo-Italian Protocols as to the other treaties cited in Article 1 of the Tripartite agreement Italian claims to Ethiopia had been strengthened. The Italians themselves had no doubt about this. Tittoni, the Italian Foreign Minister, told the Italian chambers that the Tripartite Treaty had opened a new path to Italy.[141] Whether Ethiopia would be partitioned or not, Italy had revived her rights to the country and reserved her sphere of influence. She was neither worse nor better off than her co-signatories to the agreement. This was an impressive achievement.

France had fared equally well. Whatever the British and Italian suspicions of French designs in Ethiopia, it is doubtful if France ever thought seriously of establishing a protectorate over Ethiopia. The existence of pre-ponderant British and Italian interests in that country, in any event, would have made such aims absurd and France could not have overlooked this reality. Though France aspired for both political and economic predominance in Ethiopia and hoped to achieve this through Jibuti-Addis Ababa railway she could not realize this until 1906 primarily because of Britain's opposition. Now through the Tripartite Treaty France had overcome this difficulty. Like Britain, Italy recognized the Jibuti railway as a French interests, however reluctantly, so that the constant British and Italian opposition to the railway was ended. Moreover eastern Ethiopia had been recognized as a sphere of French interests and it would fall to France if Ethiopia was partitioned. The Tripartite Treaty by harmonizing Anglo-French interests in the railway not only paved the way for direct negotiations between Menelek and the French but also strengthened the Anglo-French *entente*.

Britain gained most of all. Britain's major interests lay in the Nile and its tributaries. Through the Tripartite Treaty Britain not only widened the zone of interests which had been conceded to her in the Anglo-Italian Protocols of 1891 and 1894 but also made France recognize this as British interests. Most important she succeeded in making France relenquish her rights to build railways west of Addis Ababa. In return Britain paid very little. In withdrawing opposition to the French railway to Addis Ababa, Britain had not committed herself to support the French project. If Menelek choose to continue his opposition it was for France to settle the matter with him. Britain would have nothing to do. Likewise in providing Italy with a'territorial corridor from Eritrea to Benadir, north-south, Britain, in effect, erected a barrier against any possible French expansion towards the Nile.

So long as British rights to the Nile Valley remained undisputed and so long as the danger of French predominance in Ethiopia had been removed Britain could feel satisfied with the situation. These ends, which British had been striving since 1897, were achieved by the Tripartite Treaty. If her influence declined in Ethiopia thereafter because of her failure to support Menelek against the French Britain need not be concerned. An understanding with France, the only European power whose colonial interests had always clashed with hers, made the costly policy of building competing railways unnecessary, saved her from expensive commitments to Menelek, guaranteed Britain's interests and called off Anglo-French rivalry in the region were more to Britain's advantage than the possible temporary loss of influence in Ethiopia.

After initialling the Tripartie Agreement Britain informed Menelek of this arrangement assuring "that His Majesty's Government's great desire during proposed negotiations has been to secure in the future the integrity and independence of Abyssinia, and to promote the material development of that country. "They were convinced that the Tripartite agreement was the best possible under all circumstances and they had no hesitation in strongly recommending King Menelek to adhere it."[142] It is doubtful if this eased Menelek's mind any more than Britain's past assurances. He was sure that to protect her interests Britain had sacrificed his and had confronted him with a fait accompli. His reaction was one of long silence. Though Menelek suspected the inherent and potential threat of the agreement to Ethiopian independence, realizing the futility and possible danger of either rejecting the treaty or opposing the powers he reacted coolly. Now that Britain, France and Italy appeared to have united, Menelek lacked the scope for exploiting their differences for his own benefits. There was not much he could do. Throughout Menelek had exhibited a robust self-confidence and wisdom in handling crises and these did not fail him. With poise and dignity he told the powers: "We have received the arrangement made by the three powers. We thank them for their communication and their desire to keep and maintain the independence of our government. But let it be understood that the arrangement in no way limits what we consider our sovereignty.[143]

This was a reply befitting a great statesman who knew how to be firm without being offensive, and how to maintain composure under adversity. Menelek had fought incessantly in defence of his country's independence and he had the courage to tell the powers that he would not let them interfere with Ethiopia's sovereignty. As a result of the Tripartite agreement Britain's influence declined in Ethiopia. But the British Government was undisturbed. Influence was an ephemeral and fluctuating factor and it could be regained. Now was the time to win back Menelek's confidence and revive British influence in Ethiopia. This was what Britain set out to do.

The Tripartite Treaty was a paper partition of Ethiopia though the declared intention of the signatories was the maintenance of independence and territorial integrity of that country. It diffused tensions among the competing European powers for primacy and territory in Ethiopia, by assigning to each a sphere of influence which might be converted into a colony if the empire disintegrated as expected.

The declared objective of "maintaining independence" of Ethiopia was a political euphemism, a handy garb to cover the naked territorial imperialism of Britain France and Italy. If the paper partitioners could not get the "Ethiopian cake" it was due to the internal strength of Ethiopians and sagacity of their rulers.

REFERENCES

1. F.O. 403/346. Cromer's Memorandum, 25 June 1901.
2. F.O. 141/128. The Foreign Office Situation Report on the Sudan.
3. John Marlowe, *A History of Modern Egypt* (1984) p. 154.
4. France. Archives De La Documentatione, Ministre Des Affaires Etrange, Paris. N.S Politique Etrangers. Here after referred as N.S. Etiopie 11. Lagarde to Delcasse, 25 February 1904.
5. Archivio Storico dell ex Ministero dell Africa Italiana, hereafterwards referred as ASMAI, Rome. Italy. Pos. 35/3. Fascicolo 7. Rapporto di Ciccodicola, 8 August 1903. ASMSI. Pos. 41/1. Fascicolo 2. Genni sulla politica situaazione Italian.
6. F.O. 1/45. Sanderson's Minute, 8 September 1899.
7. ASMAI, Pos. 31/7. Fascicolo 7; Ciccodicola's Report, 8 August 1903. Foot note 3.
8. ASMAI, Pos. 38/4, Fascicolo 35; Cenni Sulla situazione ASMAI. Pos. 38/3, Fascicolo 23. Ciccodicola to the Italian Foreign Minister, 10 July 1903. ASMAI. Pos. 41/1, Fascicolo 1. Tittoni to Tornielli, 30 December 1903.
9. F.O. 1/43. Bertie to Lansdowne, 25 May 1903.

10. F.O. 1/43. Bertie to Lansdowne, 25 May 1903.
11. F.O. 1/43. Thomas Sandersons Memo on the above, 31 May 1903.
12. *Ibid*. Lansdowne's Minute on the above, 2 June 1903.
13. F.O. 1/43. Lansdowne to Bertie, 12 June 1903.
14. F.O. 45/871. Memorandum communicated by Admiral Morin, 29 August 1903 in Rodd to Lansdowne, 6 September 1903.
15. F.O. 45/871. Rodd to Lansdowne, 6 September 1903.
16. *Ibid*.
17. F.O. 800/160. Bertie to Lansdowne, 20 September 1903, Sir Francis Bertie papers.
18. F.O. 45/871. Sanderson's Minute, 28 September 1903.
19. Lansdowne to Bertie, 20 September 1903. *Ibid*.
18. F.O. 1/48. Lansdowne to Bertie, 8 October 1903.
19. F.O. 1/56. Berrtie to Lansdowne, 19 December 1903. Harrington's Memorandum, in Bertie Lansdowne. *Ibid*.
20. *Ibid*.
21. Bertie to Lansdowne, 19 December 1903. *Ibid*.
22. *Ibid*.
23. *Ibid*.
24. ASMAI, Pos. 41/1, Fascicolo. Pansa to Tittoni, 13 April 1904.
25. F.O. 403/346. Bertie to Lansdowne, 13 April 1904.
    F.O. 403/346. Lansdowne to Bertie, 14 April 1904. Tommaso Tittoni, *Sei Anni di Politica Estera* (Tornio; 1912)
26. F.O. 403/346. Lansdowne to Bertie, 20 April 1904.
27. F.O. 403/346. Lansdowne to Bertie, 5 May 1904.
    ASMAI, Pos 41/1, Fascicolo, Pansa-Horn, 16 June 1904.
28. Salisbury to Baring, 31 August 1890. Cesil, IV. Quoted by Low, *The Reluctant Imperialists;* Vol. 2, p. 69.
29. F.O. 800/160. Bertie to Lansdowne, 20 September 1906. Lansdowne to Bertie, September 1906, *Bertie Papers*.
30. F.O. 88/133. Lansdowne's Minute, 30 March 1904. *Lansdowne Papers*.
31. F.O. 1/49. The War Office to the Foreign Office, 18 May 1904.
32. F.O. 1/33. Bertie to Lansdowne, 19 December 1903, Rodd to Harrington, 19 December 1903, *Ibid*.
33. F.O. 1/40. Harrington to Lansdowne, 15 December 1902.
34. F.O. 403/346. Cromer's Memorandum, 25 January 1904.
35. F.O. 1/49. For Lansdowne's views on Ethiopian Independence, see his note on the War Office's Memorandum of 18 May 1903.
36. F.O. 403/346. Lansdowne to Bertie, 20 April 1904.
37. ASMAI, Pos. 41/1, Fascicolo, Tornielli Tittoni, 15 November 1903, Tittoni-Tornielli 30 December 1903.
38. F.O. 403/346. Lansdowne to Bertie, 1 June 1904
    F.O. 403/346. Lansdowne to Rodd, 20 July 1904.

39. F.O. 403/346. Lansdowne to Rodd 5 October 1904.
F.O. 1/56. Lansdowne to Lister, 4 January 1905.
40. F.O. 1/56. Cromer to Lansdowne, 13 May 1904.
F.O. 1/56. The War Office to the F.O. 13 May 1904.
41. F.O. 1/56. Lansdowne to Bertie, 4 January 1905
42. F.O. 401/8. Agreement between Italy and Great Britain. 18 January 1905 ASMAI, Pos 41/1 Fascicolo, Tornielli-Tittoni, 15 November 1903.
43. France D.D.F. Tome IV. No. 348, Barrere to Delcasse, 13 January 1904. Documents Diplomatique Francaise, hereinafter referred as D.D.F. Series 2, Tome IV. No., Lagarde to Delcasse, 25 February 1904.
44. F.O. 403/346. Landowne to Moson, 16 May 1904.
France D.D.F. Series 2, Tome V, No. 148. Cambon to Délcassé, 18 May 1904.
45. *Ibid.*
46. F.O. 1/56. Paul Cambon's Proposals. Lansdowne's Memo. 18 June 1904.
47. F.O. 1/56. Cambon's Proposals to Lansdowne, in Lansdowne to Monson, 18 June 1904. D.D.F. Series 2, Tome I, No. 246. Délcassé to Cambon, 28 June 1904.
48. F.O. 1/56. Lansdowne to Monson, 16 May 1904. Délcassé to Barrere, 28 June 1904, D.D.F. Series 2, Tome VI. No. 246.
49. Lansdowne to Monson, 18 June 1904. *Ibid.*
50. F.O. 1/56. Harrington to Lansdowne, 20 May 1904.
51. F.O. 1/56. Harrington to Cromer, in Cromer Lansdowne, 26 March 1905.
52. F.O. 403/346. Harrington to Lansdowne, 20 May 1904.
53. F.O. 1/50. Lansdowne to Harrington, 9 June 1904.
54. F.O. 1/50. Harrington to Lansdowne, 6 June 1904.
55. F.O. 1/50. Cromer to Lansdowne, 12 November 1904.
56. For a detailed discussion refer the previous chapter.
57. F.O. 1/56. Lansdowne to Cambon, 16 December 1904.
58. F.O. 1/56. Lansdowne to Manson, 2 November 1904.
F.O. 1/56. Cambon's Memorandum in Lansdowne to Bertie, 25 January 1905. Cambon to Délcassé, 8 November 1904, D.D.F. Series 2, Tome V. No. 246.
59. F.O. 800/160. Lansdowne to Bertie, 13 January 1905. Bertie Papers. D.D.F. Series 2, Tome VI. No. 42. Cambon to Délcassé, 21 January 1905.
60. F.O. 401/9. Lansdowne to Cambon, 13 January 1905.
61. F.O. 403/346. Lansdowne to Cambon, 16 December 1904. D.D.F. Series 2, Tome. VI. No. 48. 62. *Ibid.* Lansdowne to Cambon.
62. F.O. 1/56. Lansdowne to Monson, 28 October and 2 November 1904. F.O. 1/56. Delcasse to Cambon, 20 March 1905. D.D.F. Series 2, Tome. VI. No. 165.

63. F.O. 1/56. Lansdowne to Cambon. 13 January 1905.
    (a) NS Ethiopie. 12-13. Paul Cambon to Délcassé.
64. F.O. 1/56. Lansdowne to Bertie, 13 January 1905.
65. ASMAI. Pos. 41/2. Fas 2, Tittoni to Tornielli, 17 February 1905,
66. F.O. 1/56. Lansdowne to Cambon, 13 January 1905.
    F.O. 403/340. Monson to Lansdowne, 21 October 1904.
67. F.O. 401/8. Lansdowne to Lister, 18 January 1905.
68. NES, Ethiopie 12-15. Any future partition of Ethiopia was to be determined on the basis of the several treaties between, Britain, Italy, France and Ethiopia enumerated in article 1 of the treaty. Lagarde to Delcasse, 12 September 1905.
69. F.O. 401/8. Report of talks with Cambon, in Lansdowne to Bertie, 27 January 1905. NS Ethiopie, p. 12,13. Lagarde to Minister for Foreign Affairs, 12 September and 28 September 1905.
70. sFrance D.D.F. Series 2, Tome V. No. 246: Délcassé to Barrere, 28 June 1904. Lagarde to Delcasse, 27 January 1904 and 28 February 1904. NS. Ethiopie, XI; ASMAI, Pos. 41/1. Fas. 1 Charge D'Affires of France in London to the Italian Ambassador, 15 March 1905,

70a. France D.D.F. Series 2, Tome IV. No. 348. Lagarde to Délcassé, 25 February 1904.

71. France D.D.F. Series 2, Tome V, No. 436. Cambon to Délcassé, 13 January 1905.
72. See the chapter on the Railway.
73. F.O. 401/8. Egerton to Lansdowne, 16 April 1905.
    F.O. 410/8. Lansdowne to Bertie, 3 May 1905.
74. D.D.F. Series 2, Tome VI. No. 436. The French Charge D'Affires in Rome to Delcasse, 15 May 1905. NS. Ethiopie XII. Minister of Foreign Affairs to Cambon, 6 May 1905.
75. France D.D.F. Series 2, Tome VI. No. 431. The Charge D'Affaires of France at Rome to Délcassé, 15 May 1905,
76. France D.D.F. Series 2, Tome VI. No. 456 and 466. Barrere to Délcassé, 27 and 29 May 1905.
77. *Ibid* Barrere to Rouvier, 27 May 1905. D.D.F. Series 2, Tome VI. No. 456.; Same to same 29 May 1905. *Ibid*. No. 466.
78. F.O. 401/8. Egerton to Lansdowne, 16 April 1905.
79. F.O. 401/8. Lansdowne to Bertie, 19 April and 26 May 1905.
80. F.O. 1/48. Lansdowne to Bertie, 31 May 1905.
81. F.O. 1/48. The French Minister of Foreign Affairs to London, 19 November 1905. NS. Ethiopie. Telegram No. 315, Lansdowne to Bertie, 7 June 1905.
82. *Ibid*.
83. F.O. 401/8. Lansdowne to Bertie, 9 June 1905.
84. F.O. 633/8. *Cromer Papers*. Cromer to Gorst, 13 January 1905.
85. F.O. 1/56. Sir George Clerk's Memo. 25 January 1905.

86. F.O. 1/56. Lansdowne's Minute on the above. 25 January 1905.
87. F.O. 401/8. Lansdowne to Cambon, 27 June 1905.
    F.O. 401/8. Lansdowne to Bertie, 4 January 1905.
88. F.O. 401/8. Egerton to Lansdowne, 31 July 1905.
89. F.O. 403/346. Gleischen to Whithead in Whitehead to Lansdowne, 9 December 1904.
90. F.O. 633/7. Lansdowne to Cromer, 3 April 1905. Cromer Papers.
91. F.O. 401/8. Lansdowne to Bertie, 19 April 1905.
92. F.O. 401/8. Louis Mallet to Bertie, 13 April 1905.
93. Gooch. G.P. and Temperley (Eds) *British Documents on the Origin of the War 1898 to 1914*. (London; 1927). Lascelles to Lansdowne, April 1905, No. 79, Volm 3.
94. N.S. Etiopie, XIV, Note Per la Ministre intervention eventual allemagre Cambon to Delcasse, 27 March 1905. D.D.F. Serie 2, Tome VI. No. 196. NS. Etiopie 14. Note per le Ministre per intervention eventualle de Allemagne, 17 March 1906.
95. F.O. 401/8. Lansdowne to Bertie, 5 April 1905.
96. France D.D.F. Series 2, Tome VII. No 201. Note Du Department, French Foreign Ministry, 7 December 1905.
97. France D.D.F. Series 2, Tome VI. No. 214. Paul Deschenel, President of the Commision for Foreign Affairs of the French Chamber of Deputies.
98. France D.D.F. Series 2, Tome VII. No. 105. Rouvier to Barrere, 28 November
99. France D.D.F. Series 2, Tome VII. No. 40. Barrere to Rouvier, 19 November 1905.
100. France D.D.F. Series 2, Tome VII. 9. 1. Rouvier to the French Ambassadors in London, Paris, Berlin and St Petersburg, 20 June 1905.
101. Barrere to Rouvier, 26 January 1906. NS. Etiopie 14.
102. *Ibid.*
103. F.O. 401/8. Lansdowne to Bertie, 22 November 1905. D.D.F. Series 2, Tome VIII. No. 212: D.D.F. Series 2, Tome VIII. No. 215. Rouvier to Barrere, 11 December 1905. Rouvier to Cambon, 11 December 1905.
104. Rouvier to Barrere, 10 November 1905. D.D.F. Series 2, Tome VIII. No. 120.
105. F.O. 401/8. This Agreement which harmonized French and Italian interests in the Mediterranean had set a new direction to Franco Italian relations nearly twenty years of rivalry over the Tunis question. Lansdowne to Bertie April 1905.
106. F.O. 401/8. Lansdowne to Lister, 12 August 1905.
107. NS. Ethiopie 12. Rouvier to Lagarde, 9 November, 1905. Lagarde to Rouvier, 17 June 1905; XL-XIV/No. 2, No. 64.

108. F.O. 401/8. Lansdowne to De Graz 27 September 1905. Gorst's Memo, 18 November 1905.
109. France D.D.F. Series 2, Tome VIII, No. 130. Geoffrey to Rouvier, 18 November 1805.
110. *Ibid.*
111. France D.D.F. Series 2, Tome VIII. No. 130. F.O. 401/8. Ferry to Rouvier, 18 November 1905, Lansdowne to Bertie, 22 November 1905.
112. Barrere to Rouvier, 11 December 1905. D.D.F. Series 2. Tome VIII. No. 215.
113. Rouvier to Barrere, 11 December 1905. *D.D.F. Series 2. Tome VIII.* No. 212. Note per le Minister, 20 November, 1905. *N.S. Etiopie 14.*
114. Barrere to Rouvier, 6 January 1906. *Series 2, Tome VIII. No. 334.*
115. D.D.F. Series 2, Tome IX No. 65. Barrere to Rouvier, 26 January 1906. NS. Etiopie. 14. Cambon to Rouvier, 24 January 1906.
116. Berthelot, Secretary to the Cabinet, to Lousi, Director of Political Affairs. French Foreign Ministry. *D.D.F. Series 2, 27 January 1906.* D.D.F. Series 2. Tome IX. No. 71. Cambon to Rouvier, 24 January 1906. *NS. Etiopie XIV.*
117. Lagarde to the French Foreign Minister, 19 March 1906: NS. Etiopie XIII; Minister of Foreign Affairs to Lagarde 9 May 1906. No. 33. NS. Ethiopie XIV.
118. F.O. 1/52. Harrington to Lansdowne, 7 March 1905.
119. F.O. 371/1. For instance see Clerk's note on Cromer to Grey. 1 January 1906.
120. Italy ASMAI, Pos. 38/4. Cenni, Della situatione dell'Italia in Etiopie, 1906.
121. F.O. 800/46. *Sir. Edward Grey Paperes.* Grey to Egerton, 25 December 1905. Grey's Minute of January 1906.
122. F.O. 800/46. *Grey Paperes.* Cromer to Grey, 17 January 1906. ASMAI. Fascicolo. 1. Pos. 38/1. Memo of the Under Secretary to the Foreign Minister of Italy. 24 March 1905.
123. Fascicolo 1. Pos 38/1. Foreign Minister of Italy to F.O. April 1906.
124. F.O. 371/1. Tittoni to Grey. 12 April 1906. Pansa to the Italian Ambassador in London. April 1906. *ASMAI. Pos. 41/1. Fasicolo 8.*
125. F.O. 371/1. Grey to Tittoni, 12 April 1906.
126. F.O. 371/1. Tittoni to Grey, 19 April 1906. Cambon to Boutgeois, 18 May 1906. *NS. Etiopie 14.*
127. F.O. 371/1. Cambon to Rouvier, 28 February 1906. *D.D.F. Series 2,* Tome IX. Grey to Bertie, 21 May 1906.
128. F.O. 371/1. Grey to Egerton, 23 May 1906; France N.S. Etiopie, XIV Cambon to Bourgeis, 18 May 1906.
129. F.O. 371/34. Harrington's letter in Cromer to Grey, 27 May 1906. ASMAI. 41/8 Fasicolo 8. Annatozione circa la progetto d'Covenzione la Francia la Agelterra Alla Abyssinia.

130. F.O. 371/1. Grey to Bertie, 19 June 1906.
131. F.O. 371/1. Bertie to Grey. 21 June 1906.
132. Cambon to Bourgcois, 7 June 1906. D.D.F. Series 2. Tome X. No. 93.
133. *Ibid.*
134. Cambon to Bourgcouis, 20 June 1906. D.D.F. Series 2. Tome X.
135. Bourgcouis to Cambon, 26 June 1906. D.D.F. Series 2. Tome X.
136. D.D.F. Series 2 Tome X. No. 94. Cambon tó Bourgeois, 8 June 1906.
137. D.D.F. Series 2 Tome X. No. 81. Bourgeios to Cambon, 28 May 1905.
138. D.D.F. Series 2, Tome X. No. 136. Cambon to Bourgeois.
139. F.O. 401/9. Grey to Harrington, 6 July 1906.
140. Hertslet, The Map of Africa by Treaty, 3 Volume. (London; 1965) Vol 3. pp. 440-444.
141. Tittoni's reply to De Marinis in the Chamber of Deputies, 15 March 1907. Italian Parliament. *ASMAI, Fas. Pos. 41/2.*
142. F.O. 371/1. Grey to Harrington, 6 July 1906.
143. F.O. 371/1. Enclousre in Clerk to Grey, 10 December 1906.

Conclusion

From 1839 when Britain established a naval base at Aden, Ethiopia came to be regarded as a strategically sensitive region by British policy-makers. Washed on the east by the Red Sea, the oceanic link to India and flanked on the West by the Nile River, the lifeblood of Egypt, and surrounded by British colonial possession in East and North-East Africa Ethiopia was strategically important to Britain. Britain did not wish to see any European power achieve predominance in Ethiopia lest British interest in the region be endangered. British policy during the 1869-1906 period was designed to prevent the achievement of primacy by any European power in Ethiopia. This objective remained constant throughout the period though the means adopted to secure the objective was changed in response to changing situations and political pressures in the Nile Valley and the Red Sea region. Three distinct stages can be identified in British policy of the period in Ethiopia: 1869 to 1884; 1884 to 1887 and from 1897 to 1906.

By 1869, the starting point of this study, Britain was disillusioned with Ethiopia. Economically frustrated and politically embarrassed Britain had very little interest in Ethiopia. Only the Red Sea shore of Ethiopia was of concern to Britain and on this Ethiopia had no control having lost it to Turkey since the 15th Century. In the circumstances Britain choose to attempt disengagement. So long as other European powers kept away from Ethiopia so would Britain. However Britain enjoyed abundant goodwill and influence with Ethiopia chiefs, having voluntarily withdrawn from the country after the victory achieved at Magdala in 1868; she could rely on this to serve her interests. British policy in Ethiopia was also profoundly influenced by the nature of British relations with Egypt and changes in Britain's diplomatic alignments in Europe.

In contrast to the situation in Ethiopia, Britain had vital financial and commercial interest in Egypt. To those the Suez Canal was added in 1869. The extension of the Egyptian authority to the Western Red Sea ports in the 1870's further enhanced Egypt's importance to Britain. To forestall rival European powers from establishing bases on the Western Red Sea shore Britain recognized Egyptian Rights to the Region under Turkey's suzerainty on the condition of non-alienation of the territories without London's consent. Egypt was thus made Britain's watch-dog in the region.

These developments had a significant impact on British relations with Ethiopia from 1869 to 1884. Tilting towards Egypt and virtually condoning her aggression on Ethiopia in the 1870's Britain ignored Ethiopian grievances against Cairo. Though bonds of common Christian faith occasionally prompted Britain to sympathise Ethiopia these did not translate themselves into British support for that country. Moslem Egypt served British interest better than Christian Ethiopia and Ethiopian interest were sacrificed.

With the occupation of Egypt in 1882 the security of that country became a vital British concern. To protect Egypt's southern borders from a possible Ethiopian attack Britain signed Hewett Treaty with Ethiopia restoring to her the Egyptian occupied Bogos while denying the much sought coastal territory. The collapse of Egypt in 1882 and her withdrawal from the Red Sea following the financial and military debacle ended her role as Britain's surrogate. Britain picked up Italy as new watch-dog to substitute Egypt and planted her in Massawa. Apparently a masterly diplomatic manoeuvre aimed to pre-empt France from Massawa, to safeguard the eastern approach to Nile Valley and ensure continued Italian support in Egypt. However this was by no means a new strategy. There are strong parallel to this in other areas of Africa where Britain used weaker powers as "Surrogates" to advance her interests. In the mid-1880's in

Congo Britain used Portugal to check the French expansion and to protect British interest and free trade; in East Africa Britain used the Sultanate of Zanzibar to protect British interest on the mainland of East Africa. But the strategy failed to serve British interest in the Ethiopian region for long. On the contrary the strategy failed. It ensured Britain the contempt of Ethiopia which felt cheated out of Massawa, the political embarrassment of the Surrogate Italy challenging Anglo-Egyptain rights to the Sudan and intensified French rivalry. The pre-emption of France from Massawa was a poor consolation to Britain.

Concern for the security of the eastern Nile Valley shaped British policy toward Ethiopia from 1882. Determined to keep all Europeans powers out of the Nile Valley lest British interest be jeopardized Britain preferred the continuance of an indigenous Government in Ethiopia to any European one. However when Italy claimed a protectorate over Ethiopia Britain recognized the surrogate's claim and concluded the Anglo-Italian Protocols demarcating British and Italian spheres in the region. These arrangements kept Italy out of the Sudan, blocked France from the Eastern Nile Valley and safeguarded British interest in the region temporarily.

This strategy to ensure British interest in the Ethiopian region collapsed with the forced annulment of Italy's Ethiopian Protectorate following her disastrous rout at Adwa in 1896. The humilitating and unexpected defeats of Britian's "Surrogates" Egypt and Italy by Ethiopia had significant impact on British attitudes towards Ethiopia-Ethiopia's-ability to field thousand of solders at a short notice against her external invaders the ability of Ethiopian rules to provide confident leadership to their people in times of external challenges to their Independence and their diplomatic abilities impressed Britian. Ethiopia was seen as a strong power in the region which, if antagonized could Jeopardise British interest in the British East Africa and the Sudan. Both the militarily weak British East African Protectorate and the unpacified Anglo-Egyptian Sudan could be targets of Ethiopian attack and expansion. The British preferred to cultivate friendly relations with Emperor Menelek than to have him as a unfriendly adversary; maintaining peace with Ethiopia was seen as more important to Britain that the acquisition of few square kilometers of disputed territory from her. Worse still having won predominant influence in Ethiopia by supporting Menelek against Italy France seemed to be threatening British interests in the region. To checkmate France and humor Ethiopia, Britain hastened to cultivate friendly relation with Menelek. Britain achieved this by yielding to some extent to Ethiopian territorial claims in the three frontier treaties concluded with that power between 1897 and 1907 and by supporting Menelek's opposition to the French controlled Jibuti Railway. During this phase of intense Anglo-French rivalry from 1897 to 1904 Britain used both Ethiopia and Italy to frustrate France. Notwithstanding the tensions caused by the Italian territorial ambitions in the Sudan friendship with Italy remained a constant feature of British policy. Encouraging Ethiopia to oppose the French with implied British support, Britain let down that power badly to suit her *post-enete* friendly policy with France. To protect British imperial interest in the Nile Valley and Western Ethiopia, and to achieve a friendly accord with France and Italy Britain concluded the paper partition of Ethiopia in the Tripartite Treaty of December 1906 cynically disregarding Ethiopia's Independence.

What is very striking in this policy is Britain's singleminded pursuit of strategical interests to the exclusion of economic interests. Though Ethiopia was among the first of Tropical African countries with which Britain established relations, hardly any British economic interest existed there. No British trader ever visited Ethiopia; no British merchantman ever called at a Red Sea Port to trade with Ethiopia. No London, Liverpool or Manchester firm ever sent a representative to Ethiopia to exploit its markets. Though one or two gold mining concessions were won by British nationals to exploit gold in western Ethiopia, nothing was done to work these concessions. Even Menelek's railway concession to build a railway from the British Somali Protectorate to the Sudan through Ethiopia was seen by Britain as a political weapon to intimidate the French to make concessions to British strategic interests and not as a means to exploit Ethiopia economically. The British Government did not support private British investors wishing to exploit the French Ethiopian Railway Company economically on the contrary they were abandoned to the whims of the French Government to facilitate an Anglo-French diplomatic accord on Ethiopia to protect Britain's strategic interest. Likewise the Bank of Abyssinia a private British financial institution, was pressed to serve Britain's strategically oriented policy to the detriment of its financial interest. "If economic imperialism implies a political function to integrate new regions into an expanding metropolitan economy" then there are no proofs of Britain's economic imperialism in Ethiopia in the period covered by this study. British policy was motivated and guided by strategic considerations only. It was supported by a diplomacy marked by desertion and duplicity as it was applied to Ethiopia.

Select Bibliography

Manuscript Sources Public Record Office, London.
Foreign Office Correspondence

1.	Abyssinia (Political and Diplomatic) (1869-1905)	F.O. 1
2.	Abyssinia (Political) after 1905	F.O. 371
3.	Abyssinia (Consular)	F.O. 368
4.	Abyssinia (Commercial)	F.O. 369
5.	Egypt until 1905 Classified under Turkey	F.O. 78
6.	Egypt after 1905	F.O. 371
7.	Cairo Agency Archives 1868-1908	F.O. 141
8.	France	F.O. 27
9.	Italy	F.O. 45
10.	Africa-General	F.O. 2, F.O. 802
11.	Protocols	F.O. 93
12.	Maps and Plans	F.O. 925

War Office

Precise Information regarding the British Mission to Ethiopia

Military Report on Abyssinia 1902	W.O. 33/251
Military Report on Eritrea	W.O. 33/410
Military Report on Somaliland	W.O. 33/465

The Board of Trade

The return of the New African and the International Trust and Construction Companies from 1900 onwards B.T. 31.

The Treasury

Out Letters to the Foreign Office	T/12

Private Papers

Lord Cromer Papers	F.O. 633
Sir Edward Grey Papers	F.O. 800
Sir Francis Bertie Papers	F.O. 800
Lansdowne Papers	F.O. 800
Sir Thomas Sanderson Papers	F.O. 800
Papers of the Third Marquess of Salisbury	
Christ Church, Oxford	

India Office Library and Records London

Records of British Administrator in Aden	R/20/A.I.A
Artificial Collections: Selections from	
Bombay Political Department	L/P&5/85
Correspondence Relating to the Egyptian	L/P&3/18/
Evacuation of the Somali Coast	132.
Political and Secret	L/P&3/18
Political and Secret Department Bombay Files	R/20/F.I.A

France

Archiveds du la Documentation Ministre
Des Affaires Etrange, Quid' Arsay, Paris.
Etiopie, NS Politique Etrange.

1. NS Etiopie 11, Jan-May 1905
2. NS Etiopie 12, June to November 1905
3. NS Etiopie 13, December 1905 to April 1906
4. NS Etiopie 14, June to December 1906.

Italy

Archivio Storico dell' ex Ministero dell' Africa Italiana. Rome. Posizione, 37 to 50
Questione Etiopiche
Missione Ciccodicola
Accordo Tripartito del 1906
Azione Inglese
Banco Circolozione

Printed Primary Sources

1.	Colonial Office Confidential Prints East African Protectorate Affairs and Correspondence 1905-1906	C.O. 879/88
2.	Uganda Protectorate	C.O. 879/87

Foreign Office Confidential Prints

North East Africa and the Sudan 1898-1905	F.O. 403
Abyssinia 1905-1908	F.O. 401
Egypt 1905-1908	F.O. 407
The Red Sea and the Somali Coast	F.O. 881

Cabinet Papers

Red Sea Ports by Tyron, February 1884.	Cab/37/10
Evacuation of the Red Sea Ports	Cab/37/63/165
French Railway from Jibuti to Harar and British Railway from Berbera to Harar	Cab/37/62/119
Anglo-Italian Attitude towards Abyssinia	Cab/37/71/

Published Documents

Carlo Rosetti, *Storia Diplomatica Dell' Italia Il Regno di Menelek II. Accordi, Trattati, Atti di Converzione e Alti Documenti Relativi all' Ethiopia. (Torino: 1910).*

E.T.S. Dugdale, *German Diplomatic Documents 1871-1914,* IV. Volumes, (London: 1928).

France, Ministers des, Affairs Etrangers Documents Diplomatiques Francais 1 & 2 Series (Paris: 1938).

Gooch G. P. and Temperley Harold, British Documents on the Origins of War 1898-1934 (London: 1937).

Hertslet, E., The Map of Africa by Treaty 3 Volumes (London: 1967).

Italy, Ministero degli Affari Esteri, Documenti Diplomatici Italiani, Series 2 (Roma: 1953).

Contemporary Memoirs and Accounts

Burton, Richard, *First Footsteps in East Africa* (Reprint: New York: 1966)

Brickbeck and Hill, Gordon in Central Africa (London: 1881).

Cromer, *The Earl of Modern Egypt* (London: 1908).

Dye, Mc E, *Moslem Egypt Cristian Abyssinia* Reprint (Negroe University Press: 1969).

Gilmour, Lennox, *Abyssinia, Ethiopian Railway and the Powers* (London: 1906).
Giolitti, Giovanni, *Memorie Della Mia Vita* (Garzanti: 1922).
Gleischen, Edward, *With the Mission to Melenek* (London: 1898).
Grey, Sir Edward. *Twenty Five Years 1989-1916*, 2 Volumes (London: 1920). *Letters of Queen Victoria* 3rd Series, 3 Volumes, (London: 1932).
Mantegazza, Vico, *Menelek L'Italia E L' Ethiopia* (Milano: 1910).
Maritini, Ferdinando, *Diario Eritreo*, 3 Volumes (Firenze: 1943).
Portal, Sir Gerald. *My Mission to Abyssinia* (London: 1892).
Rodd, Rennel. *Social and Diplomatic Memories*, 3 Volumes (London: 1923/25).
Skinner, R. *Abyssinia of Today* (New York: 1969) (Reprint) Negroe University Press first published, Longman Greens Co. New York, 1906.
Tittoni, Tommaso. *Sie Anni Di Politica Estera* (Torino: 1912).
Vivian, Herbert. *Abyssinia* (Reprint 'Newyork: 1969).
Wellby, Captain. *"Twixt Sirdar and Menelek* (London: 1901)
Winstanley. *A Visit to Abyssinia*, 2 Volumes London: 1881. Reprint (Negroe University Press New York 1961).
Wylde, A.B.*"83 to the"87 in the Sudan*, 2 Volumes (London: 1888).

Secondary Works

Albert Carrie, Rene. *A Diplomatic History of Europe Since the Congrees of Vienna* (Methuen & Co., London: 1958).
Alf, Andrew Hagoy. *The African Politics of Garbiel Hanotaux* (University of Georgia: 1972).
Andrew, Christopher. *Theophilus Delcasse and Making of Entente Cordiale* (London: 1968).
Anthony, Nutting. *Gordon Martyr and Misfit* (London: 1932).
Beach, Lady Victoria. *Life of Sir Michael Hicks Beach* (London: 1932).
Berkeley, G.F.N. *Tha Campaign of Adwa and the Reign of Menelek* (London: 1935).
Budge, Wallace. *History of Ethiopia, Nubia & Abyssinia* (London: 1922).
Bissolati, L. *La Politica Estera Dell'Italia Dal 1897 Al 1920* (Milano: 1922)
Canuti, Giuseppe. *L' Italian in Afirca La Guerre Con L' Abyssinia* (Firenze: 1932).
Carrier, Albrecht Rene. *A Diplomatic History of Europe from the Congress of Vienna* (London: 1965)
Cesil, Lady Gwendolin. *Life of Robert Marquess of Salisbury*, 4 Volumes (London: 1932).
Dye, W.M. *Moslem Egypt and Christian Ethiopia* (New York).
Duin, C. *Histoire Du Regne Di Khedive Ismail*, 3 Volumes, (Paris: 1939).
Bairu, Tafla. *A Ethiopia and Germany* Cultural, Political and Economic Relation 1871-1936 (Weisbaden: 1981).

Bahru, Zewde. *A History of Modren Ethiopie* 1855-1974 (Addis Ababa University Press, Addis Ababa 1991).

Clough, Shepher. B and *A History of Modren Italy Documents.*

Saldino, Salvatore. *Readings and Commentary* (Columbia University Press: 1968).

Darkwah, Kofi. *Shewa, Menelek and the Ethiopian Empire* (Heienemann: 1979).

De Castro, Lincoln. *Ethiopia Terra, Uomini, E Cosa* (Milano: 1936).

Eubank, Keith. *Paul Cambon Master Diplomat* (University of Oklahoma: 1960).

Farer, Tom. J. *War Clouds in the Horn of Africa (Carnegie Endowments,* Washington, New York).

Gann, L.H. and Duigan, Peter. *Colonialism in Africa 1870-1960,* Vol. 1, *The History and Politics of Colonialism* (London: 1969).

Gifford, P. and Louis Roger. *Britain and Germany in Africa* (New Haven: 1967).

Giglio, Carlo. *L'Impresa di Massaua 1884-1885* (Roma: 1955).

G.Lmour *Abyssinian Railway* (London).

Glenville, T.L. *Italy's Relation with England* (Baltimore: 1934).

Greenville, *Lord Salisbury and Foreign Policy* (London: 1964).

Haggai, Erlich. *Ethiopia and the Challenge of Independence* (lynn Reiner: 1964).

Haight, Mabel V.J. *European Powers and South East Africa* (New York: 1967).

Hargreaves, John D. *Prelude to the Partition of West Africa* (Macmillan Press Ltd, London: 1963).

Hess, Robert. *Italian Colonialism in Somalia* (Chicago: 1966).

Hill, Richard. *Egypt in the Sudan* (London: 1959).

Hollis Christopher. *Italy in Africa* (London: 1941).

Holt, P.M. *The Mahdist State in the Sudan* (Oxford: 1959).

Jesman, Czeslaw. *The Russians in Ethiopia* (London: 1958).

Jardine, D. *The Mad Mullah of Somaliland.* (Negroe University Press, New York).

Keith, Bank. *Paul Cambon Master Diplomat* (Norman University, Carolina,: 1960).

Langer, W.L. *The Diplomacy of Imperialism* (New York: 1951).

Lowe, C.W. *The Reluctant Imperialists British Foreign Policy* 1879-1902 (London: 1967).

Lowe, C.J. and Marzori F. *Italy's Foreign and Colonial Policy* (London: 1975).

Marcus, G. *Life and Times of Menelek* (Oxford:).

Mario, Pigli. *L' Etiopia Nella Politica Europa* terza Edizione, (Padova: 1936).

Marlow, John. *A History of Modern Egypt* (New York: 1955).

Mathew, David. *Ethiopia, the Study of a Polity* (London: 1947).

Mungeam, G.M. *British Rule in Kenya* (Oxford: 1966).

Perham, Margery. *The Government of Ethiopia* (London: 1969).

Paul, Merab. *Impressions d'Etiopie* (Parigi: 1928).

Pierre, Alype. *L' Empire des Negus De' Le Reine de Sebe a la Societa di nations* (1925).

Prouty, Chris. *Empress Tayta Taita and Menilek II Ethiopia 1883-1910,* (London: the Red Sea Press Toronto).

Ram, K.V. *Barren Relation Britain and Ethiopia 1805-1868* (Concept Delhi: 1985).

Ramm, Agatha. *The Political Correspondence of Gladstone and Granville* 1876-82. 2 Volumes, (Cambridge University 1962).

Robinson, H.R. *England, Italy and Abyssinia* (London: 1938).

Robinson, R. and Gallagher, J. *African and the Victorians* with Denney. A (London: 1961).

Rossini, Carlo. *i' Italia e Etiopia dal trattato di Ucciali all battalgia di Adwa* (Roma: 1935).

Rubenson, Sven. *The Survival of Ethiopian Independence* (London: 1975).

Rye, C.F. *Unconquered Abyssinia* (London: 1923).

Sanderson, G.N. *England, Europe and the Upper Nile 1882-1899* (Edinburgh: 1965).

San, Saverno, Bernardo *Italy's Foregin and Colonial Policy Selected Speeches of Senator Tommaso Tittoni* (London: 1914).

Schaub. *Ethiopia, Economics, Politics and Society,* Selassie, Gebre, Z. Yohannes IV (Oxford: 1975).

Skinner, Robert. *Abyssina Today* Negroe University Press: 1969 originally published Longman Green, New York.

Theobold, A.B. *The Mahdiya, A History of the Anglo-Egyptian Sudan* (London: 1951).

Ullendorf, Edward. *The Ethiopians* (London: 1960).

Vivian, Herbert. *Abyssinia, Through the Lion Land to Court of the Lion of Judah* (Negroe University Press: 1969) originally published (London: 1901).

Watson, Seton Christopher. *Italy from Liberalism to Fascism* (London: 1967).

Woolf, Leonard. *Empire and Commerce in Africa* (London: n.d).

Work, Ernest. *Ethiopia, A Pawn in European Diplomacy* (New York: 1936).

Wortham, H.E. *Chinese Gordon* (Boston).

Wubneh Mulatu *Ethiopia Transition and Development in the Horn of Africa* (Bolder, Colarado, Avebery, England).

Unpublished Theses

Caulk, R.A. "The Origin and Development of the Foreign Policy of Menelek II, 1865-1896" (Ph.D. London University: 1966).

Christopher, J.B. "Ethiopia, the Jibuti Railway and the Powers 1899-1906" (Harvard University 1942).

Law Montgomery. "The Growth of British Influence in East African Coast & the Red Sea Coast" (M.A. Thesis, London University 1931).

Marcus, H.G. "Britian and Ethiopia 1896-1914, A Study in Diplomatic Relations" (Ph.D. Boston University 1964).

Venkatram, K. "Some Aspects of British Policy in Ethiopia 1898-1907" (Dollhouse University: 1971).

Articles

Barber, J. "The Macdonald Expedition to the Nile" *Uganda, Journal,* Vol. 27, 1964. pp. 1-44.

Berber, J.P. The Moving Frontiers of British Imperialism in Uganda" *Uganda* Journal. Vol. 29: 1965, pp. 27-43.

Cerulli, Enrica. Gli Avenimenti di Etiopia a la Questionne del Trattato di Tre 1906 *Bulletin Sicieta l" Afrca Italiana.*

Hagai, Erlich. A Political Biography of Ras Alula (Michigan: 1982) Vol. 5, 1916.

Henri Labrousse, "Rivalie enmtre l' Egypt e L' Etiopie" Proceedings of the Seventh International Conference on Ethiopian Studies. Addis Ababa.

Marcus, H.G. "The Foreign Policy of Emperor Menelek 1896-1898" *The Journal of African History"* Vol. VIII, No. 1. 1966, pp. 81-94.

Marcus, H.G. "The Ethiop-British Negotiations Concerning the borders between Ethiopia and British East Africa 1897-1914" Boston University Papers on Africa. II. *Boston University Press.*

Marcus, H.G. "Ethio-British Negotiations concerning the Western Borders with Sudan" *Journal of African History,* Vol. 6. No. 2.

Pankhurst, Richard. "The Franco-Ethiopian Railway and its History" *Ethiopia Observer.* Vol. 6 No. 2.

Pankhurst, Richard. "Italian Policy of Settlement in Eritrea 1895-1896 and its consequence" *Boston University Papers,* Vol. 1, 1996.

Ram, K.V. "The Sudan-Ethiopia Border Negotiations and its Antecedents" *Trans African Journal of History,* Vol. X, 1983.

Ram, K.V. "British Government, Finance Capitalists and the Jibuit-Harar Railway" *The Journal of Imperial and Commonwealth History,* Vol. XI, 1981.

Ramm, Agatha. "Great Britain and the Planting of Italian Power in the Red Sea 1868-1885" *English Historical Review* March 1994.

Rubenson, Sven. "The Protectorate Paragraph of the Ucciali Treaty" *Journal of African History,* Vol. XI. 1964, pp. 243-83.

Sanderson, G.N. "The Foreign Policy of Negus Menelek 1896-1898." *Journal of African History,* Vol. 1, 1962.

Tadesse, Beyene, Richard Pankhurst and Shiferaw Bakele (Eds). Kasa and Kasa Papers on the Lives, Times and Images of Tewodros II and Yohannes IV (1855-1889) (Institute of Ethiopian Studies, Addis Ababa University, Addis Ababa, 1990).

Map 1: Ethiopia in the Nineteenth Century

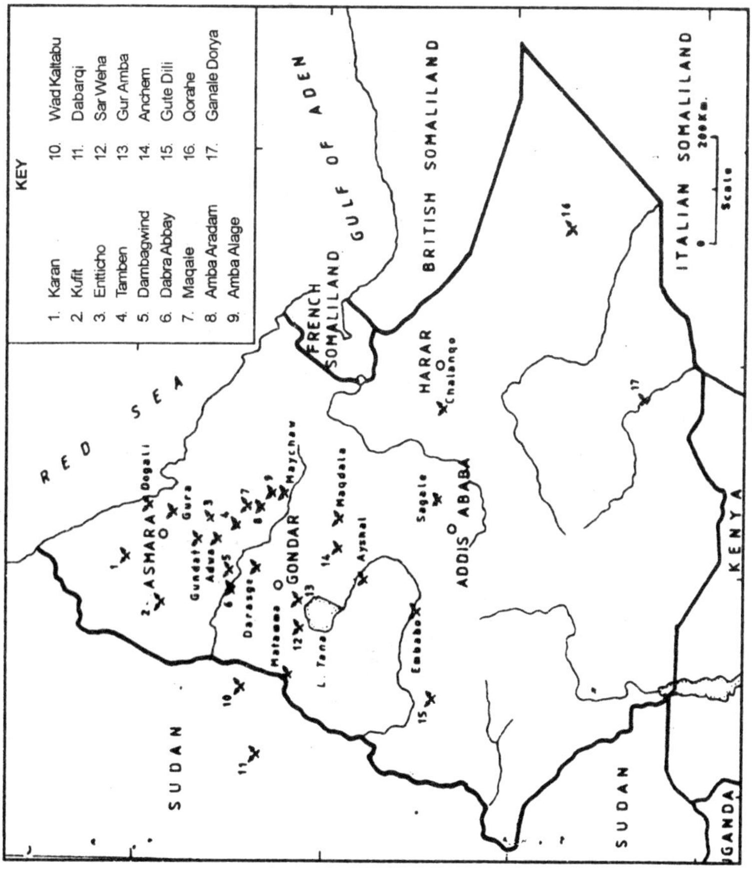

Map 4: Extent of Ethiopia as Claimed by Emperor Menelek in 1891

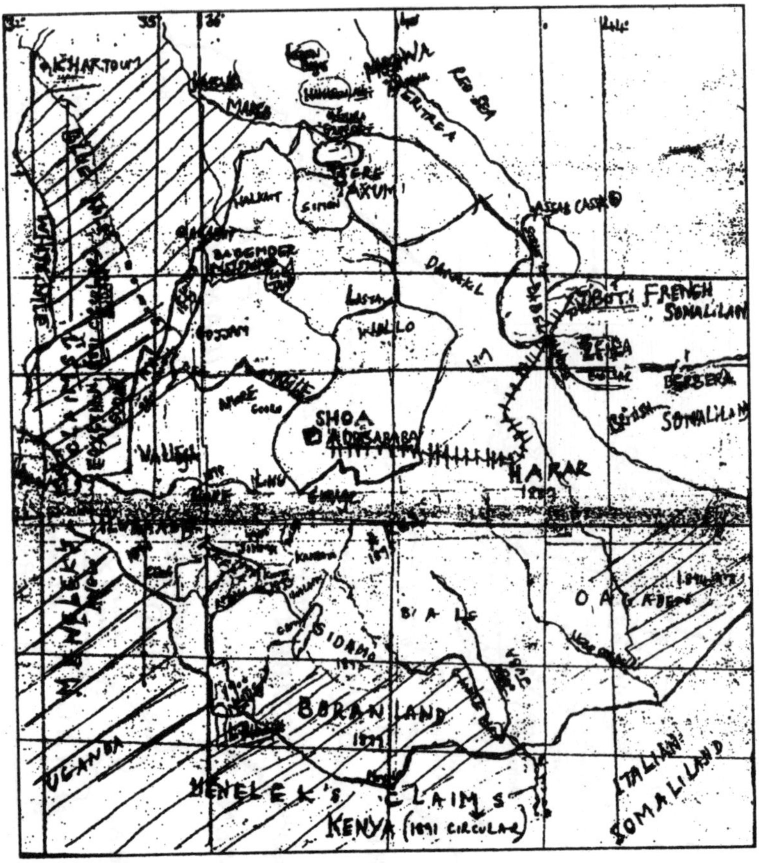

Legend:

British Claim: Tickline of demarcation between the Italian and British spheres followed from the sea. The mid-channel of the River Jiba upto Latitude 6° north of Kishau with the Territory of the Right Bank belonging to England. The line follows 6° North Latitude upto the Meridian 35° East of Greenwich upto the Blue Nile.

▨ Menelek's Claims based on 1891 circular—Menelek claimed all the territory from the 2° to 14° North Latitude and from the Sea to the White Nile for Ethiopia.

Menelek's Claim (The year of conquest Mark)—All territories outside the borders were conquered by Menelek.

Index